FEMALE GLADIATORS

SPORT AND SOCIETY

Series Editors
Benjamin G. Rader
Randy Roberts

A list of books in the series appears at the end of this book.

SARAH K. FIELDS

Female
Gladiators

Gender, Law, and
Contact Sport
in America

UNIVERSITY OF ILLINOIS PRESS

URBANA AND CHICAGO

Library of Congress Cataloging-in-Publication Data
Fields, Sarah K., 1968–
Female gladiators : gender, law, and contact sport
in America / Sarah K. Fields.
p.   cm. — (Sport and society)
Includes bibliographical references and index.
ISBN 0-252-02958-5 (cloth : alk. paper)
1. Sports for women—United States—History.
2. Sports for women—Social aspects—United States.
3. Sex discrimination in sports—Law and legislation—
United States. I. Title. II. Series.
GV709.18.U6F54   2004
796'.082'0973—dc22   2004008913

Contents

Preface

> There is no sharper example of discrimination today than that which operates against girls and women who take part in competitive sports.
>
> —*Sports Illustrated*, 28 May 1973

For American women, 1972 was a watershed year. It was a year in which liberal feminism and gender equality seemed likely to prevail because the U.S. Congress enacted Title IX and endorsed the equal rights amendment (ERA). Between these two, women believed that they would at last have all the legal rights and privileges of American citizenship that had long been available to white men and since 1868 and the enactment of the Fourteenth Amendment also available to black men. While the ERA worked its way, state by state, slowly through the country, seemingly en route to amend the U.S. Constitution, Title IX came roaring out like a tiger. Long before it had any legal standing, athletic programs cringed at its ferocity and its promise of gender equality. States changed their laws to allow girls to participate in sports previously closed to them, and the number of female athletes skyrocketed immediately following the legislation's enactment.

With regard to contact sport, however, Title IX was a paper tiger with no bite. Enforcement regulations exempted contact sport from its scope and then, adding insult to injury, defined "contact sport" so broadly as to allow some cowering athletic leagues to regroup, stand up, and stare down the beast. But before the public realized that they had overestimated the new law's legal clout, girls across America went to the courts to ask for access to sports that had excluded them. The justice system filled the gaps in Title IX's coverage with the equal protection clause of the Four-teenth Amendment of the U.S. Constitution, adding muscle and sinew as well as teeth to the tiger.

Many in the United States were not willing to let girls run unchecked across the nation's playing fields and into its gyms without a fight to keep America's culturally significant sports pure from female influence. Being a people who pride themselves on individualism and tenacity, Americans were also unwilling to concede the war after a few losses in court battles. As a result, the conflict over the gender of contact sports ranged from sport to sport in jurisdiction after jurisdiction until finally the law became clear. American girls began their assault in the 1970s, inspired by the promise of Title IX and the ERA, and they attacked the most sacred of American sports first, laying siege to baseball, football, and basketball.

The arguments in these early cases were repeated in every subsequent gender and contact sport case. Opponents of girls in contact sport argued that the biological nature of gender meant that boys, who were bigger, stronger, and faster, are better athletes than girls. Thus the presence of girls in these sports would at least lead to frustration—causing girls to quit—and, possibly, to physical injury. Even if playing contact sports did not physically or psychologically damage girls, the opposition argued, the games (and boys) would be harmed because a female presence would di-minish the quality of the sport and undermine male experience and masculine development. When girls asked to play on boys' teams, oppo-nents warned, doing so would undermine girls' athletic programs. Girls, however, maintained that they wanted to try out and that none of the arguments made by those who opposed coeducational contact sports was sufficient enough to violate their constitutional rights.

Girls lost several of the first lawsuits because some courts, having no legal precedents on which to rely, trusted their instincts and were swayed by cultural representations of the sport as male and of females as physically vulnerable. In the end, however, courts moved beyond cultural arguments and rejected these stereotypes, ordering leagues ei-ther to give girls a chance to try out with boys or to provide them with leagues of their own.

This book examines the legal and social history of the U.S. school-girls who filed lawsuits in order to gain access to contact sports and the pockets of U.S. communities that resisted their efforts. The book only explores published court decisions, not the untold numbers of lawsuits that were threatened, settled, or concluded without written judicial de-cisions. It considers lawsuits over access, the opportunity to try out, rath-er than issues of equity. It also focuses on schoolgirls, usually those under the age of twenty and not in college. It does not discuss the numerous Title IX suits filed against various colleges and universities.

The first chapter, primarily historical, begins by briefly summarizing the long history of women in sport. Then it describes the political history of American women's rights after World War II and the evolution of the equal protection clause of the Fourteenth Amendment of the U.S. Constitution, which guarantees that "no state shall . . . deny to any person within its jurisdiction the equal protection of the laws."[1] It surveys the history of Title IX and its enforcement regulations as well as the controversy that surrounded that legislation.

In 1972 President Richard Nixon signed Title IX, a law stating that "no person in the United States shall, on the basis of sex, be excluded from participation in, be denied the benefits of, or be subjected to discrimination under any education program or activity receiving federal financial assistance."[2] No one at the time anticipated the firestorm of debate that would follow. Several years later, enforcement regulations were released that stated, "Where a recipient [of federal funding] operates or sponsors a team in a particular sport for members of one sex but operates or sponsors no such team for members of the other sex, and athletic opportunities for members of that sex have previously been limited, members of the excluded sex must be allowed to try-out for the team offered *unless the sport involved is a contact sport* [emphasis added]."[3] A "contact sport" was defined as "boxing, wrestling, rugby, ice hockey, football, basketball and other sports the purpose or major activity of which involved bodily contact."[4] The law and these regulations opened the floodgates for lawsuits involving gender and access to sports.

The next three chapters examine the published decisions involving the most traditionally popular American sports: baseball, football, and basketball. Baseball, America's pastime, was the first sport to be contested (lawsuits began in 1973), and it was the sport that spawned the most litigation. Chapter 2 begins with a description of baseball and its role in American culture, and attempts by women in the nineteenth and early twentieth century to infiltrate the game, and continues through youth baseball's unsuccessful fight to protect itself from a female invasion.

Although baseball is only arguably a contact sport, football is the quintessential contact sport, and its history in America is one plagued by death and injury. The struggle over gender and youth football began just after the baseball cases, and court decisions were fairly consistent (chapter 3). Everywhere except in Texas, courts ruled that girls had to have an opportunity to try out for their schools' teams. The conflict over football is also significant because it marked the first time the equal rights amendment, as contained in state constitutions, was used, warning of the potential power should the federal version of the equal rights amendment be enacted. Even after the courts ruled that girls could try out for football teams, the social battle has continued. Girls in football are so rare that local media often covers their participation as a human interest story.

Chapter 4 explores basketball, a sport that only relatively recently assumed a prominent position in American culture. Basketball was defined as a contact sport in the Title IX enforcement regulations and thus excluded from the legislation's power, but despite this exclusion, girls repeatedly filed suit under Title IX to accomplish two ends. First, girls in states where a modified half-court version of the game with six players was still played wanted access to a full-court version. Second, some girls wanted the chance to play on boys' teams. Although they succeeded in changing from a half-court to a full-court game, one of the most liberal Supreme Court justices rejected a girl's attempt to play on a boys' basketball team instead of the girls' team.

The fifth chapter looks at a sport that has only a limited American past: soccer. In 1977 soccer was new to most Americans, a game played by immigrant men in parks. As social concerns grew about the pressures (both psychological and physical) that faced boys in youth baseball and football, however, soccer in the United States reinvented itself as a less-dangerous, more player-friendly game—one for smaller, weaker, more timid boys as well as a game for girls. Soccer in Colorado, however, was defined as a contact sport until one high school girl sued in federal district court for the right to try out. Her victory led to a national enthusiasm that has caused huge numbers of girls to play soccer and spawned a very successful women's national team.

Chapters 6 and 7 examine two less culturally significant American sports: wrestling and boxing. Wrestling, like football, is a designated contact sport that clearly involves constant bodily contact. Unlike football, however, wrestling is divided by weight classes, and people of similar sizes are matched against each other. Also, unlike baseball, basketball, and football, wrestling is a minor sport in American culture. In American mythology the football captain, not the wrestler, is usually king of the school and society. Thus, not surprisingly, fewer lawsuits were filed and published regarding girls' access to wrestling. The suits also came chronologically later, in the 1980s and 1990s, after the law concerning contact sport and the Fourteenth Amendment had been more fully explored. The wrestling cases are significant, however, because issues of sex and sexuality were raised for the first time in popular media and in published court decisions. Female wrestlers were often portrayed as either (and sometimes both) sexual sirens leading the boys astray or as lesbians seeking to be more masculine.

The dispute over boxing, unlike the other sports addressed thus far, was low-key. When a federal district court ordered Golden Gloves competitions to open a female division, only a local newspaper reported the decision. Yet female boxing, especially female professional boxing, now holds a prominent place in the American popular press, and some are unsure if the sport is a sign of gender equity or the end of American civilization.

The eighth chapter discusses field hockey, the only traditionally American female contact sport and the only one in which boys sued to play on girls' teams. The suits occurred only on the East Coast, where the game is most popular. The boys were faced with the same arguments their female counterparts had encountered—issues of safety and female participation. Unlike the girls, however, the boys lost. Three courts rejected their arguments and concluded that if boys did play field hockey they would take over the game and eliminate positions and playing time for girls.

The ninth chapter, the book's conclusion, considers contact sports that traditionally have been at the periphery of American consciousness. Baseball, soccer, and field hockey were contested in the courtrooms despite not being included the Title IX enforcement regulations, and yet other sports like ice hockey and rugby were not contested in lawsuits despite being listed as contact sports. Ice hockey, although rapidly growing in popularity, was in the twentieth century considered more of a Canadian sport, and rugby remains a very minor club sport with only a few participants. The fact that these two sports were not litigated suggests that the social and legal battle over keeping contact sport male was limited to sports more firmly entrenched in the broader American identity. The final chapter also addresses why many in American society resist the presence of girls in contact sport and why, when courts have let girls on teams, some communities have relied on social control to continue to exclude them. Finally, chapter nine describes the current state of gender and contact sport and explores the legal and social ramifications of separate but equal sports programs for boys and girls.

This book debunks the mythologized power of Title IX, and it lauds the legal might of the equal protection clause. It is a work of legal history that examines the narrow field of gender and contact sport. The book is also about social conflict in the United States—the conflict between a judicial system banning gender discrimination and a society not always ready for gender equality in sport, the last bastion of male prerogative.

Mostly, however, this is a book of stories: stories about parents who filed and paid for lawsuits and judges who made difficult decisions, sometimes in the face of strong social opposition. These are tales of children who just wanted an opportunity to try out for, and perhaps play, the sports they loved and how difficult it was for them to do so.

My fascination with sports began as a child, when I first started playing catch with my father almost before I could walk. My first encounter with contact sports and Title IX came when I was seven, but I had no idea that my parents' threat of legal action was what got me onto the second grade soccer team at my public school. I was the only girl on the team, and most of the time I never really thought about it—I just felt I was part of the team. Only occasionally would I hear murmurs from the crowd, questioning whether a girl should be out there among the boys.

After decades of playing any sport with any team that would take an enthusiastic but not terribly gifted athlete, I discovered in graduate school that not only could I play and watch sports but I could also somehow turn that love into part of my career. This book began as a seminar paper for Catriona "Tina" Parratt's "History of Women in Sport" class during my first semester as a doctoral student at the University of Iowa. My American studies department chair, John Raeburn, directed the class to my attention with a casual "you like sports, don't you?" I liked them and the class a lot, and the combination redirected my scholarship. The paper ultimately, under Tina's guidance, turned into a dissertation with the assistance of the other members of the committee, especially Susan Birrell and Richard Horwitz. There would be no book without all they taught me.

This book would not have been possible without the financial support of two institutions. An Iowa Fellowship at the University of Iowa provided funds for a year of uninterrupted dissertation writing at the end of my coursework, and a Faculty Research Grant from the University of Georgia Research Foundation provided funds for a summer of writing in 2002.

Substantively, the dissertation and the book could not have been written without the aid and advice of a large number of people and organizations. My cohort of graduate students at the University of Iowa in American studies and sport studies helped make my work and my life better. Stephen G. Wieting, a member of my dissertation committee, included an earlier version of the baseball chapter in his anthology *Sport and Memory in North America* (2001). The members of the North American Society for Sport History, especially Mel Adelman, and members of the North American Society for Sport Sociology heard many of these chapters as conference presentations and were gracious enough to provide suggestions and encouragement. Steven Reiss and the Chicago Seminar on Sport and Culture invited me to speak on the topic of separate but equal for gender in sport, and the resulting discussion ultimately helped deepen my understanding on the topic. The fellows of the 2003 J. Willard Hurst Summer Institute in Legal History at the University of Wisconsin School of Law under the guidance of Robert W. Gordon and Lawrence Friedman commented on sections of the book and helped me better grasp how my work fits into the world of legal history. My colleagues at Washington University in St. Louis and the University of Georgia offered support and advice along the way, and my students at UGA have helped me refine and articulate my arguments and ideas. Occasionally, they even let me play on their intramural teams.

A large number of individual scholars, editors, and friends also deserve thanks. I am grateful to Shelley Lucas and Theresa Walton, who share my interest in gender and contact sports and whose own work in basketball and wrestling respectively has greatly influenced my understanding of these sports. Anne DeMartini, my graduate research assistant at UGA, read the manuscript and made comments and then did extensive research and edits. Susan Cahn and Steve Ross were the initial readers for this book, and their comments and suggestions made it a vastly better work. Ben Rader, the series editor, showed me how the book could be more reader-friendly. Richard Wentworth and the staff at the University of Illinois Press, especially Mary Giles, have made this possible. Dick found me after my first presentation at a national conference and told me to contact him after I finished the dissertation. I did.

Finally, I thank my family. My brother, Aaron Fields, was not only my childhood training partner but he also, fortunately, married Kathleen, a freelance editor who patiently answered my questions, even on her honeymoon. My sister Elizabeth Brooks, a librarian, has kept me up to date on new books and distracted me with an unending stream of mysteries, which her husband, Matt, encourages me to keep rather than return. My parents, Wayne and Karen Fields, who introduced me to sports and encouraged me to play when girls often were not so encouraged, have read every draft and listened to every idea since this book began long ago as a seminar paper. Dawn Comstock has also read each draft and been subjected to hours of lectures on the topic. She has responded with good humor and insightful suggestions and, more important, has reminded me that it is not enough to watch and critique. You must, at least occasionally, get in the game and play. Thank you.

FEMALE GLADIATORS

1 The History of American Women in Sport, Society, and Law

This book traces the stories and the lawsuits of the school-aged girls who fought to compete in contact sports and the communities that sometimes supported but often resisted their efforts. The vast majority of these cases began after 1972, and to understand the significance of the legal and social changes marked by that landmark year one must remember what happened before and during it. The girls in this book were not the first female athletes in the world or even in the United States; they were just the newest generation. Their legal struggles built on the work of mothers and grandmothers who had struggled for legal and political equality in America for generations. These girls wrestled with the changing interpretations of the equal protection clause and pushed Title IX into a realm its framers' had not entirely envisioned. They were links in a chain of people who struggled for gender equality, and hence their stories must be contextualized in the social, political, and legal history of women.

An Introduction to Women in Sport

Historically, sports have been a primarily male prerogative, but some women, to varying degrees and in different cultures, have participated in athletic activities. Gender differentiation may have occurred in part because sports often served as a form of mock warfare that trained young boys for battle and maintained young men's readiness as warriors. The

Duke of Wellington allegedly credited the victory of English forces at Waterloo to the playing fields of Eton. Allen Guttmann has explored how some ancient cultures segregated sporting events. The Greeks, for example, had all-male Olympic Games and dedicated all-female games to Hera. Others, however, allowed their young to compete against each other, regardless of gender, in races or wrestling matches, but those cultures seem to have been overwhelmingly outnumbered by ones that segregated games.[1]

One reason for gender segregation in contemporary sport has been explained as a male need for a masculine preserve, a space in which boys could learn to be men away from the interference of their mothers and in which men could bond without the distraction of women. That reasoning assumes males to be defined in opposition to females and male betterment to occur away from the influence of women. Underlying this need for segregation is an assumption of male physical superiority. In other words, by competing against other males, a boy became stronger and quicker and more manly: win or lose, he could improve and continue to separate himself physically from women. If females were to compete in the same arena, then the competition would be diminished. On the one hand, if the boy won he gained nothing because he was expected to defeat the less physically gifted female; on the other hand, if the boy lost he learned he was weaker than the "lesser" female and, therefore, even less a man than before the competition.[2]

Historians such as Reet Howell and Nancy Struna argue that women in the eighteenth- and nineteenth-century United States were not encouraged to become involved in athletics, and, except for a few extraordinary individuals, females were excluded from physical sports.[3] Although physical exercise and sport for American men had long been encouraged as a way to build strength of body and in turn strength of character, many considered strenuous exercise beyond housework to be physically dangerous for middle- and upper-class white women. As Helen Lenskyj has documented, the medical profession warned of uterine displacement and other female reproductive failures if women jumped excessively or exerted themselves too vigorously, a reflection of doctors' beliefs that women were physically unique—different from men and much more frail. Toward the end of the nineteenth century, however, doctors observed that robust women produced healthy babies. Although contact and strenuous exercise were still deemed physically risky, limited exercise was at this point encouraged as long as women avoided excessive activity while menstruating.[4]

Light exercise, conventional wisdom suggested, made women healthy

and attractive; too much exercise, however, made them les
Doctors warned that excess exercise at the wrong time in the
cycle would inhibit pregnancy, making women unable to fulfill t.
feminine capacity. Underscoring that point was the belief, as Sus.
explains, that excess activity caused a "mannish" appearance. At.
for women, if it was to become acceptable, had to be justified as a means
of enhancing physical beauty and reproductive capacity. Exercise in excess or of the wrong sort could ultimately lead, some segments of society
warned, to female athletes who were "muscle molls" and lesbians.[5]

As more women began participating in sports during the early twentieth century, certain sports and styles of play were encouraged over others. Women were not supposed to be overly competitive (a masculine
trait), and they were to avoid contact that could lead to injury and unnecessary exuberance. Thus games like tennis, golf, and swimming were,
on an amateur level, acceptable. When women in the twentieth century
did try to become professional athletes in these sports, their efforts, although ultimately successful, were initially resisted.[6] Team sports were
also socially questionable in the early twentieth century. Field hockey,
with its female tradition, was one of the few exceptions until basketball
became acceptable, but only after basketball was modified to a less-stren-
uous half-court game that prohibited even incidental contact.

As the twentieth century progressed, women and girls began to participate more widely in sports, but that participation was still restricted. Some events in the modern Olympic Games, like sprints and gym-
nastics, opened to women in the 1920s, for example, whereas women
were still excluded from more strenuous track and field activities such
as the decathlon, the marathon, and the pole vault until near the end of
the twentieth century.[7] At the local level, although the number of female
athletes was still small compared to male athletes, certain girls' sports
were encouraged in some regions. In rural areas of Iowa, for example, high
school girls' six-on-six basketball drew enthusiastic statewide interest,
and the girls' state tournament significantly outdrew that of the boys'.[8]

But rural Iowa was an exception. In most regions, including more
urban areas of Iowa, girls' sports placed a distant second to the boys' program and received little or no funding. By the 1960s and 1970s people were
beginning to ask why that discrepancy, especially among school children,
needed to continue. In Iowa City, for example, the school district bud-
geted $60,000 in 1971 for twelve boys' varsity teams and about $200 for
girls' tennis and swim teams. When parents complained, the district offered to increase the girls' athletic budget by $2,000, however that in-
crease was not enough for many who declared that their daughters should

get half of what their sons did—even if it meant cutting the budget for boys' sports.[9]

Historically, American athletic contests were for American boys, regardless of what a few parents in Iowa believed. For school-aged girls to get half of what boys did in sports, whether money, facilities, coaching, or athletic opportunities, there would have to be a revolution, and one battle in that rebellion would involve allowing girls to play the same sports by the same rules as boys. Although in isolated instances a few extraordinary female athletes like Babe Didrikson Zaharias continued to be allowed to compete with and against men, league rules prohibited most from competing with boys in every sport from golf to football. As women and girls became more athletically accomplished, however, they began to demand access to those forbidden sports. The result was a sporting revolution that dovetailed with a social revolution.

Women's Rights in America after World War II

The women's movement arose directly from the civil rights movement, which began during World War II when African Americans actively opposed racial discrimination in the military and in other areas of American society. In a series of decisions, the Supreme Court responded to African American demands that racial injustice in the form of Jim Crow laws be overturned. Outside the courts, members of the civil rights movement were vocal and active: Demonstrations, sit-ins, and riots became commonplace during the 1960s.[10] Joining many African Americans in their quest to gain access to political, social, and economic power were women, both white and black, who supported racial equality.

While working toward political changes that would make black men the legal equal of white men, many women came to realize that their own position in society also warranted examination. The women's movement of the 1960s and 1970s was, like the civil rights movement, a response to earlier historical shifts, especially to the pivotal changes in American society of the World War II era. When men had gone off to war, women were encouraged, if not required, to enter the public arena of work and sport to fill the void. One result was Rosie the Riveter and the All-American Girls Professional Baseball League. Yet after the war ended, women were supposed to return to their old roles in the private sphere. Even those who, of financial necessity, were forced to continue to work did so without societal approval and with economic discrimination, their worth undermined by the assumption that men supported the family while women worked for luxuries. As a result, the 1950s were a decade of frustration for women. When Betty Friedan published *The Feminine Mystique* in 1963, validating the sense of isolation that many women of her generation felt, her work suggested that anomie was a reflection of the problematic place of women in society rather than an individual failing.[11] Her best seller touched a chord in many women and inspired them to seek better conditions for themselves and their daughters. That growing disquiet, working in conjunction with civil rights activism and its emphasis on equality, resulted in a women's movement that began during the 1960s and lasted through the 1970s.

A major focal point for liberal feminists was a political agenda designed to push for legislative initiatives that would make women the legal, if not social, equals of men.[12] Their first success, occurring in the early days of the women's movement and providing a paradigm for the legislative agenda, was the Equal Pay Act, which President John F. Kennedy signed into law in 1963. The law amended the 1938 Fair Labor Standards and required that men and women receive equal pay for equal work, but it excluded executives, professionals, and administrative employees, allowing courts arbitrarily to distinguish among the job descriptions of men and women.

The next legislative step linked the civil rights movement directly with the women's movement. The 1964 Civil Rights Act included Title VII, which banned discrimination in employment and advancement on the basis of sex as well as race.[13] Unfortunately for those convinced that legislating equality would change the way things worked, the Department of Labor and the Equal Employment Opportunity Commission (EEOC) failed to respond to early complaints. As a result, the National Organization of Women (NOW) was formed in 1966 to pressure governmental enforcement of the law.

The pinnacle of congressional involvement in mandating equal treatment came in 1972. Title IX, which banned gender-based discrimination in public-supported educational settings, was the next, and for athletics the most significant, piece of legislation. At the time, however, Title IX was overshadowed by its more powerful cousin the equal rights amendment (ERA), which Congress also endorsed in 1972. The ERA was not a legislative change but rather an amendment to the U.S. Constitution that stated that "equality of rights under the law shall not be abridged by the United States or by any state on account of sex." If passed by both chambers of Congress and ratified by two-thirds of the states, it would amend the Constitution and thus most significantly affect the rights of women.[14]

The ERA's history before 1972 was rocky. It had initially passed out of a Senate committee and was sent to the floor for a vote in 1964, but it had many opponents both in the Senate and the public, including many women's groups who feared that the ERA would undermine protective laws that they believed helped women. Between 1964 and 1972, however, the Supreme Court began to invalidate many protective laws, such as those limiting the hours women could work, and as a result some women's groups and previously reluctant senators grew to believe that the ERA would help protect women. In 1972 both the House of Representatives and the Senate passed the measure by wide margins, and within a year twenty-eight states ratified it. Proponents were confident that ten more states would ratify the amendment within seven years and thus, with two-thirds of the states' approval, the Constitution would be amended accordingly.[15]

Had the ERA been ratified it would have, at least theoretically, ended all forms of gender discrimination in the United States and rendered Title IX and Title VII redundant. Even ERA supporters, however, recognized that passage was at best several years away, and until then Title IX became the focal point for women interested in sport. When the ERA failed to gain the necessary ratification from ten additional states within the required time-frame and disappeared from the public agenda, many believed that Title IX was the only hope for women in sport. The combination of the women's movement and legislative intervention led to a number of lawsuits through which women tried to gain equal access to civic life and sport.

The Intersection of the Fourteenth Amendment and Title IX

After the U.S. women's soccer team won the 1999 World Cup, most journalists and commentators suggested that the victory was proof of Title IX's success. *Newsweek* reported that "World Cup Fever seemed to signal that twenty-seven years after Title IX legislation mandated equal financing for girls' athletics, women's team sports have truly arrived."[16] *Time* credited the legislation with even broader powers: "Daughters of Title IX, they've [the U.S. women's soccer team] never been told what they cannot do."[17] The hoopla celebrating the team's victory and the success of Title IX continued unabashedly and with no apparent awareness of the actual limited power of the legislation. Even the scholarship about Title IX has focused mainly on the increased numbers of female athletes and the financial divide between male and female sports. Only law review articles have evaluated the legal limitations of the legislation with regard to contact sport.[18] The universal, uncritical acceptance of

Title IX's decisive influence, however, restricted as that influence legally was, suggests how the act has been mythologized in the American imagination.

Although Title IX has been critically important in opening sport to women, its power with regard to contact sport has been practically nonexistent. The equal protection clause of the Fourteenth Amendment has actually provided the legal mechanism that opened these sports, including soccer, to women. The equal protection clause states that "no state shall . . . deny to any person within its jurisdiction the equal protection of the laws."[19] Although the Fourteenth Amendment was adopted in 1868, only after Title IX was enacted more than a hundred years later did the courts conclude that the equal protection clause allowed girls equal access to sports.[20] Title IX and the cultural climate that created it triggered the suits; the clause filled the gaps in Title IX's protection.

One of two amendments to the U.S. Constitution ratified after the Civil War, the Fourteenth Amendment was designed to provide basic civil rights to newly freed male slaves. The framers of the equal protection clause did not intend to provide all civil rights to all people—discussion on the floor of the House and Senate made it clear that the right to vote, to serve on juries, to receive an education, and to marry white women were not to be included in the Fourteenth Amendment's protections and that it was to apply to male African Americans and not to any women of any race.[21] The Supreme Court would not apply equal protection to women until the middle of the twentieth century, and even then the amendment was not used literally.

The equal protection clause has never been applied on face value: Not all people are treated equally under the law. The law discriminates against ten-year-olds, for example, limiting their right to drink alcohol, join the military, drive, and vote. Therefore, to accommodate necessary distinctions between groups of people, courts have been asked to balance the equal protection of the laws with the ability of the law to classify individuals. The courts must decide when a classification fails to treat similarly situated people similarly.[22] To do that, the Supreme Court has created certain tests for equal protection questions regarding different categories of people (categories like race or age). The test for evaluating when gender classifications violated the equal protection clause, however, has changed over time.

The first Supreme Court case to examine gender and equal protection was in 1948. *Goesaert v. Cleary* challenged a Michigan state law that provided that no woman could obtain a bartender's license unless she was the wife or daughter of the male owner of a licensed liquor establishment.[23] Valentine Goesaert had purchased a bar and wanted to run it with her daughter and two other female employees. She sued claiming that the state statute violated her equal protection rights by classifying wives and daughters of bar owners differently from wives and daughters of those in other professions. To decide the issue the Supreme Court relied on the rational basis test, the simplest way to justify a state's right to discriminate against certain groups. The test requires that the state have a legitimate governmental interest and that the classification upon which the discrimination is based be rationally related to that state interest. In this case the Court concluded that Michigan had a rational interest in protecting women and that the classification quite reasonably minimized the risks that a female bartender might face by ensuring a husband or father be nearby.

In 1971 the Supreme Court revisited gender and equal protection in *Reed v. Reed*.[24] In that case, the two parties were the adoptive parents of a deceased minor child, and they both wanted to be named administrator of the child's estate. The probate court appointed the father because of an Idaho state law that gave preference to men as administrators over women. The mother sued, claiming that gender preference was a violation of the equal protection clause. The Supreme Court agreed in a unanimous decision, noting that although the state's desire to reduce the workload of probate courts was legitimate, the use of gender was not rationally related to that legitimate end. The Court maintained that the use of the sex-based classification to avoid probate court hearings was an arbitrary choice prohibited by the Fourteenth Amendment. The *Reed* decision, which appeared to continue the rational basis test, seemed less deferential to the state's justification than the reasoning in *Goesaert*, suggesting that the Court was now more inclined to be more critical of gender classifications.

In 1973 the Court declared a federal law permitting male members of the armed services an automatic dependency allowance for their wives but requiring female service members to prove that their husbands actually were dependents to be a violation of the equal protection clause. Four Supreme Court justices argued that sex-based classifications were inherently suspect and should be treated with the same rigorous examination as race and other immutable characteristics that received close judicial scrutiny and, moreover, that the rational relation test was unacceptable.[25] In matters of racial classifications, the strict scrutiny test required that the government prove the classification necessary for achieving a compelling governmental interest. In other words, the means must be narrowly tailored to meet the end. Four other justices concurred in the judgment but were unwilling to base their conclusions on a strict scrutiny test, finding that the government had failed to pass the rational basis test. Because of the lack of a majority ruling, legal scholars were unsure of what the test for gender discrimination would be.

The question of how to review gender and equal protection would be answered in 1976. *Craig v. Boren* involved an Oklahoma state statute that allowed females over the age of eighteen to purchase 3.2 percent beer but prohibited the sale of the same beer to males until the age of twenty-one.[26] The state claimed that their classification was acceptable because men under twenty-one were more likely than women under twenty-one to be involved in traffic accidents and that, in addition, the state wanted to protect the public health of its citizens by ensuring the sobriety of a high-risk driving group.

The Supreme Court rejected the state's claim, and a majority of the Court agreed on a new test for gender classifications: intermediate scrutiny. The majority concluded that the government must have an important objective and that gender classification must be substantially related to achievement of that objective so as not to violate the Fourteenth Amendment. In addition, the Court concluded that "archaic and overbroad" generalizations about gender would not justify the use of gender segregation.

Intermediate scrutiny would eventually become the standard used to evaluate gender-based discrimination, but it would take several subsequent decisions in the 1980s to clearly establish itself.[27] As a result, throughout the 1970s lower courts dealing with gender and equal protection claims in contact sports were never completely certain what standard should be applied, forcing the courts to anticipate the Supreme Court's next decision.

The test for gender classification continued to evolve. In 1996 the Supreme Court was asked to determine if the state of Virginia could continue to fund the Virginia Military Institute, a male-only state university.[28] In 1990, after the state attorney general received complaints about VMI's refusal to admit women, the United States filed an equal protection suit against the state of Virginia for funding VMI. The Fourth Circuit Court of Appeals ruled that the existence of VMI caused the state to violate the Fourteenth Amendment and gave Virginia three options: admit women to VMI, discontinue state support of the institution, or establish a separate, parallel institution for women. Virginia established the Virginia Women's Institute for Leadership (VWIL), but the program was significantly different from VMI. The VWIL did not follow the adversative method (systematic physical and psychological abuse designed to instill character and camaraderie), its students did not live a militaristic lifestyle, and the institute did not have the endowment and budget that VMI had. Six years later the United States renewed its suit, contending that the VWIL was not a parallel institution to VMI and hence Virginia was still violating the equal protection rights of female citizens.

The Supreme Court heard the case in 1996, and Justice Ruth Bader Ginsberg wrote the majority decision on behalf of five other justices, holding that the admissions policies of VMI violated the Fourteenth Amendment.[29] The majority relied on the intermediate level of scrutiny but emphasized the necessity for an "exceedingly persuasive" justification for gender segregation. Most of the gender and sport cases, however, occurred before the VMI decision.

The issue of when the girls discussed in this book filed lawsuits to play on contact sport teams is, therefore, critically important. When a lawsuit went to trial determined what test the court applied, and earlier cases relied on the rational basis test (a classification being rationally related to a legitimate governmental interest)—the lowest level of scrutiny. Some cases in the early 1980s came when the Supreme Court itself was uncertain of how to evaluate gender classifications, leaving lower courts to guess or fashion their own tests. For cases in the 1990s, the state had the increased burden of proving that their classification was substantially related to an important governmental objective.

Just as the Fourteenth Amendment was the result of a specific crisis in American history, Title IX was enacted after the social and political protests of women in the 1960s, and—just like the equal protection clause—Title IX seemed to promise equality for both men and women. In 1972 President Richard Nixon signed Title IX, which stated that "no person in the United States shall, on the basis of sex, be excluded from participation in, be denied the benefits of, or be subjected to discrimination under any education program or activity receiving federal financial assistance."[30] On its surface, the language seemed to cover all athletic activities in educational settings from grade school through college, but the literal language of the legislation could not stand alone. Like every piece of legislation, it needed enforcement regulations.

After Title IX became law, the Department of Health, Education, and Welfare (HEW) undertook the complicated task of promulgating enforcement regulations for Title IX. It took HEW three years to accomplish this task, an extraordinary length of time explained in part by the fact that Congress was still struggling with how to conceptualize the legislation. Title IX's primary purpose was to prevent discrimination in the classroom. For example, it would stop schools from excluding girls from physics and wood-working classes and ensure that all students, regardless of gender, had the opportunity to acquire financial aid. The legislation's implication for athletics was never really discussed during congressional debate. At the time, the only record of discussion of sport and Title IX was the comment by Sen. Birch Bayh, the bill's co-sponsor, that the law would mandate neither the desegregation of football fields nor men's locker rooms.[31]

Soon after Title IX was enacted, however, the issue of athletics came to the fore. In 1973 Gwen Gregory, an attorney in the Office of Civil Rights, the HEW division charged with drafting the regulations, told *Sports Illustrated* that HEW was debating two options: The guidelines could open all sports and teams to everyone, or they could order funds and facilities equally divided between men and women. *Sports Illustrated* supported the second choice, suggesting that if all teams were open to everyone there would be no girls' teams, and most girls would not be good enough to win positions away from boys.[32] The choice was between a unisex sports program (which was likely to exclude most girls who did not have the same experience and advantages that boys did and would be beaten out in merit-based tryouts) or two different programs based on a premise of separate but equal.

Congress's inability, however, to decide how Title IX applied to athletics made HEW's decisions more difficult. Soon after enacting it, many in Congress became concerned that the legislation would put girls in baseball dugouts or (more disconcerting to collegiate sports fans) on college gridirons. In an attempt to clarify the scope of Title IX, both houses of Congress debated how to direct HEW's attempts to draft enforcement regulations. Neither, however, could decide how to do this. In 1974 the Tower Amendment, which stated that Title IX would not apply to revenue-producing intercollegiate sports at all, was defeated, and in 1975 the Javits Amendment was adopted instead. It instructed HEW to create a provision in the regulations that would "include with respect to intercollegiate athletic activities reasonable provisions considering the nature of the particular sports."[33] Thus Congress seemed to be asking HEW not to take Title IX literally but to guard male collegiate sport from women. The Javits Amendment and the threatened Tower Amendment warned HEW that enforcement regulations for Title IX needed somehow to protect collegiate football fields from a female invasion.

Almost everyone felt compelled to comment on HEW's internal debate. In June of 1974 HEW published a set of proposed regulations and began a four-month comment period, a much longer time for consideration than the usual ninety days. It took more than six months to sort through the more than ten thousand written messages forwarded to HEW.[34] Women's groups such as the Association of Intercollegiate Athletics for Women (AIAW), which oversaw women's collegiate sport, were frustrated with regulations that would dilute the literal language of Title IX. Other groups, however, notably the National Collegiate Athletic Association (NCAA), responsible for men's collegiate sport, feared that even those regulations would allow women too much access. Although the athletic regulations were just two of the document's forty sections, they received the overwhelming majority of comment, prompting HEW Secretary Casper Weinberger later to comment that "athletics . . . [are] without question the most important issue before the American public today."[35]

The final version of the regulations was even weaker than expected. Without explanation but probably in response to the Javits Amendment, which had been adopted after the initial proposed regulations, HEW chose to distinguish between contact and noncontact sports.[36] In a statement at the 1975 regulations presentation, Secretary Weinberger rationalized the distinction: "We wanted to eliminate the very evident and obvious discrimination which has taken place against women in athletics and sports over the years, mostly unconsciously, I think, by the schools. At the same time we did not want to disrupt the entire pattern of American college life, or indeed a larger part of American life itself. . . . I think this regulation will . . . enhance markedly the opportunities for women in athletics. But it will also allow schools certain flexibility."[37]

Weinberger's statement actually referred to the Javits Amendment in which Congress asked HEW not to disrupt college sport, that is college football and basketball, too significantly. He also identified the link between sport and society and suggested that to allow women into men's collegiate sport would disrupt not just college life but "American life itself." His comments clearly indicated the compromise HEW had reached with college athletics: Any past discrimination had been unintentional, and any future discrimination would be for the good of the country. The enforcement regulations completely ignored the breadth of the literal language of Title IX, which prohibited any gender-based discrimination, and instead exempted contact sports from Title IX, explicitly stating "where a recipient [of federal funding] operates or sponsors a team in a particular sport for members of one sex but operates or sponsors no such team for members of the other sex, and athletic opportunities for members of that sex have previously been limited, members of the excluded sex must be allowed to try-out for the team offered *unless the sport involved is a contact sport* [emphasis added]."[38]

HEW's definition of contact sport managed to be both specific and nebulous: "boxing, wrestling, rugby, ice hockey, football, basketball and other sports the purpose or major activity of which involved bodily contact."[39] Clearly, revenue-producing sports like football and basketball were protected from a female invasion, but the vague definition would also allow leagues to classify soccer and baseball as contact sports and exclude girls from those activities as well.

Although schools were given until July 1978 to comply with the Title IX regulations, athletic departments immediately challenged the language of Title IX and its regulations. First, they questioned whether an individual had a private right of action under Title IX. In other words, nothing in the language of the statute or the regulations specifically said that an individual, Jane Doe, had the right to sue State University for not allowing her to play a sport, but rather the regulations suggested that she could instigate an Office of Civil Rights' investigation of the school. Courts rejected several causes of action resting on Title IX claims on precisely these grounds until the Supreme Court ruled in 1979 in *Cannon v. University of Chicago* that Title IX had an implied right of action that allowed individuals to sue their schools.[40]

Title IX and its enforcement regulations also failed to define exactly who had to receive federal financial assistance in order for its provisions to apply. That provided another loophole for those who did not want Title IX to affect athletic departments. One group argued that if any department of an educational institution received federal money, the entire school had to comply with Title IX. Thus, if students received federal aid in the form of student loans and grants, the athletic department had to act in accordance with Title IX. The other side argued that this interpretation was too broad. If the financial aid office received federal money then, yes, Title IX pertained to that office, but it did not apply to the athletic department unless the athletic department itself received federal money. Because few athletic departments receive direct governmental aid, the argument would have effectively cut athletics out of Title IX's domain.

The Supreme Court agreed with the narrow, program-specific interpretation, and in 1984 most athletic departments were exempted from Title IX.[41] In 1988, however, Congress passed the Civil Rights Restoration Act of 1987 (1988 Amendments) over President Ronald Reagan's veto.[42] The Restoration Act reaffirmed that Congress intended the institution-specific approach the Supreme Court had rejected, and as a result, only sixteen years after Title IX was enacted, it finally, clearly, applied to athletic departments.

Title IX had no direct legal impact on sport during the 1970s, but it did have an immediate social impact, evident in a dramatic increase in the numbers of female athletes. During the 1970–71 academic year, before Title IX's enactment, high school girls composed 7 percent of the pool of athletes; only 268,591 played on their schools' teams, compared to 3,473,883 boys. In the 1972–73 academic year, immediately after the enactment of Title IX, those numbers changed dramatically. Some 743,958 girls (17 percent of the athletes) played on high school teams, compared to 3,553,084 boys.[43] The huge increase came after Title IX was signed into law but long before the courts and Congress had determined whether it applied to athletic departments, well before its regulations went into effect, and even before the regulations had been drafted.

Because of the increased number of females in high school and collegiate athletics, and because of increased spending on behalf of those female athletes, in July of 1974 *Sports Illustrated* proclaimed, "This year has been the Year of the Woman in Sports." The authors cited the impending threat of Title IX with greater spending on the growing number of female athletes.[44] Sports scholars examining the legislation agreed, crediting Title IX with increasing opportunities for female athletes. Peg Burke, president of the AIAW, suggested that "since Title IX, women and girls in the United States have moved out of the Dark Ages of Athletics."[45] Joan S. Hult, a sport historian, called it "the single most significant piece of legislation to affect the direction and philosophical tenets of women in sport. Much of the growth of girls' high school athletics . . . resulted from the act's implementation."[46]

These numbers suggest the profound effect of Title IX on women and girls involved with sport, an influence that began even before the law legally applied to athletic departments. Title IX was a catalyst for change, but it was not the sole explanation for the changing landscape in sport. On the contrary, the role of females was changing in society, and a corresponding change in the sporting world would seem only logical. During this evolution Title IX, especially because it applied to school- and college-aged females, took on social and psychological significance for people on both sides of the struggle over women's place in American sport as well as in America more generally.

An Introduction to the Legal Cases

Title IX would trigger countless lawsuits over access to sports after its enactment in 1972, but at least one went to trial in 1971, and the language of the judge foreshadowed the rhetoric in the conflict over sports that would follow in years to come. In 1971 a high school girl in Connecticut wanted to run cross-country and indoor track. Unfortunately for her, her school only had a boys' team in these sports, and the league prohibited coeducational sports in any form. The lawsuit she filed failed, but the words the judge uttered in announcing the decision embodied many of the "arguments" against females in sport. The judge's comments reflected the significance of the cultural influences in law, because his arguments were based on assumptions and prejudices about women and sport rather than on rational legal suppositions. The court announced:

> The present generation of our male population has not become so decadent that boys will experience a thrill in defeating girls in running contests. . . . It could well be that many boys would feel compelled to forgo entering track events if they were required to compete with girls on their own teams or adversary teams. . . . In a world of sports, there is ever present as a challenge, the psychology to win. With boys vying with girls in cross-country running and indoor track, the challenge to win, and the glory of achievement, at least for many boys, would lose incentive and become nullified. Athletic competition builds character in our boys. We do not need that kind of character in our girls, the women of tomorrow.[47]

If girls really wanted to run, the court suggested, they should compete against each other, taking advantage of times when male athletes were not using the facilities and equipment. This judge suggested that girls were not physically capable of competing with boys and that if they did, their presence would diminish the sport, their femininity, and the male psyche. Separate, the court ruled, was the best girls could hope for.

The ruling was overturned by Title IX, which ordered equal access for boys and girls to all noncontact sports. These sentiments, however, foreshadowed arguments made by those who would exclude girls from contact sports. Although Title IX, promising separate but equal, avoided the judge's form of paternalism for noncontact sports, it left open the door for female exclusion from contact sports because of the same kind of cultural assumptions and prejudices about females and their athletic capabilities.

The general public seemed unaware of Title IX's legal limitations, endowing it with a mythic power despite its lack of any real "teeth." It was up to the Fourteenth Amendment to provide the practical legal bite for the paper tiger that was Title IX. In 1973 the first in a long series of published court decisions involving attempts by high school or collegiate female athletes to gain access to a contact sport, as defined by either Title IX regulations or state athletic association rules, was released.[48]

During the 1970s, girls used the Fourteenth Amendment to gain access to the most popular American sports—baseball, football, and basketball. Their attempts to use Title IX, however, were rebuffed because it excluded contact sports. In the 1980s and early 1990s, girls sued to participate in more exotic sports such as wrestling and boxing, while boys did so to play field hockey. Not until 1999 would a court finally rule that Title IX might provide legal recourse for a girl involved in a contact sport; even then it could only force schools not to discriminate on the ground of gender against the females who tried out for male teams.[49] The courts repeatedly rejected attempts to use Title IX in these suits, making their final decision on other grounds such as the equal protection clause.

The cultural opposition to females in contact sports resulted in struggles in jurisdiction after jurisdiction and sport after sport as girls gradually gained access to traditionally male games. When a girl would sue for access to a contact sport, the courts often had limited legal precedent on which to rely. Their situation was complicated by the fact that the Supreme Court, until the 1980s, did not clearly delineate how to deal with gender discrimination under the Fourteenth Amendment, thus forcing lower courts to guess at the high court's standard. Further, before 1973 no contact sports decisions existed for school- and college-aged girls. Almost every decision would be one of first impression for a court, and that court would be forced to look outside legal precedents for support. The result was a wide array of cases that had a range of decisions influenced by the cultural significance of each sport.

Although the cases had certain similarities, their differences can be measured in several ways. First, the language of deciding judges varied from case to case because in the absence of legal precedents they were forced to rely on their own instincts and close readings of each case. Ultimately, they developed a new line of decisions that gave lawyers a new line of law to study. Second, public interest in opening a particular sport to girls can be inferred from the number of cases filed about the activity as well as the media rhetoric the cases generated. Thousands of articles and books, for example, have been written about the role of baseball in American society. Not surprisingly, more suits were filed to open baseball to girls than any other sport. Almost nothing, however, has been written about the importance of rugby to American society, and no published decision about a girl's attempt to play rugby exists, perhaps because no one cared if a few played that game. In the end, the legal and societal duel over contact sports would be limited to those most important to the American national identity.

2 Baseball

In the flood of lawsuits seeking to open contact sports to girls in 1973, the first sport contested was baseball, a fact significant for the importance of baseball's role to American culture and the fact that it is not a quintessential contact sport, nor is it included in Title IX's enforcement regulation list of enumerated contact sports. Baseball, the national pastime, has long been inseparably intertwined with American identity and been part of what it means to be American. Yet it has traditionally been a game for men—fathers and sons. When society changed, however, and daughters asked to play with their brothers, America was divided over whether girls should play baseball or whether a feminine presence would somehow undermine the sport's role in defining American manhood. To emphasize the masculine quality of the game and help justify the exclusion of girls, youth baseball officials declared that baseball was a contact sport and implied that girls were either not tough enough to play or that their presence would dilute the game's manly aspects.

Although Title IX and the equal protection clause seemed to imply gender equality, those who controlled youth baseball wanted to exclude girls, so girls went to court and sued for the right to try out for youth baseball leagues. The timing of these lawsuits supports the claim that Title IX's enactment in 1972 instigated the suits, because no published baseball decision existed before 1973. The lawyers in these lawsuits, though, recognized that Title IX might have inspired their clients to come forward but could not be used as the basis for any legal action because enforcement regulations were not yet in place. Consequently, they used other legal mechanisms, particularly the equal protection clause, to try to gain girls' access to baseball. The dispute over baseball was long and fierce. Finally, however, after mixed results in court and despite continued misgivings of the leagues and the culture, youth baseball was opened to any child qualified to play.

Baseball and Its Role in American Culture

Until at least the 1950s no other sport came close to challenging baseball's supremacy in the American imagination. The game has inspired cultural critics to comment on baseball and its role in society. Walt Whitman said, "It's our game: that's the chief fact in connection with it: America's game; it has the snap, go, fling of the American atmosphere; it belongs as much to our institutions, fits into them as significantly as our Constitution's laws; is just as important in the sum total of our historic life."[1] Mark Twain had his Connecticut Yankee teach baseball to the knights of King Arthur's Court, normally cynical commentators like George F. Will have waxed sentimental about baseball, and academics such as A. Bartlett Giamatti left the solitude of ivy towers for the ivy of Wrigley Field. Baseball is as American as mom and apple pie, although both mom and the pie have been relegated to the back burner during pennant races. But if baseball is America's game, it is preeminantly a man's game.

Baseball's cultural significance arises in part because it reflects aspects of America's image of itself. Many believe the myth that the game was invented in, by, and for Americans—that like America itself, baseball is exceptional. In 1907 a commission led by sporting goods magnate Albert Spalding officially concluded that Abner Doubleday had created the game in Cooperstown, New York, in 1839. The commission countered suggestions that baseball derived from the British game of rounders because, after all, an American power needed an all-American game.[2] Baseball also seemed reflective of a mythologized world, providing both heroes and tragedies. On the one hand, Babe Ruth was a larger-than-life hero who was molded into the American dream, a poor boy who through his own talent gained fame and fortune. Young boys throughout the country could dream of pulling themselves up by their bootstraps and being the next Ruth. On the other hand, when heroes failed, when the mighty Casey struck out, when the Boston Red Sox sent Babe Ruth to the Yankees, the tragic side of baseball appealed to Americans' appreciation of struggle. One must, it is believed, overcome obstacles in order to succeed.[3]

Women and girls were not formally banished from the game and the culture of baseball as a whole. On the contrary, the occasional female has crossed the baseline and stepped onto the diamond. In 1866, just a year after Vassar College's establishment, that college's women formed two teams.[4] In the beginning of the 1890s, women interested in playing professionally could join the Bloomer Girls, barnstormers who played any team willing to compete, and between 1943 and 1954 women could compete in the All American Girls Professional Baseball League (AAGPBL). Even those options, though, were limited. The Bloomer Girls were rare, and the AAGPBL came into being only because of the manpower drain of World War II and the financial threat to the business of sport.[5]

Generally, however, females have not been welcomed with open arms into the dugout. Girls were expected to play other games and not infringe on this aspect of American culture, and those who tried were subsequently forbidden. After five women joined in a baseball game at the University of Pennsylvania in 1904, for example, the university took swift action and ordered the men not to play on campus and the women not to play at all.[6] In 1928 Margaret Gisolo, age fourteen, was a pitcher for Blanford, Indiana's American Legion Junior Baseball team. After Gisolo singled in the game-winning run-in to lead her team to the Junior World Series, the opposing and losing team challenged her eligibility because she was a girl. A lengthy debate ensued among league officials in consultation with major league baseball's commissioner Kennesaw Mountain Landis, and Gisolo was allowed to play because nothing in the rules stated that the league was only for boys.[7] The next year, however, the league amended the rules and prohibited girls from playing.[8]

In 1931 Jackie Mitchell, seventeen, signed a minor league contact. After she struck out Babe Ruth and Lou Gehrig in an exhibition game, Commissioner Landis voided the agreement on the grounds that life in baseball was "too strenuous" for women. Babe Ruth said that he had no idea what would happen if women were allowed in the game because "of course they will never make good. Why? Because they are too delicate. It would kill them to play ball every day."[9] In 1952, after Eleanor Engle signed a minor league baseball contract, Commissioner Ford Frick voided the contract and banned women from playing professional baseball.[10]

Generally, the rules against women's participation in the game were unwritten—until women tried to play. At that point rules intended to ensure that the American pastime remained a masculine one were written.[11] As a sportswriter observed in 1974, "Baseball is a serious business. It is also clearly understood to be a man's business."[12] It was the business side of the sport that built the women's league when men were away in World War II, and it was business that caused female players to be dropped when peace was restored.

As women and girls struggled to gain access to baseball, the game was being formally propagated among American boys.[13] Little League Baseball, begun in 1939 as a summer program for boys in Pennsylvania, was designed to teach baseball, Americanism, and masculinity. The organization grew exponentially, and by 1964 more than 1.25 million boys played in approximately six thousand leagues in the United States, Canada, Japan, and Australia. In 1964 Congress designated the organization a federal corporation when President Lyndon B. Johnson signed the federal charter of incorporation that granted the group tax-exempt status and encouraged the league to "promote Americanism." According to sociologists Lewis Yablonsky and Jonathan Brower, to learn baseball in Little League was to learn to be a man. "Softball is for girls, old people and those who do not have the skill or inclination to prepare for baseball" they quote a Little League manager as saying. Baseball requires toughness, dedication, and discipline, all attributes of a good man.[14] Robert Stirrat, league vice president in 1974, said, "We've always assumed baseball was a boy's sport. We think most people have always felt that way. We assume they've accepted baseball as a male prerogative of some sort."[15]

Even the rhetoric of Little League reflected a text of masculinity. The official motto stated "from the ranks of boys who stand now on the morning side of the hill will come the leaders, the future strength and the character of the nation."[16] The charter articulated the league's goals in its statement of objectives and purposes: "(1) To promote . . . the interest of boys who will participate in Little League Baseball. (2) To assist . . . boys in developing qualities of citizenship, sportsmanship, and manhood."[17] The language of Little League referred only to males and boys. By the early 1970s Little League was solidly entrenched as an American Institution, but the charter limiting that institution to boys was about to be challenged.

Baseball and the Law

Legally, the "baseball cases" were filed when U.S. law on gender equity was not well defined. The Title IX legislation that prohibited gender discrimination in educational settings had been enacted and signed into law on June 23, 1972, but its enforcement regulations were still in the drafting stage when the baseball lawsuits were first filed. Although those enforcement regulations would ultimately exclude contact sport from Title IX's protection, they were not approved until 1975. Even after being affirmed, the regulations failed to adequately define contact sport, stating that "contact sports include boxing, wrestling, rugby, ice hockey, football, basketball, and other sports the purpose or major activity of which involved bodily contact."[18]

Although not legally applicable until 1978 after most of the baseball decisions, the enforcement regulations created a legal distinction between contact and noncontact sports, and baseball leagues seized on that distinction as a means of excluding girls from their ranks. By limiting girls' opportunities in contact sport, the regulations underscored the old notions (the same given by Babe Ruth and Kennesaw Mountain Landis to keep women out of baseball) that women and girls were not physically capable of playing sports, particularly tough contact sports.[19] By arguing that baseball was a contact sport, an argument difficult to support under the rules of the game, youth baseball could bridge the stereotypes with the soon-to-be legal distinctions of Title IX's enforcement regulations.

The baseball cases also occurred at a time when the Supreme Court had not yet clarified the tests by which to judge gender classifications under the Fourteenth Amendment's equal protection clause. In the years before 1972 the Court repeatedly ruled that gender was a benign classification, like height or age, and that the test was to see whether the classification was rationally related to a legitimate governmental interest. If it was, the classification was allowed to stand under the equal protection clause. In 1973, however, the Court shifted positions and classed gender with race as an immutable characteristic; to survive, the classification must be necessary to attaining a compelling governmental interest. For the next eight years legal scholars and lower courts were uncertain which test the Supreme Court would apply to gender classifications. In terms of legal precedents the waters were murky.

As if the status of gender classification was not complicated enough, judges who examined baseball cases had exactly two gender and sport precedents to consider, and neither precedent was published.[20] Both occurred before Title IX's enactment, and both rejected attempts by girls to compete on noncontact sport teams. Although Title IX was not yet enforceable, judges were aware of its existence and suspected—and knew for certain after the release of the enforcement regulations—that Title IX required that girls be allowed to try out for noncontact sport teams. These precedents were legally useless, and as a result judges worked essentially in a legal vacuum. Any precedents they could use were by analogy only. Therefore, they seemed particularly susceptible to cultural forces as well as their own experiences while making these decisions.

The Baseball Cases

The legal floodgates opened in 1973 when the first of five major base-ball cases was published.[21] Pamela Magill was ten years old, and she wanted to play baseball in the Avonworth Baseball Conference (ABC) in her western Pennsylvania hometown, but her application had been re-jected because the league did not allow girls to play.[22] Her parents sued the ABC on her behalf, claiming that her equal protection rights had been violated.[23]

In order to claim protection under the Fourteenth Amendment, a plaintiff must establish that the defendant, if not a direct branch of the state or local government, is acting as a representative of that govern-ment. Without some evidence that the defendant is acting under the auspices of state law, the Fourteenth Amendment usually does not ap-ply. The ABC claimed that it was not a state actor but rather a private organization, and the federal district court judge agreed.[24] At this point the decision made sense. Determining state action is somewhat subjec-tive, but the judge had ample legal precedent to justify the decision. Had the decision ended there the case would not have been terribly interest-ing, and determining whether the court really believed its decision or was merely fabricating an excuse to exclude girls from baseball would have been impossible to conclude.[25]

The district court did not stop there, however. The judge felt strong-ly enough about the issues to write more than a page of dicta discussing how the case would turn out if the ABC had in fact been a state actor.[26] This language, especially the language considering Magill's Fourteenth Amendment claim, indicated that the judge personally believed girls should not play baseball. The ABC had argued that it excluded girls for two reasons. First, they would get hurt playing baseball, and, second, if they played, boys would quit.[27] Although the court did not address the second justification, the mere idea that the ABC suggested it as a ratio-nale is significant. The ABC believed it more important for American boys to play baseball than for girls to play. Thus the league believed it was better to deliberately exclude one-half of the youth population than risk having a few boys voluntarily quit the league. The court, however, focused on the league's first claim that girls would get hurt if they played baseball because baseball was a contact sport.

The directors of the ABC claimed that baseball was a contact sport, and the court agreed. Establishing that fact was critical in justifying the division between contact sports and noncontact sports and in protecting the masculine status of baseball. The judge explained the conclusion, noting, "There is no question that a runner who tries to beat a throw to the plate is frequently blocked by a catcher. The contact is severe if not violent. The directors spoke of their concern with wild pitchers and, of course, we know the consequences of trying to steal second or third."[28]

The court never commented on medical evidence, relying instead on the testimony of the directors of the league who were being sued, trusting that those wise patriarchs would know what was best for their players. Further, the court seemed unaware of the irony of claiming "of course, we know the consequences." The judge could only be speaking to males who had played baseball because a person who had never tried to steal a base would not know from experience what the consequences would be. Because this decision would exclude girls from playing baseball, it would exclude girls and women from even understanding the language of the decision.[29] The lengthy dicta is significant because it indicates the cultural forces influencing the legal decisions, expressing the judge's conviction that baseball was too rough for girls and that the presence of girls would dilute the masculinity of the game.

The second major baseball decision arose after eleven-year-old Maria Pepe won a position on her local Little League team. When the leaders of the national organization, Little League Baseball, Inc. (LLB) learned of her success, they ordered her removed from the team. If she was not, they threatened to revoke the team's charter, causing the team to lose insurance, funding, and access to other LLB teams.[30] When the team cut Maria, the local chapter of the National Organization for Women (NOW) sued LLB for violating her equal protection rights as guaranteed under the New Jersey constitution. The lawsuit was instigated just two months after President Nixon signed Title IX into law.

After Examiner Sylvia B. Pressler ordered LLB to admit girls aged eight to twelve into the league, LLB appealed.[31] The verdict of the appellate court was anxiously awaited by Little League officials across the country, some of whom seemed to see a female conspiracy to take over the sport. One official in Houston, explaining why his league would wait for the appellate decision before changing its policy, said, "It was a lady judge who ruled in favor of the girls. The case hasn't moved up to male judges yet."[32] The Superior Court of New Jersey upheld the lower court order, and in the decision the court described and commented on LLB arguments against girls' participation in conjunction with NOW's arguments.[33]

LLB argued primarily that girls were too physically frail to play baseball. Unlike the defendant in *Magill*, however, LLB relied on some medical evidence to prove its point. Unfortunately for Little League, that evidence was based on research examining bone strength in Japanese cadavers of people between the ages of eighteen and eighty. NOW's medical expert countered with the argument that between the ages of eight and twelve boys and girls are physiologically very similar. LLB's expert claimed that girls who suffered contact to the chest or breast would have breast cancer as an adult, but NOW's expert completely disagreed. The court concluded that NOW's evidence that girls were physically capable of playing baseball was more compelling. LLB also argued that boys and girls needed "islands of privateness" to engage in same-sex social activities, or they would risk later psychological problems. NOW maintained that sex-integrated baseball would, in fact, teach girls and boys to work together. The court thought both theories far-fetched but rejected LLB's suggestion that girls should be excluded for psychological reasons.[34]

LLB also made a series of arguments justifying gender segregation that the court found particularly unpersuasive. LLB claimed that coed baseball would threaten the bodily privacy of girls. If a girl were injured, for example, her presumably male coach would have to give first aid and hence perhaps be forced to touch her. The court called this contention "frivolous." LLB asserted that after puberty girls would lose interest in baseball and would, in fact, be unable to play well because of their physiological changes. Therefore, LLB thought it best not to waste time teaching the game to those who would not play for long. Further, if girls were squandering coaches' efforts, boys who could gain "permanent baseball skills" would suffer, so LLB generously encouraged girls to take up a sport they could enjoy for the rest of their lives. The court was no more persuaded by that argument than the others, noting that the purpose of sex discrimination legislation was to "emancipate the female sex from stereotyped conceptions as to its limitations embedded in our *mores* but discordant with current rational views." The court saw no reason not to teach girls to play and found no evidence that boys would suffer if girls did join a team.[35]

Finally, LLB pointed to its national charter as evidence. The charter, LLB suggested, called for improving the qualities of "citizenship, sportsmanship, and manhood," and admitting females to the league would foil that effort. The court equated manhood with maturity of character and concluded that girls, too, should have these qualities developed. The court also rejected LLB's argument that no court should tamper with Congress's decree that LLB be for boys. The court noted that Congress could not create legal corporations, and thus the charter was more symbolic than significant. Although Congress seemed to deem LLB for boys, no evidence indicated a deliberate intent to exclude girls. Therefore, the New Jersey court rejected LLB's arguments and ordered it to admit girls.[36]

After the decision, many Americans were distraught. *Newsweek* reported that "the battle has reached new levels of chauvinism and near hysteria" and, referring to LLB's safety concerns, added that the "real 'traumatic impact' in the case was on the adults."[37] An official with the New Jersey chapter of NOW claimed just two years after the emotional *Roe v. Wade* decision legalized abortion, "This particular issue is as fraught with emotional backlash as any I've ever seen."[38]

The importance of baseball as both a man's game and as America's game was highlighted by the violent public reaction to the court's decision. Many feared what would happen were girls to intrude on a masculine preserve.[39] While LLB considered appealing to the New Jersey Supreme Court, most individual teams voted to suspend play rather than admit girls. Two thousand teams in New Jersey alone refused to play if they had to open their dugouts to girls.[40] The New Jersey Assembly was presented with fifty thousand signatures on a petition supporting a proposed law to keep girls off diamonds, but after an emotional debate the bill lost by three votes.[41] The *New York Times Magazine* emphasized that the conflict was about gender as much as baseball: "The challenge [of girls gaining access to baseball] is not merely to male supremacy but to an established institution in American life [Little League]."[42] Sportswriter Frank Deford, trying to explain the emotional outcry, wrote that "the real dispute is social"; girls were not just "monkeying with men's baseball but with men's childhood."[43]

The legal precedent of the New Jersey decision was strong, but it was not binding on courts outside New Jersey. Despite the precedent, perhaps because of the social reaction to it, the third major baseball decision, released two months later, disagreed with the New Jersey decision. The U.S. District Court of Rhode Island decided in 1974 that the Darlington Little League could exclude ten-year-old Allison "Pookie" Fortin from the league because of her gender.[44] Pookie had sued on equal protection grounds, and the court reached a decision quickly. The league was a state actor, it ruled, because public fields were designed for the league and controlled by the league. The court added, however, that the league was correct: Baseball was a contact sport, and girls would get hurt playing with boys. The court noted the *Magill* decision's dicta and quoted it approvingly; safety, the court said, was a legitimate reason for the gender-based classification.[45] This district court was willing to ignore its New Jersey counterpart (which had no binding value as precedence) and to rely on the legally useless dicta of an earlier case to prop up a more socially popular decision.

On appeal, however, the U.S. Court of Appeals First Circuit overruled the district court. Ironically, after the lower court decision in 1974, Congress had amended the federal charter for Little League Baseball, striking the words *boys* and *manhood* and inserting *young people.* Little League Baseball had given up the fight and admitted girls.[46] The Darlington Little League, however, refused to surrender. It also refused to assure the court that the league would admit girls despite the shift in the national organization's position. Hence, the First Circuit heard the appeal and ruled in favor of Pookie Fortin.

Unlike the lower court, the First Circuit dedicated much of the written decision to describing the trial's testimony and explaining which evidence was most compelling and why. The debate was strikingly similar to the *Magill* case and the New Jersey *NOW* decision. Darlington argued that baseball was too dangerous for girls. The court summarized the evidence from both sides. Pookie's father, a physician, testified that his daughter was physically fit and capable of playing the game, and another expert, a pediatrician, testified that girls and boys from the age of eight to twelve were physically similar, although girls were often bigger and stronger at that point. Another expert, a radiologist, presented evidence that girls' bones were no different from boys' and that structurally no skeletal conditions suggested that girls were more prone to injury. Darlington's expert witness, an orthopedist at Brown University who worked overwhelmingly with male athletes and had never actually seen girls play baseball, testified to the contrary. He believed, like many in society, that girls could not throw overhand, that girls' bones were more likely to be damaged by exercise, and that girls' pelvises made their gait unstable. The court condemned Darlington's expert, noting that the doctor's opinions "rested mostly on the observation that girls, being more sedentary, were likely to be in poorer condition than boys." The court also questioned whether the doctor's testimony was based on scientific study or his own personal views, which, he apparently admitted, included that "it was the normal activity of a young lady to keep off baseball fields and play with dolls." After examining Darlington's expert's testimony, the First Circuit questioned the lower court's decision to ignore the plaintiff's experts, whom the First Circuit had found compelling. The First Circuit also noted that girls were playing baseball with the blessing of Congress and their parents—neither of whom would deliberately endanger American girls. Finally, because Darlington allowed physically disabled boys to play, the court determined that the physical dangers of playing in the league were minimal.[47]

After dismissing the physical safety arguments, the court of appeals also dismissed Darlington's other justifications for excluding girls. Darlington claimed to be concerned that the presence of girls would detract from the quality of the game and from training boys with a future in baseball. At the same time, Darlington feared that if girls played, then boys would quit. Further, if girls did play (presuming enough boys stayed to field a team) they would get hurt, and they and the male coaches would be embarrassed should first aid be necessary. Finally, apparently believing Pookie was a bizarre aberration from the typical American girl, Darlington suggested that girls really wanted to play with other girls and not boys. The court, citing the New Jersey decision with approval, rejected all of these arguments as being "archaic and overbroad generalizations" and devoted less than a paragraph to dismissing them.[48]

The last major baseball decision came less than a year later, in 1976. The earlier decisions opened Little League and youth baseball to girls, but the final one opened the door for girls to play on high school boys' teams. Jo Ann Carnes was a high school senior in Wartburg, Tennessee, who tried out and was selected for her school's baseball team. The Tennessee Secondary School Athletic Association (TSSAA), however, told the school that she could not play because TSSAA regulations stated that baseball was a contact sport and hence coed teams were not allowed. Carnes, just like the girls before her, filed suit, claiming that her equal protection rights had been violated.[49]

The TSSAA argued that it had enacted the rule excluding girls for two reasons: to protect females from the physical dangers of contact and to protect female sports programs from male intrusion. The federal district court was unimpressed with the relationship between the rule and the rationales. The judge found the first justification to be overbroad, noting that some girls were likely to be physically capable of playing and emphasizing that even Carnes's coach believed she was a competent player. The judge also doubted that baseball really was a contact sport, given that collisions were infrequent and often incidental or accidental, but failed to make a legal ruling specifically on the issue of contact. With regard to the TSSAA's claim to be protecting female teams, the judge dismissed that assertion by noting that no female baseball teams existed for males to take over. Carnes, the court asserted, either played baseball with the boys or not at all. Not playing, the court believed, was a violation of the equal protection clause of the Constitution, and Carnes was allowed back on the team.[50]

These five decisions, two opposing coed baseball and three supporting it, have certain similarities. The courts that would continue to exclude girls from baseball were convinced that baseball was a contact sport and that girls would somehow be injured playing the game. When the enforcement regulations of Title IX created an arbitrary line between contact and noncontact sports, baseball was not included as a definitive contact sport. For those who wanted to keep baseball masculine, however, proving that the sport involved contact was important to their case. Ultimately under the Fourteenth Amendment, whether or not baseball was a contact sport was irrelevant. At this early stage of litigation no one was quite sure of the significance of the legal status of a sport, contact or noncontact, so it became a social, if not legal, distinction. For many in society, however, declaring baseball a contact sport also emphasized the American pastime's tradition of manliness.

Cultural Identity, Baseball, and Gender

The fight over baseball was fought on multiple fronts in the courtroom and in the arena of public opinion. Regardless of the location of the skirmish, though, the arguments were similar. No one who wanted to keep baseball a masculine institution suggested that girls be excluded for any reason except that they were not boys.

The underlying position of supporters of all-male baseball was that baseball was a contact sport, which meant that girls could be excluded because they would be hurt playing the game. Although the legal definition of baseball as a contact sport was important in arguing their case in court, emphasizing that the leagues only wanted to protect frail young females from the risks of a physically dangerous game was important as well in trying to sway public opinion. To that end, defendants argued that girls did not have the right bone structure to play safely and further that breast cancer would result from any contact with their chests. For these arguments the defendants relied, although often unsuccessfully, on old medical myths and unsubstantiated medical opinions. Some in the public and the courts, however, accepted the tenets. Little League manager and sociologist David Q. Voight wrote in 1974 that although his teams never had any female players, he would have accepted them if they wanted to play. The league president worried, however, that if girls played the league would "get sued if they [female players] get breast cancer from getting tagged out on the boobs."[51] Further, New Jersey State Assemblyman Christopher Jackman introduced the bill to keep girls off baseball diamonds so they would not get "hurt in their vital parts."[52]

Little League's contention that baseball was a dangerous contact sport was ironic, however, because its own 1967 study determined that Little League players, if one defined injury as harm sufficient to warrant medical attention, had an injury rate of 1.96 percent. Creighton Hale, the

Little League executive who testified from 1973 onward that girls were too frail to play, had characterized the injury rate in 1967 as "low."[53]

Youth league officials, however, did not seem nearly as anxious about collisions between players as about potential contact between female players and their male coaches. A major concern often seemed to be how a female player should be congratulated for a good play. Apparently, patting a boy on the buttocks was the most traditional manner of letting him know he had done well, and coaches and players worried about what to do with female players. One coach in New Jersey lamented to his star player, who happened to be a girl, "I can't even pat you on the back side."[54] A twelve-year-old boy told of conflicted feelings after a female teammate hit a home run. He wanted to pat her on her rear, but, he said, "I didn't want her to think I was getting fresh," so he patted her shoulder instead.[55] Creighton Hale, who had a Ph.D. in physical education in addition to being a Little League executive, argued that the league must exclude girls because "it just wouldn't be proper for coaches to pat girls on the rear end the way they naturally do boys. And suppose a girl gets hurt on the legs? Why that's not going to go over—some grown man rubbing a little girl's leg."[56] If girls played, the league reasoned, they would get hurt, and everyone would be embarrassed if a man (because presumably only men would want to coach baseball) gave first aid to a girl. In fact, when New Jersey's Little League program in Union accepted girls it did so with a caveat: If a girl was on the field, her parent or guardian must be in the stands so if she was injured, "Coaches [would] not have to suffer the 'embarrassment' of unbuttoning a girl's uniform."[57]

In case physiological arguments failed to work, opponents of coed baseball relied both on psychological and organizational arguments. When Dr. Joyce Brothers, a popular psychologist of the era, argued that boys and girls required homosocial activity to develop islands of privateness and become well-adjusted adults, Little League Baseball cheered and quickly incorporated her theory into their arguments.[58] Along those same lines, youth baseball suggested that if girls were allowed to play on all-boy baseball squads, the entire system of girls' sport would collapse. Thus a few particularly athletic girls would get to play, but average, presumably nonathletic, girls would have no outlet. Others outside the leagues agreed. Dr. Melvin L. Thornton, for example, argued that girls should participate in more endurance-building forms of exercise to improve their health. Baseball, he believed, did not provide enough exercise. He never suggested disbanding youth baseball, so either he did not care about boys' health or he assumed that boys who played baseball engaged in other, more strenuous activities. Further, Thornton feared that if communities saw a few girls in youth baseball, they would claim to have programs adequate to meet girls' physical needs. "There is," he suggested, "no game for the other 230 girls in town who cannot swing a bat as smoothly as Dorothy Dombrowski or who, unlike Ellen Vetromile, don't care about being as good as or better than the boys down the block."[59] Thornton seemed to assume that only athletically talented girls would want or be allowed to play baseball.

Despite youth baseball's self-righteous assertion that it protected little girls from the rigors of the game—and its contention that girls' sports in general would collapse if a few girls played—it was abundantly clear that actual fears concerned how girls' presence would affect boys who played the game, the manly aspect of baseball, and the future of the game itself. Many seemed to believe that somehow the experience of male players would be diminished. After thirteen-year-old Yvonne Burch was removed from a Babe Ruth League team in North Carolina because the national organization threatened to revoke the local league's charter, the league president said, "It was a matter of depriving either Yvonne or two hundred boys."[60] The fact that Yvonne represented countless girls already being deprived seemed never to have occurred to the man. In the converse, a vice president of a New Jersey little league system said, "Most of us didn't want the girls playing but we figured rather than penalize five hundred or so boys by not having any baseball at all, we would let girls play."[61]

The leagues and many of the public seemed to believe that having girls on teams would diminish the quality of the coaching for male players, who had a better chance of playing longer and, at least theoretically, professionally. The implication was that a future Joe DiMaggio might not get the coaching he needed in Little League because the coach was busy working with the boy's sister, who would never play pro ball and probably would not even continue playing into high school. One manager claimed that coaching girls was a "waste of time" because when they got older they would quit playing to do, presumably, "girl-things."[62] The arguments leagues made, that girls were too physically frail to play or that teaching them the game was pointless because they would never play professionally, seemed particularly illogical in light of the fact that many leagues, including Darlington, allowed physically handicapped boys to play.

Another concern of Little League Baseball officials was the impact that admitting girls to the game would have on male volunteers. Accounts in the *New York Times* from 1973 to 1978 repeatedly referred to Little League's fears that volunteer coaches and administrators would quit because they did not want to work with girls. Volunteers themselves were quoted as saying they did not want the government or the courts to tell them who they could or could not coach, and many thought their rights were being violated. A *New York Times* article suggested that after girls "muscled their way" into Little League baseball, "a lot of middle-aged men in windbreakers caught a glimpse of their future and didn't like what they saw."[63]

A major fear for youth baseball and for the men who ran the leagues was that the presence of girls would diminish the masculinity of the game and the masculine egos of boys who played. Robert Stirrat, a Little League Baseball vice president, argued that "baseball is traditionally a boy's game. To admit girls would certainly cripple the program."[64] If girls played, boys might quit, and that would be the end of America's pastime. A New Jersey Little League manager said, "I want girls to play ball, and I would have been glad to take an all-girl team in a separate division. What I'm afraid of is that if you have a girl who is good and plays more than some of the boys, it's bad for the boys. The kid's friends may get on him and say, 'Hey, how come a girl is playing more than you?'"[65] Another manager said, "I think in most instances men are afraid the girls are going to play better than their sons or compete better than boys in general."[66] Rather than risk jarring their sons' egos, many New Jersey teams chose not to play at all.

As violent as the reaction of many to the court's decisions, some people were shocked by the opposition to girls playing America's game. In New Jersey, Judge George Gelman, a former Little League manager, ordered the Ridgefield Boys Athletic Organization to allow an eleven-year-old female shortstop to play in 1974. When the counsel for Ridgefield announced that the league would fold first, Judge Gelman exclaimed from the bench, "I don't understand. What's the big deal?"[67] Frank Deford of *Sports Illustrated* openly mocked youth baseball's arguments against girls on the diamond, even describing Creighton Hale as "an otherwise rational man" so long as he was not talking about girls in baseball.[68] Gov. Brendan Thomas Byrne of New Jersey, whose state was at the center of much of the turmoil, voiced his support of "qualified" girls in baseball, adding "I know very few boys—including my own son—who would object to being beaten out by a better girl."[69] The Martha Griffith Little League Bill was introduced in March 1974 in the U.S. Congress to expand the Little League organizational charter to include all children, both boys and girls.[70] The bill eventually passed, indicating that the majority of the House of Representatives and the Senate either believed, or believed their constituents believed, that girls should have the chance to play ball.

Now, more than twenty-five years after the first case for girls to play was decided, change in the gender of baseball has remained slow. When Little League opened the door for girls, it emphasized that the change simply meant girls could try out. "The girls," said a league official, "would have to prove equal competency in baseball skills, physical endowments, and other attributes."[71] This statement set the tone with the inference that only an exceptional girl could play with boys, and indeed boys still vastly outnumber girls in youth baseball.[72] The game remains a macho one as well. As late as 1987, sociologists studied youth baseball in order to "describe and analyze how the sport makes men out of boys."[73] Only a handful of women have played college ball, and since the days of the AAGBL only one professional female team, the Silver Bullets, survived for any length of time or with any publicity.[74] Softball is more generally considered a girls' sport, and as Title IX and equal protection cases more clearly underline the prevailing philosophy of "separate but equal" with regard to sporting programs, softball is usually seen as baseball's female counterpart despite the significant differences between the two games.[75]

The struggle to encourage girls to play baseball was hotly contested in numerous jurisdictions because Americans are passionate about their national pastime. Some girls felt strongly about playing Babe Ruth's game, and other people held just as strongly that the Babe should be the only babe in baseball. Little League teams in New Jersey rebelled against the court orders and the national organization mandate for years.[76] Baseball spawned an astonishing number of lawsuits about whether girls could play the game. Twenty-two lawsuits were filed against the official national Little League Baseball Association; even more were filed about other youth and high school baseball leagues.[77] They arose because America's identity was very specifically and intentionally linked to baseball and to allow females access to America's game was to foreshadow female access to all aspects of American society. Not all of America was ready to change without a fight.

The baseball dispute was specifically linked to the historical moment of social change. The first lawsuits in the early 1970s came at the height of the feminist movement, immediately after the moment of liberal feminism's victory of Title IX and in the days when the equal rights amendment seemed inevitable. Not surprisingly, the National Organization of Women, founded to pressure government to enforce laws prohibiting gender discrimination, recognized the symbolism of girls invading the dugout and took an active role in the lawsuits. Baseball was America's sport, and females gaining access to baseball was representative of gaining access to other positions of power, prestige, and identity in American culture.

In some ways baseball was the riskiest sport to attack first. Although its status as a contact sport was clearly dubious, the legal void in which courts were forced to work, in conjunction with a society divided on the questions of girls in baseball and equality for women, generally gave a great deal of discretion to judges. Of these cases, two courts would have continued to exclude girls and, had it not been for the one overruled by a higher court, girls' access to the game might have been even slower. The pitched fever of battle, both in courtrooms of law and in public opinion, would not be matched in any other sport. But the fall of baseball as a male preserve did not mean other culturally significant sports capitulated without a fight.

3   *Football*

Although baseball has traditionally been America's pastime, football has been its rival in the affections of Americans, especially American males, since the 1960s. Like baseball, football evolved primarily in America and even more than baseball has grown in popularity with players and spectators alike thanks in large part to television. Unlike baseball, however, football is clearly a contact sport with emphasis on tackles and blocking, and the Title IX enforcement regulations list the game as one of the definitive contact sports exempt from Title IX.[1]

After baseball, football was the second sport subjected to court action. The first gender and football decision was published in 1974. The speed with which the lawsuits were filed after the enactment of Title IX suggests that football, like baseball, carried great symbolic importance in the United States. Americans somehow understand themselves to be uniquely defined by the games they claim to have invented—baseball and football. Football was fiercely and continuously contested because of its cultural significance as a game unique to America and because of its significance as the quintessential masculine American game.

Despite its role as a manly sport, however, some girls want to participate in the extensive youth leagues that exist for football, just as some want to play baseball. The courts, with the exception of the state of Texas, consistently opened the gridiron to girls, and yet the public continued to oppose their presence and manifested that opposition in the form of continued exclusion (disregarding judicial decisions in other parts of the country) and alleged discrimination during tryouts.

Unlike baseball, however, where courtroom battles over access to the sport ended after just two years, disagreement over girls' access to football spanned the years from 1974 to 1985, and the controversy over whether girls were really given a fair chance to make teams continued throughout the remainder of the twentieth century. Those who wanted to play football used three legal tools to try to gain access to the sport: Title IX, the equal protection clause, and state equal rights amendments. The result was two almost competing discourses between courts that would allow girls to play football and segments of the public that resisted judicial orders.

The History of the Game and Its Masculine Roots

The origins of American football contained the serious contact and physical exertion that would mark the game as a builder of men, and the sport's popularity grew rapidly. As early as the 1840s, men from Yale and Harvard colleges competed against one another in rivalries so fierce that the administrators of both schools suspended the intramural games during the Civil War. The contests resumed after the war (and enactment of the Fourteenth Amendment to the U.S. Constitution), and more Ivy League schools began participating. Most played a game similar to British soccer in which players were only allowed to kick the ball, but Harvard played a game that more resembled the modern game of rugby in which players were allowed to pick up the ball and run with it.[2] In 1874 the captain of Montreal's McGill University, whose team played a more advanced form of rugby, challenged the Harvard team to a three-game series. The Harvard team learned more rugby techniques, incorporated them into its game, and then challenged Yale to a match. In 1875 the first intercollegiate match of rugby was played in America. Its several thousand spectators were watching the inception of American football.[3] Each college had its own set of rules and its own mongrelization of soccer and rugby, a lack of common rules that frustrated players when they competed in intercollegiate matches.

American football formally began in the 1880s when representatives from Yale, Harvard, Princeton, and Columbia universities gathered to hammer out more consistent rules in an effort to standardize the game. Two rules differentiated American football from its British ancestors. First, play began with a snap backward to the quarterback, who could not rush forward; second, if the team with the ball had not advanced at least five yards, possession would switch to the defending team. Rules would change dramatically over the next hundred years (and they continue to evolve), but the snapped ball and deliberate change of possession essentialized the game. American college men loved it.[4]

Football grew rapidly in popularity, especially in the South, where fans envisioned the game as rewarding bravery and strategy despite the fact that it and its coaches were northern imports. Football was well-established at southern colleges by the 1890s.[5]

Not everyone, however, loved the game. Opposition to football was generated by both the lifestyle that some religious leaders perceived to surround it and by the physical dangers of the game itself. Opposition was especially virulent in southern churches. Evangelicals in the 1890s lobbied for football's demise, citing the violence that would later concern President Theodore Roosevelt and the sins they related to the game. Churches feared that students would succumb to the dangers of drinking and gambling associated with football and further claimed that even if a student or athlete could fight off the associated sins of the game, the contest was itself an enormous waste of time for players and fans alike. The church insisted that time could be better spent than in watching or playing this brutal game. By the Jazz Age of the 1920s, however, southern churches had given up on that particular fight. With new dangers of public nudity and growing alcohol consumption, football seemed a lesser evil.[6]

Southern churches were not alone in objecting to football. The sport was arguably more dangerous physically than its rugby and soccer counterparts, and contemporary press accounts deplored the violence on the field, especially the punching and kicking that accompanied tackles. In 1905, after nineteen deaths were attributed to tackle football, some sportswriters and university administrators called for the discontinuation of the game. President Roosevelt, who had long endorsed the strenuous life and embraced the notion of muscular Christianity, pressed for reforms to bring the violence to a level acceptable to the American public. The rules reform committee concluded that instituting the forward pass would open up the field and help disband the mass-group plays that caused the most injuries.[7]

The game, despite rule reforms that lowered the death rate, remained a violent contact or collision sport. A key component of football is the ability to knock the other player to the ground. Success favors size, strength, and speed—the bigger, the stronger, the faster, the better. It is a game suited for aggressive "manliness" and deemed a means of teaching young boys to become men.[8] As Robert F. Kennedy, U.S. attorney general in the early 1960s said, "Except for war, there is nothing in American life—nothing—which trains a boy better for life than football."[9]

As the twentieth century passed and women gained more rights and privileges, football remained the ultimate masculine preserve, a stronghold against changes in the structure of American society. "I may work for a woman," a man told sports studies scholar Michael Messner, "a woman may even be my boss, but I'll be damned if she can take a hit from [NFL Hall of Fame Member] Ronnie Lott."[10] Regardless of whether most people could safely absorb a tackle from an all-pro professional football player in the prime of his career, the sentiment indicated that many people, despite changes in American society, believed it critical to protect football and what they perceived to be its undiluted masculinity.

Legal Cases involving Girls' Access to Football

As in baseball, after the enactment of Title IX girls wanted to play football regardless of its masculine status, and they sued for the right to do so. The arguments used by those who wanted to exclude them were typically based on at least one of three positions: the girls would be hurt, girls' athletic programs would be hurt, and the game of football would be hurt. Because football is clearly more violent than baseball, safety arguments carried more weight, especially with the public, but some defendants had apparently learned from the lawsuits in baseball and shifted their arguments more to the issue of increasing athletic opportunities.

Although debates in "football cases" were similar to those with other sports, girls who wanted to play used slightly different legal positions. Most did not bother filing Title IX claims, even before enforcement regulations exempted football from the legislation in 1975, because their lawyers recognized that constitutional claims would provide better remedies. The public misperception of Title IX's power continued, as evidenced in 1983 when one school board argued that Title IX enforcement regulations forbid coeducational contact sports and again in 1985 when a girl argued that Title IX gave her the right to play contact sports.[11] Given that these lawsuits were filed after the enactment of Title IX, however, the legislation still seems to have contributed to girls' increased involvement in contact sport.

Football cases are legally distinctive because, first, equal protection clause claims about football were evaluated by two different tests, rational relationship and intermediate scrutiny (because the court cases dragged on so long); and, second, for the first time in sport and gender cases girls relied on the equal rights amendment (ERA) as enacted by their state constitutions. The results of ERA claims, however, were different in Texas than in the rest of America.

CLINTON V. NAGY: THE SAFETY ARGUMENT

The first football decision was published in 1974, the same year that Little League Baseball, Inc., capitulated and officially opened the league to girls. Brenda Clinton, a twelve-year-old who lived in Cleveland, told her mother in September 1974 that she wanted to play football. She then went to William Thomas, coach of the Ninety-seventh Street Bulldogs, and asked for an opportunity to play on his team, which was licensed by the city as part of the Cleveland Browns Muny Football Association.

Neither Brenda's mother nor her coach objected to her playing with the Bulldogs, and at the end of the month her mother filled out the necessary forms required of all league participants. Although Brenda suited up to play on Saturday, September 28, 1974, the director of the Bulldogs' division refused to let the coach put her in the game because she was female. In mid-October, at the request of the Muny League director, Brenda's mother signed a waiver absolving the city, the league, and anyone associated with Cleveland Muny football of all liability—a waiver that no boys were required to sign. Although the director told Brenda's mother that the girl would be allowed to play after the waiver was signed, the day before the next game he announced that she could not play because "that was the law."[12] He said that the league had based its rules on Ohio High School Athletic Association rules, which said that "boys' teams must be composed of boys only, in all contact sports."[13] Brenda, through her mother, filed a lawsuit based on the equal protection clause of the Fourteenth Amendment, seeking permission to play in the team's final two games of the season.

To discriminate on the basis of gender when this case was decided in 1974, the league, a state actor because it was organized by the city of Cleveland's Division of Recreation, needed only to establish that its classification bore a rational relationship to a legitimate objective.[14] The league argued that its gender-based classification was rationally related to its legitimate interest in providing for the safety and welfare of females. The league claimed to have medical experts who would testify that boys, even by the age of ten, were bigger, faster, and stronger than girls of the same age.[15]

Judge Thomas D. Lambros, the federal district court judge who ruled, was skeptical of the paternalistic safety claim because the league never argued that Brenda as an individual was in any greater danger from the game than her male teammates. Lambros was unwilling to ban Brenda, the individual, from a game because the league and the state thought that girls, as a class, were in danger from the experience, although he was more than willing to admit that football was a "rough and sometimes brutal contest," one that was dangerous for all kids. Nevertheless, the judge concluded, football and other contact sports are played, and "those individuals who encourage young men to participate . . . seem to do so with a sincere belief that although the game is potentially dangerous, the rewards which will be reaped from participation . . . offset the potential dangers." Lambros noted that sports were intended to develop "strength of character, leadership qualities and to provide competitive situations." He believed those characteristics would help any young person, even though society had traditionally limited access to these events to young men. The district court found such distinctions between genders "irrational" and insisted that the focus needed to be on the capability of the individual and not the class. Brenda, the judge said, could suit up for the final games because applying a rule to girls as a class was irrational if the state's interest was the safety of its children. Lambros did not believe the state would care only about the safety of little girls and not that of little boys; therefore, he broadened the legitimate state interest to the safety of all children. The court cautioned, however, that the coach was under no obligation to play the girl if he believed her unqualified or lesser qualified than another player on the day of the game.[16]

The power of this case lies in early analysis of the safety argument for gender and contact sports. In 1974, after just a few baseball cases had been decided, the federal district court rejected the argument that football, the most violent of the major American sports, was too dangerous for girls to play. The court reached its decision under the least rigorous level of analysis ever used for discrimination cases under the Fourteenth Amendment and concluded that if the state's goal was to protect its children, prohibiting all girls from playing a sport would be irrational.

In 1974, when the case was argued and decided, little legal precedent existed. When Brenda Clinton offered legal precedents in which courts had allowed girls to join boys' tennis teams, the defendants were quick to distinguish between contact and noncontact sports. In fact, on appeal of one tennis case the Sixth Circuit Court of Appeals emphasized that the decision held only for noncontact sports because that was the only kind of sport challenged.[17] The court in the *Clinton* case, however, noted that the Sixth Circuit had not claimed that the Fourteenth Amendment did not allow girls to play contact sports but merely reserved the question for a case more directly on point. Football, the *Clinton* court concluded, was such a case, and the judge laid groundwork for any subsequent decisions regarding gender and football, or gender and contact sports, for those who wanted to argue that excluding girls from football for reasons of safety was irrational. Many in the public, however, were not convinced by the Ohio judge's decision and continued to oppose girls' participation, relying on methods of social control to keep them off the gridiron.

EQUAL RIGHTS AMENDMENT DECISIONS IN THE UNITED STATES

Football was the first contact sport in which girls used claims under the equal rights amendments to state constitutions. In 1972 the U.S. Senate passed the national ERA, and had two-thirds of the states ratified it the legislation would have been added to the federal constitution. The ERA, if adopted, was expected to render Title IX moot because its coverage was much broader than just education. Conventional wisdom in 1972 suggested that the national ERA would be ratified, which did not occur. Many states, however, did endorse it and went so far as to incorporate it, or a version of it, into their constitutions. During the mid-1970s, when the football ERA cases went to court, the equal rights amendment was on many minds as the national effort was waged for ratification.

The first ERA decision was published in 1975 in the state of Washington. Carol Darrin was a sixteen-year-old junior who stood 5'6" tall and weighed 170 pounds, and her sister, Delores, was a 5'9" fourteen-year-old freshman who weighed 212 pounds. The sisters wanted to play tackle football. During the fall of 1973 the coach had both fill out the required medical forms and allowed them to practice with their high school team. The coach later testified that the Darrin sisters held their own in practice with the boys and that he would have allowed both to play in games. Just before to the start of the season, however, the Washington Interscholastic Activities Association (WIAA) informed the coach that their rules prohibited coed tackle football teams. Through their parents, the girls sued the league under the auspices of the Washington state constitution's ERA.[18]

The Washington State Supreme Court heard the case in 1975 after a lower court had rejected the Darrin girls' claim. The WIAA claimed that it excluded girls in an effort to protect them from the rigors of the game and save the integrity of the girls' athletic program. The court summarily dismissed the second argument, calling it conjecture without evidence.[19] Instead, Justice Charles Horowitz, who wrote for the majority, considered the safety argument in light of the national ERA, which was adopted in 1972 and incorporated into the state constitution. The ERA stated "equality of rights and responsibility under the law shall not be denied or abridged on account of sex."[20] Although Horowitz allowed for the possibility of excluding individual girls who were "too weak, injury-prone or unskilled" to participate, the justice was annoyed that the WIAA only worried about the safety of girls. The Washington court, like the *Clinton* court in Ohio, emphasized that boys also risked physical injury in football but were still allowed to play the game. Horowitz seemed surprised that the WIAA allowed "small, slightly built young boys, prone to injury, to play football without proper training to prevent injury." The state supreme court, therefore, opened the gridiron to anyone qualified to play.[21]

Similarly, state courts in Pennsylvania and Massachusetts rejected attempts by their state legislators to prohibit coed sports in general and in football particularly because of their own state equal rights amendments. In 1975 the Supreme Court in Pennsylvania invalidated a clause in the Pennsylvania Interscholastic Athletic Association by-laws that prohibited any coeducational sporting events. The Pennsylvania attorney general had asked the court to invalidate the clause for noncontact sport, but it invalidated the clause entirely because the court ruled that the distinction between contact and noncontact sport was arbitrary. Only the existence of separate teams for boys and girls in the same sport would be an acceptable reason to gender segregate sports under the state's equal rights amendment.[22] The Supreme Judicial Court in Massachusetts also rejected a bill that would have excluded girls from football and wrestling teams. Like the Pennsylvania court and for the same reasons, the Massachusetts court found the provision to be a violation of the state's equal rights amendment.[23]

This series of decisions indicates the power of the equal rights amendment. The *Darrin* court in Washington directly addressed the distinction between the ERA and the equal protection clause. The Darrin girls had actually argued, in addition to their ERA claims, that their constitutional rights under the Fourteenth Amendment had been violated. Before examining the ERA claim the Washington Supreme Court summarized the case law surrounding equal protection arguments and acknowledged that the appropriate test for gender-based classifications was unclear at the time. The court noted, however, that many cases involving girls and sport had invalidated gender classifications under the rational relation test. But the court also recognized that, using the same test, other courts had upheld those gender classifications. Because none of the other cases had occurred in Washington and the precedents conflicted, the court chose to examine the state constitution–based claim and rest its decision on those grounds, avoiding the entire equal protection clause debate.[24]

Finally, in his majority decision Justice Horowitz acknowledged that although the Darrins' right to play football under the Fourteenth Amendment of the U.S. Constitution might be questionable, their right was absolute under the ERA in lieu of conflicting precedents in other jurisdictions and the lack of rigor of the rational relation test. Because, on the surface, the language of the ERA seemed to be repeating that of the equal protection clause, the court concluded that the intent of the ERA was to outlaw any interpretation of the Fourteenth Amendment that allowed exceptions to the prohibition of gender discrimination. Thus the Washington Supreme Court maintained that a wholesale prohibition against all females participating in an activity violated the ERA.[25]

Had the federal ERA been ratified by the required number of states, it rather than the Fourteenth Amendment and Title IX would likely have been the power behind changing women's sports. Its failure to pass nationally, however, left gaps in the protection of females' rights to athletic opportunities, depending on how tolerant a judge was of a league's justification of gender discrimination under the Fourteenth Amendment.

Although the power of the ERA seemed clear, not every member of the judiciary was comfortable with that power. The Washington Supreme Court clearly outlined the power of the ERA in its unanimous *Darrin* decision, but even some jurists felt a certain ambivalence about the power they were investing in the ERA. One justice wrote a concurrence in which he agreed with the outcome of the case but added a point the majority had neglected, highlighting the conflict between societal pressures to exclude girls from football and legal realities of the ERA that required inclusion. The concurring justice wrote that although he agreed, "with some qualms," with the majority in the result, he questioned whether the "people in enacting the ERA fully contemplated and appreciated the result here reached."[26] He believed that the people who voted the ERA into law never imagined or intended for the law to give equal access to football. At least two judges in the state of Texas might have agreed with that sentiment, but they never allowed gender and football to go to trial.

THE ERA IN TEXAS

Two decisions were published in the state of Texas during the 1970s that radically differed from every other ERA-based decision in football and every other published decision about football in general. In 1976 Renota Gaudet asked for an injunction from the Texas courts that would allow her to play junior (pee-wee) football. A lower court gave her that injunction on the grounds that the Texas Constitution's equal rights amendment provided that "equality under the law shall not be denied or abridged because of sex, race, color, creed, or national origin."[27] The lower court said she could play junior football until she reached puberty, but the court of appeals overruled the lower court. The Texas Court of Appeals concluded that although the league was a nonprofit corporation licensed by the state and its games and practices were held on either school grounds or in city parks, no state action existed because the local government was not sufficiently involved with the league. Thus the Texas Constitution did not apply to the junior football league.[28]

Three years later Kathy Lincoln encountered a similar situation. The eight-year-old had played tackle football along with three other girls in a boys' pee-wee league for one season. She came through this experience unscathed, and her coach described her as an average player. In the off-season the league decided it would limit teams to one gender and create a parallel girls' division. After only eight signed up, however, the league canceled the girls' schedule but refused to let Kathy or the other girls play in the boys' division. She sued under the Texas equal rights amendment, just as Renota had and with similar results. A court of appeals relied on the earlier *Gaudet* decision and concluded that no state action existed and Kathy had no grounds to sue.[29]

Texas's decisions were contrary to those made by every other court in America looking at football and gender; they were also out of line with most courts examining contact sports and gender. Although no contact sport cases had yet been decided in Texas, courts nationwide had already opened baseball to girls under the Fourteenth Amendment, and several other sports, including basketball and soccer, had been contested by 1979 when the *Lincoln* case was dismissed. Youth teams are often operated by private associations, but courts have frequently concluded that these athletic associations act in the stead of the state. The state, the courts have held, has an interest in the education of its children. Because athletics are part of that education, the reasoning holds, the athletic association acts on behalf of the state. Relatively few courts in dealing with gender and contact sport issues have found a lack of governmental involvement in youth sports leagues.[30] Little League Baseball, Inc., for example, was held to be a state actor because recruiting was done in schools and games were played in public parks without the league paying more than a nominal fee for their usage.[31] Yet neither Texas decision cited any precedents regarding state action and youth leagues, leaving it unclear whether they were swayed by legal precedents and analysis or by the serious opposition in the state of Texas to girls playing football.

Football is generally thought to have played an important role in shaping masculinity in America, but in Texas the sport seems to have had a singular impact not just in making men but especially in making "manly" men. Football is something of a religion in Texas, and people revere their football teams at every level. The Dallas Cowboys, a professional team, were so popular throughout the 1970s that they were referred to as "America's team." At Texas A&M University the football team has no formal cheerleaders. Freshman arrive at school a week before the start of the fall semester to learn school cheers; at games, leaders from the field signal the next cheer to the crowd, so choreographed cheers reverberate from all the students and alumni in the stands. If the football team loses, students stay after the game to practice cheering because, surely, the loss can be blamed on their lack of enthusiasm. Schoolboy football is just as popular. A winning team is often more important to a high school than its students' SAT scores, and the travel budget for a football team might exceed the entire budget of the English department.[32] Football mattered then and now in Texas, and it mattered especially as a masculine game. Thus it was important to keep it masculine. In refusing to hear girls' ERA claims, Texas courts, at least inadvertently, did their part to limit the game to men and boys, regardless of what rest of the nation was doing.

FOOTBALL AND INTERMEDIATE SCRUTINY

Despite Texas's reluctance to open the gridiron to girls, future courts would be significantly less willing to exclude them. The next cases involving girls and football were published in the mid-1980s and arose, ironically, after the U.S. Supreme Court had ratcheted up the Equal Protection test for gender discrimination to intermediate scrutiny. Now the state actor, instead of proving a rational relationship, needed to establish that gender classification was substantially related to an important objective. Yet despite these stricter standards and the precedent of the *Clinton* case, the issue of gender and football again went to court.

The next case was published in 1983 when Nichole Force was a thirteen-year-old in Missouri who wanted to play on her eighth-grade football team.[33] Her school district offered her the opportunity to play girls' volleyball, but Nichole had grown up playing football with two older brothers, and that was the sport she wanted to play. The school had a no-cut policy, so, usually, no student was refused the opportunity at least to practice with the team. Before the season started, Nichole's mother, Renee, contacted the football coach to ask if he had a problem with Nichole participating. If the administration approved, he replied, so did he. School administrators told Nichole's mother to talk to the school board. After much debate, the board told her that although they all agreed Nichole would be a good football player, if they let her play they would have to let other girls play. That would be the end of the girls' volleyball team because boys, consequently, would have to be allowed to play volleyball.

Furthermore, the board was concerned with issues of safety and with such administrative complexities as locker rooms. Some board members even believed that Title IX prohibited coeducational contact sport teams. Therefore, the board unanimously rejected Nichole's request, and she sued, claiming that her equal protection rights had been violated.[34]

The *Force* case was the first time a federal district court hearing a gender and contact sports case relied on the intermediate level of scrutiny for equal protection violations. The U.S. Supreme Court had announced the new test in 1979 and reiterated it in several 1981 decisions, but no gender and contact sports cases were published between 1981 and the *Force* decision in 1983. Under the new test, the district had to prove that the gender classification was substantially related to important government objectives instead of rationally related to reasonable objectives. The school board argued that it had four important objectives: first, to maximize athletic opportunities for all students; second, to keep participants safe; third, to comply with Title IX, which the board said forbid coeducational contact sports; and, fourth, to comply with Missouri State High School Activities Association (MSHSAA) rules, which prohibited coed football. The district court summarily rejected the last two arguments, noting that Title IX regulations on contact sports rendered Title IX neutral and MSHSAA regulations could not transcend the U.S. Constitution.[35]

U.S. District Court Judge Ross T. Roberts agreed that the school board's first two objectives, maximizing athletic opportunities and keeping students safe, were important, but he questioned whether gender segregation was substantially related to attaining those goals. Although Roberts was initially confused by the idea that allowing girls to play football would actually limit their athletic opportunities, he was willing to consider the district's complicated argument. This was composed of three claims. First, males as a class are better athletes than females as a class, and the best way to maximize opportunities for both would be separate leagues. Second, if Nichole played football, then any student must be allowed to play any sport. And, third, the best female athletes would play football, while boys not interested in playing football would take over the volleyball team, and thus overall female participation (at least in games because of the no-cut policy) would dwindle. Judge Roberts said that although he did not completely accept the first claim, some evidence suggested the possibility that boys after puberty are physically bigger, stronger, and faster. He found, however, no evidence that girls would defect to football and added that if boys in fact are better athletes, few girls would want to play football. The problem would be self-correcting. The court also suggested that if large numbers of girls wanted to play football and large numbers of boys wanted to play volleyball, the district should consider forming girls' football and boys' volleyball teams. Although the judge felt that separate leagues were acceptable, he believed that designating certain sports as gender-specific was wrong. "Volleyball," he observed, "is *not* football; and baseball is *not* hockey; and swimming is *not* tennis."[36]

Safety, the court conceded, was also an important state objective, but the judge heard no evidence that Nichole as an individual was more likely to be injured playing football than the average eighth-grade boy. Judge Roberts found that a prophylactic gender-based classification was unacceptable for reaching the goal of student safety because the school let any male, regardless of size, speed, and physical build, play football while prohibiting all girls from playing. The judge added that his decision was consistent with almost every other gender and sport case that dealt with issues of safety. Like the judge in the *Clinton* case in Ohio, he emphasized that his decision did not entitle Nichole to a starting position (which she had not asked for) but merely a chance to compete. Roberts noted that Nichole sought "simply a chance, like her male counterparts, to display . . . [her football] abilities. She ask[ed], in short, only the right to try." The judge did not suggest that there was a constitutional right to try, but he did conclude that "the idea that one should be allowed to try—to succeed or fail as one's abilities and fortunes may dictate, but in the process at least to profit by those things which are learned in the trying—is a concept deeply ingrained in our way of thinking; and it should indeed require a 'substantial' justification to deny that privilege to someone simply because she is a female rather than a male." He found no such justification in this case.[37]

The final decision involving girls' access to football was published in 1985. Jacqueline Lantz, a sixteen-year-old junior in Yonkers, New York, wanted to play for her high school team. She claimed that her Title IX rights and her Fourteenth Amendment rights were violated by a New York State Board of Regents rule that prohibited coed football, basketball, boxing, ice hockey, rugby, and wrestling. The federal district court rejected the Title IX argument, ruling that it was unclear if Title IX applied to any nonfederally funded division and, further, that Title IX, as the court in *Force* ruled, was neutral with regard to contact sports, but it considered her equal protection clause claims.[38]

Unlike the 1983 *Force* case in Missouri, the regents of New York rested their arguments solely on the issue of safety, presenting evidence that senior high boys are bigger, stronger, and faster than senior high girls. The state argued that it was irrelevant if a few girls are more physically prepared to play football than a few boys because the rule was based on more general data and designed to protect the general population and not to deal with exceptions. The New York court, like the *Force* court of two years before, applied the intermediate level of scrutiny and agreed that the safety of girls was an important objective, but it rejected the idea that the classification was reasonably related to the goal. This court scoffed at the notion that a rule based on broad generalities really protected girls and suggested the rules instead assumed girls had an "inherent handicap or [were] innately inferior to boys."[39]

The struggle over access to football was notable for the consistency of the legal rhetoric and the courts' decisions. Every court outside the state of Texas consistently ruled under the equal protection clause and state equal rights amendments that girls had a right to try out for youth football teams. This legal discourse rejected arguments that girls' participation would cause them injury or devastate the separate girls' athletic program, but all the courts also emphasized that their decisions were only to let girls have the same opportunity to try out and participate as boys did. Each judgment specifically stated that it did not expect the ruling to give a girl a starting position or even game time—just a chance to try.

Although the legal precedent was clear, the dispute over girls and football went to court eight times in five states over eleven years because many Americans were not ready to accept girls playing the most dramatically masculine of manly sports. Astonishingly, two of the gender and football cases occurred after the Supreme Court made it more difficult to discriminate on the basis of gender and after a district court had allowed girls on the football field under an older, more lenient standard of evaluating gender discrimination.

So great was the opposition to girls playing football that the battle dragged on in multiple jurisdictions. The legal discourse prevailed, however, and state after state opened high school football to those girls who wanted to try out. Eventually, in 1993 even Texas officially opened football to girls. Many in the public, however, continued to oppose girls' presence in football, opposition that was reflected in media representations of those who did play. As a result, lawsuits involving gender and football did not stop once girls gained the right to try out.

Acceptance of and Opportunity for Girls in Football

Although cultural pride in baseball seems to stem from its Americaness, cultural pride in football seems linked to the sport's manly qualities—and that manliness seems connected to the idealized violence of the game. Football is described with warlike images. Lineman battle over the line of scrimmage, and commentators refer to particularly tough and scrappy players as warriors. Wars, for Americans, are traditionally fought by men because they are assumed to be bigger, stronger, and tougher than women—the same qualities prized in a football player.[40] Although youth leagues in football legal cases often argued that they wanted to protect the integrity of girls' athletic programs, the perception of the public, as reflected in media accounts, suggested that the real concern was about protecting girls from the physical dangers of the sport and keeping them away from the combatlike violence of the game. As a result, regardless of the legal rhetoric many in the public were reluctant to accept girls on the gridiron. Contemporary accounts focused on safety and size, and although girls seemed to be getting the chance to try out like the courts had ordered, many claimed to face discrimination during the tryouts.

PUBLIC PERCEPTIONS OF FOOTBALL AND GIRLS' LAWSUITS

Media accounts of girls in football throughout the 1980s were captivated by the notion of petite girls trying to play, and stories were devoted to the girls' physical appearance and the risks they took in the sport. A contemporary media report of the *Force* decision focused on the safety aspect of the decision despite the fact that the bulk of the defendant's argument had been based on protecting girls' athletic opportunities. Nichole's size was reported—5'1" and 110 pounds—as was the length of her hair, which had recently been cut to fit under a helmet. Her mother was quoted as saying that although she knew of the physical risks on the football field, Nichole "should be allowed to take those risks if she [chose]," and that as a mother she was no more concerned about her daughter's safety than she had been about her son's when he played football.[41]

National media accounts of Jacqueline Lantz's story were also eager to mention her size—4'11" and 119 pounds—and equally careful to mention that she would not be allowed to play until after a thorough evaluation of her skills. Her coach was quoted as saying that with only three games left in the season, he was unsure if she would play but that he would "take it on a day-to-day basis and see what happens." The coach also reported that Jacqueline's male teammates were concerned less with her gender and more with the fact that she had not been practicing with them since August, and "that would bother them with anyone."[42] Jacqueline was not likely to be welcomed onto the team at that stage of the season, but she was reportedly still excited about winning the case because she felt it opened the door for other girls to play and hoped to play the next

year. Her chances were not good, however. The *New York Times* reported that school officials had found that her "performance in various sprints
and distance runs was not sufficient to allow her to begin contact drills."[43]
The clippings implied that although the law might allow girls to try out,
their diminutive size (which, newspapers implied, all girls shared) and
relative inexperience would keep them from making the team and certainly keep them from ever playing in a high school game.

Other football access issues were discussed in other newspapers. In
the summer of 1985, the same year Jacqueline Lantz went to court for a
chance to try out for her football team, Elizabeth Balsey announced in
New Jersey that she wanted to try out for her high school football team.
Although the *Balsey* decision was not published in court proceedings, the
media covered the case.[44] Like the other press reports covering girls' efforts to play football, Beth's size was always mentioned. As a 5'5", 125–
pound, fifteen-year-old sophomore, she wanted to try out as a wide receiver or a defensive back, but the coach turned her down because he did
not "want to see anyone injured." The school's athletic department supported his decision and added, "To admit girls to boys' sports defeats what
we're trying to do." The local newspaper that printed the quotation concluded that the district wanted to "promote girls' sports."[45] Beth, however, won her duel with the district in front of an administrative law
judge, and the district declined to appeal. The board decided to continue
its unwritten practice of not letting girls play on boys' teams and vice-
versa until the state made a general rule, but Beth was to be an exception.[46] The next year, 1986, a fifteen-year-old girl in Nebraska challenged
the Nebraska School Activities Association's ban on coed football. Newspaper accounts reported her size, 5'5" and 137 pounds, and her position,
guard. The town in which she wanted to play barely had enough students
to field a football team, and the girl was sure she would play. The local
athletic association capitulated without a court battle because its lawyers advised that the rule had been held unconstitutional.[47] Coverage of
these two cases, with emphasis on size and playing opportunities, indicated that safety remained the matter of greatest public concern, and the
diminutive female was the preeminent image they had of girls involved.

The media sometimes did not even feign objectivity when reporting
on girls playing football. In 1986 the *Los Angeles Times* ran an extensive
update on a girl who had played high school football two years earlier:
"Girls in Football; It Isn't Working Out; They Worry about Broken Bones
More Than Broken Fingernails, Not to Mention Coaches and Players with
Chips on Their Shoulders; Impressions from a Short Career; Jarring Hit
Helped Cyndi Bays Find Place Out of Football."[48] The centerpiece of the

article concerned a hit the girl took while fielding a punt, with the implication that had she known more about football she would have known to call a fair catch. The title of the piece was an indication that the *Los Angeles Times* was not keen on girls playing football, and the story that followed was an account of the young woman's "bad and real bad" memories of the experience. The article stressed that she never fit in with her male teammates and had contributed nothing to the team because she was not athletic enough to compete; even in practice, she rarely could catch the ball. The players explained that their lack of friendliness stemmed from antagonism toward her weakness as a player. Cyndi described her teammates as nonsupportive "jerks" whom she ignored after the season; she even claimed one of them had threatened during the season to beat her up. She also discussed how football changed her and made her more aggressive off the field—a trait that worried her and that she tried to lose after she quit playing. She suspected that aggressiveness made her unattractive to male classmates and had limited her social life while she was on the team, a point her best girlfriend confirmed while emphasizing that Cyndi had "grown out" of that aggressive, unattractive, tomboy behavior. The article noted that the football helmet had left her hair "matted and dirty," which, one must assume, lowered her dating value. The article also emphasized the danger of the game, describing the hits Cyndi took when she did occasionally play and the pain she recalled them inflicting. The piece concluded with a discussion of Cyndi being from a single-parent home and having practically no contact with her father, a man whom the newspaper claimed she missed desperately. The entire article reinforced the notion that football is physically dangerous for girls, that girls are not good athletes, that football makes girls less feminine and attractive, and that only girls with a history of family instability would want to play. It echoed the public discourse that football should remain a game for males only.

LAWSUITS OVER PARTICIPATION AND FAIR TRYOUTS

Judges who opened football to girls repeatedly emphasized that the Fourteenth Amendment only gave the girls the right to try out for a team; it made no guarantees about their right to play. Perhaps not surprisingly given the cultural opposition to girls on the gridiron, even after girls were allowed to try out they encountered problems with practice opportunities and the fairness of tryouts themselves. As a result, the litigation did not end with the court decisions allowing girls to try out for football.

One lawsuit highlighted the question of who was responsible for a girl's safety when she did qualify for a football team. In 1998 a girl on a football team in San Diego, California, sued for the opportunity to participate in contact drills in practice. Kymberly Ketchum was a senior with three years of high school football experience. She weighed 160 pounds and was a member of the offensive line, but the coach would not allow her to participate in contact drills at practice; as a result, she never had a chance to play in a varsity game. Kymberly had undergone arthroscopic surgery on a knee and could no longer match her 325–pound best squat-lift. In part because of the injury and her weakness, the coach believed that contact drills would put her in an "unsafe position." The local newspaper speculated that making that decision about safety was difficult for a coach but "had she blown out the same knee trying to block a defensive lineman who outweighed her by a hundred pounds, the school district might have been facing litigation of an entirely different nature." Kymberly filed a discrimination lawsuit, but the San Diego County judge dismissed the case because he felt player safety was a decision for the coach.[49]

As the San Diego court decision suggests, the question of when a coach is legitimately concerned about a female player's safety as a player and when a coach is paternalistically and patronizingly concerned about a female player's safety as a girl remains complicated. Coaches are generally in the best position to determine the quality, fitness, and capabilities of a potential player and are usually entrusted with deciding who should make the team and who should play in what circumstances. Coaches owe a duty of care to their athletes to protect their safety by providing medical treatment and teaching proper technique, and a few coaches have been held liable for breaching that duty.[50] Therefore, strong deference to the decisions of coaches seems reasonable, because very few have been held liable for risking their players' safety. On occasion, however, coaches have been charged with abusing their authority and making personnel decisions on the basis of factors other than the individual's talents and performance.[51] In these situations, courts are forced to balance the knowledge that the coach is the expert with the possibility that the coach may have discriminated on impermissible grounds. The American court system has had ample opportunity to balance these questions of fact throughout the history of discrimination and employment law and would likely do so in these kinds of cases.

To respond to such injustices, in 1999 the Fourth Circuit Court of Appeals created a new tool for girls to use in situations in which they perceive gender discrimination. Although almost every court in America has read the Title IX enforcement regulations to exclude contact sports from the legislation's jurisdiction, in 1999 the Fourth Circuit ruled that

Title IX did prohibit gender discrimination during a tryout for any team—including a contact sports team.[52]

Heather Sue Mercer had been the placekicker on her New York state high school football championship team. In the fall of 1994, as a freshman at Duke University, she was given a private tryout by the coaching staff and allowed to practice the rest of the season with the other kickers on the team. She was never allowed to practice with the team, however, or suit up for home games like other walk-on kickers, and she claimed that this was part of a pattern of gender discrimination she endured while ostensibly on the Duke football team. She maintained that when she asked to suit up for games, the head coach told her to sit in the stands with her boyfriend. She was allowed to play in the spring scrimmage of 1995 and kicked the winning field goal, after which she was told she had made the team for the next season. The Duke coaching staff even told the national media that she had made the team, but several weeks later the coach told her she had not made the team and would not be allowed to practice with them. After she asked why she could not attend summer practice with the team in 1995, she alleged that the coach asked her why she wanted to play football and why she did not want to be in beauty pageants instead.[53] She was officially cut from the team in the fall of 1996.

The next fall she sued, claiming that Title IX protected her from gender discrimination in educational settings. After a lower court dismissed the claim, relying on the precedent that said Title IX regulations exempted contact sports, the Fourth Circuit Court of Appeals ruled that Title IX did not force schools to let females try out for contact sports, but if they chose to allow females to do so, the school and its staff could not discriminate against them on the basis of gender. The decision does not claim that a court can run a football team, but it prohibits blatant discrimination and allows the question of whether gender discrimination occurred to be determined by a jury.[54] In October 2000, a jury awarded Mercer $2 million in punitive damages after concluding that the Duke football staff had discriminated against her because of her gender.[55] The decision suggests that although courts cannot and should not run sports teams, the legal system can be used to curb the most blatant abuses by coaches.

Concluding Thoughts on Football

The discourse of the legal system has been very clear: Girls and women have every right to try out for their school football teams under the equal protection clause and any state equal rights amendments. Popular opposition to girls in this masculine sport, however, has resulted in continued social opposition and in more legal cases involving the equity of the tryouts for football teams. As a result, court conflicts over football lasted far longer than those for any other sport, from the beginning of the contact sport battles in 1974 through 1999.

Football has had an extremely antagonistic relationship with Title IX proponents, with football proponents blaming Title IX for the budget and scholarship cutbacks that football suffered in the preceding twenty-five years. Although Title IX has never been used successfully by a girl to gain access to a team, the *Mercer v. Duke University* case was the first sign that Title IX might influence the gender of football teams. Title IX, aside from the *Mercer* decision, has had an affect on football, just as on every other sport, in that its enactment and ratification of the equal rights amendment seemed to inspire girls to demand their right to try out.

Football's unique status in American culture as a game that makes men, however, does complicate the issue of access. It is the only traditionally popular American sport that does not have an even remotely female counterpart of the sort baseball has in softball and boys' basketball has in girls' basketball.[56] Perhaps its isolated status stems in part from the fact that it is a game based upon violence, a trait in turn envisioned in America as a masculine attribute. Football is proud of its toughness, and creating a parallel female sport might undermine the basic masculine construction of the game. Because no parallel game exists, to give girls equal access to football almost always means letting them try out for the male team, subjecting them to physical dangers of playing with bigger, faster, stronger players and the possibility of gender discrimination and social disapproval.

The answer, some suggest, is to create and introduce female football, usually flag or touch. In 1977, however, a federal district court in Chicago concluded that touch football is not the same game as tackle football. A twelve-year-old girl had been refused permission to play in the local (boys') tackle league because the league offered a comparable girls' touch league. The court ruled that to offer a sport to one gender and not the other was a violation of the equal protection clause.[57] Yet despite this ruling, some schools are beginning to offer varsity flag football for high school girls as an alternative to varsity tackle football with the boys.[58] Women and girls do play both tackle and flag football. Like their male teammates, some are injured and some are injured severely, but it is not clear that the rate of injury is higher than for boys, and there is no record of a female dying as a result of playing tackle football.

Regardless of the clarity of the law, though, many communities in

America still try to exclude girls from football. After Texas opened grid-irons to girls, for example, the coach of the Odessa, Texas, Permian High School football powerhouse mused that "football is a very violent sport, and I don't know if there are any young ladies that are physically and mentally prepared for that."[59] As late as 1996 a church league refused to let two girls play in a youth-tackle football league because, the church league said, the sport was too dangerous for girls.[60] These attitudes demonstrate that although American courts may have opened football to girls, much of America remains opposed to putting girls on the gridiron.

4   *Basketball*

Basketball, like baseball and football, plays an important role in the broader American culture. It is the third major sport in most schools, the winter game for the athletically inclined. It is a game, like football, which rewards size and strength, elements that help emphasize masculinity and toughness. Although its rules forbid contact, punishing it through a system of fouls and penalties, interpretation and enforcement of the rules has created a game in which physical contact is a major component. As a result, under the enforcement regulations of Title IX, basketball, like football, is plainly, legally a contact sport and thus exempt from Title IX.[1]

Despite the legal exclusion of basketball from Title IX, however, the legislation still triggered a number of lawsuits involving school girls and their access to the game. Title IX was enacted in 1972, and three different baseball decisions and a football decision had already been published by August 1975 when the first basketball case appeared in print.[2] In June 1975 the Title IX enforcement regulations had been published, clearly excluding basketball from the protection of that legislation, yet some subsequent basketball cases would try to claim protection under Title IX. The law seems to have inspired "basketball suits," and when Title IX provided inadequate, the Fourteenth Amendment filled its legal gaps.

Published legal decisions fell essentially into two camps. One set was related to the rules of the sport and the idea that girls should have equal access to the same game as boys. Historically, women and girls played different versions with different rules that excluded any and all contact, required six players, and used only half the court. The right most girls sought by 1975 was the opportunity to play the same full-court game as their male classmates. They did not ask to join boys' teams; they wanted to play with other girls but by boys' rules. Another set of lawsuits, however, did involve access to boys' teams and resulted when either no girls' basketball team existed or when girls believed that boys played a higher-quality game to which they could also aspire.

Despite its legal weaknesses, Title IX seemed to have encouraged both categories of lawsuits; all arose after its 1972 enactment. Further, the sheer number of lawsuits and appeals suggests that "girls' rules" basketball is profoundly important to the identities of communities that support the game and consider full-court basketball as an exclusively masculine sport. Lawsuits aimed at creating coed teams (suits unrelated to the issue of rules) also met resistance from those who believed that because basketball is a contact sport, girls are not capable of playing safely with boys.

Full Court versus Six-on-Six

When James Naismith nailed up two peach baskets in 1891 and invented the game of basketball he did not outline different rules for different genders. Nonetheless, basketball split quickly into two games, one for males and one for females. It took almost eighty years, the women's liberation movement, the enactment of Title IX, the U.S. Constitution, and four federal court decisions before basketball players across America, regardless of gender, would play by essentially the same rules. Even though enforcement regulations exempted basketball from Title IX, almost every lawsuit filed or threatened in order to allow girls to play by the same rules as boys tried to name Title IX as a cause of action.

By 1891, just a year after basketball's invention, girls and women across America were enthusiastic participants. The popularity of the game for females was evident from the number of reported matches, but media accounts of the game were often critical of what they felt to be the excessive level of competition and physical exertion. Senda Berenson, the women's athletic director at Smith College, was concerned about rough play and negative publicity. Although at that time, for males as well as females, the rules of the game varied dramatically from location to location, Berenson was instrumental in changing the rules for females and making them more consistent across the country. By 1901 she had convinced Spalding Sporting Goods to publish the first basketball guide for women.[3]

The rules in that guide called for the court to be divided into three zones (front, center, and back-court), with six players on each team to be split evenly among the zones. Players were limited to one dribble (later changed to three) and forbidden to leave their zones. Contact was strictly prohibited. By contrast, basketball rules for boys allowed five players per team, and they could range the court with unlimited dribbles.[4] By 1936 girls' rules had further evolved so the court was divided in half, with three forwards (front-court players who could shoot) and three guards (back-court defensive players).[5]

Although girls' rules would continue to vary according to region, the common theme was six players instead of five, with most, if not all, limited to a certain area of the court. The rules were established to limit the physical exertion required by female basketball and keep contact to an absolute minimum, complying with the then-popular notion that too much vigorous exercise would harm girls.[6]

In the first half of this century, girls' rules basketball was practically the only way for most girls, especially high school–aged players, to play the game. Although some teams, most of them in semi-pro and industrial leagues, did play five-on-five boys' rules, the official governing bodies at all levels sanctioned the girls' six-on-six game.[7] As the years passed, however, the rules of girls' basketball continued to evolve. In 1966 the Division for Girls' and Women's Sports (DGWS) adopted the unlimited dribble. By 1969 the DGWS and the Amateur Athletic Union (AAU) agreed to approve the five-player game on a limited basis, and in 1971 it was formally adopted by the DGWS and the AAU.[8] A number of high school programs across the country also switched to the full-court five-player game, but others remained with the time-tested, and in some regions extremely popular, six-on-six version. Although most states and all the colleges and universities made the shift to the full-court game fairly quickly, in 1976 junior high- and high-school girls in five states—Tennessee, Iowa, Arkansas, Texas, and Oklahoma—still played six-on-six basketball.[9] Beginning in 1976, three girls in three of these states commenced lawsuits demanding that their state athletic unions open the full-court game to girls.

THE GIRLS' RULES BASKETBALL CASES

The lawsuits in this category were inspired by the 1972 enactment of Title IX prohibiting gender discrimination in educational settings. All of these lawsuits were waged against the governing bodies of public school athletic leagues in order to gain access to a game that male members of the league played. All of these cases tried to claim a right of action under Title IX despite the fact that enforcement regulations, announced in 1975 before any of the lawsuits were filed, specifically defined basketball as a contact sport and made it exempt from Title IX. Further, Title IX and its regulations made no mention or provision whatsoever for different rules for the two genders. For those girls living in a state that played girls' rules basketball but who wanted to play the same game as their brothers, Title IX offered no direct recourse. Yet many seemed to believe that Title IX was a useful tool and gave it the power in social imagination that it lacked in legal reality. Fortunately for the girls who wanted to play full-court basketball, their lawyers also filed lawsuits under the equal protection clause of the Fourteenth Amendment, which provided the protection that the public seemed to believe to be available from Title IX.

By the time the first case was published in 1976, the status of law concerning gender and sport was slowly assuming a clearer form while the status of gender and the equal protection clause was becoming more obscure. By 1976 most of the baseball cases had been decided (and in favor of the girls).[10] The first two football decisions allowing girls on the gridiron had also been published.[11] Although none of these cases provided binding precedent for judges deciding the half-court cases, they did suggest a trend that the Fourteenth Amendment allowed girls to play contact sports, even with boys. At the same time, the Supreme Court was reexamining how to determine the constitutionality of gender classifications under the equal protection clause.

Although other sport and gender cases had been evaluated under the rational relationship test (in which the classification must be shown to be rationally related to a legitimate governmental interest), in December 1976 the Supreme Court announced a new test for gender—intermediate scrutiny—which asked whether gender classification was substantially related to important governmental interests.[12] That single Supreme Court decision was not sufficient, however, to establish intermediate scrutiny as the definitive test for gender classifications, and therefore judges were often uncertain how to test gender classifications for rules in half-court cases.

The first girls' rules lawsuit to reach a verdict occurred in 1976 when Victoria Cape sued the Tennessee Secondary School Athletic Association (TSSAA), calling for access to full-court basketball.[13] Victoria was a 5'10" high school junior who had been a starting guard (back-court player) as a sophomore. The summer after her sophomore year she had gone to a basketball camp and played center on a five-on-five team. She loved being an offensive player and at the end of the summer went home and asked her coach to allow her to play forward (front-court player), but the coach wanted her to stay at guard. Victoria sued, challenging the rules that limited her to just offense or defense, on the grounds that her rights under

Title IX and the equal protection clause had been violated. Federal District Court Judge Robert L. Taylor summarily rejected the Title IX claim, however, on technical grounds. Title IX did not seem to grant an individual the right to bring suit.[14] Even if it did, Title IX had an extensive administrative procedure that Victoria had failed to exhaust before filing suit. Taylor, though, gave much more weight to her equal protection claims.

Judge Taylor relied on the traditional rational relation test to evaluate the case. To save girls' rules basketball the TSSAA needed to prove that its gender-based classification was reasonably related to a legitimate purpose. Victoria Cape, however, as the plaintiff, argued that she suffered from the TSSAA's distinction between boys' and girls' basketball. She asserted that she, unlike her male counterparts in Tennessee, was denied the full benefits of playing basketball because she was female. She could not participate in the offensive strategy or execution and claimed that she could not reach her full physical development because she only ran half the length of the court. She further maintained that it was virtually impossible for her, as a guard, to obtain an athletic scholarship to college because colleges preferred players who grew up playing full-court basketball. On the rare occasions schools did recruit half-court players, they usually signed forwards who could shoot. Victoria's witnesses included coaches who testified that the full-court game was not too strenuous for girls and who agreed that, as a guard, Victoria's limited knowledge of offense would greatly reduce her collegiate opportunities, even in Tennessee state schools. Pat Head, the University of Tennessee's women's basketball coach, testified that ten of the eleven Tennesseans on her team had played forward in high school. The TSSAA witnesses, however, testified that the full-court game was more—and according to some even too—strenuous for girls. Although Victoria's attorneys tried the progressive argument that not only were girls capable of more vigorous exercise but that their health required it, the TSSAA witnesses argued older stereotypes of female weakness and lack of athleticism. The TSSAA witnesses also expounded upon the aesthetics of the female game. For example, James Smiddy, a Tennessee high school girls' basketball coach, pronounced the "split-court game [to be] the 'prettiest thing about girls' basketball.'" Smiddy also argued that the game would be less interesting and less exciting if girls' played full-court.[15] No one, however, argued that the boys' game would be more exciting and interesting if switched to half-court, again emphasizing the implied greater athleticism of boys.

From all the testimony, Judge Taylor concluded that the state (as represented by the TSSAA) had five legitimate objectives in maintaining the separate girls' rules, and he addressed each objective and examined the rationality of gender segregation in meeting that goal in turn. First, the game was designed to protect weaker student athletes incapable of playing the full-court game. Although Taylor agreed the state had a legitimate interest in protecting the health of its young people, he concluded that assuming that all boys but no girls were strong enough to play the full-court game was irrational and overbroad. Second, the TSSAA claimed the game provided opportunity for more students to play. Although one more girl could start the game, Taylor noted, witnesses had testified that substitutions were more liberal and frequent in the boys' game. The judge refused to rule on how many youngsters played which game, commenting only that a gender classification for promoting participation was not reasonable because if one game allowed more students to participate, then the other game was not allowing as many students to play. Third, the state maintained that girls' rules allowed "awkward and clumsy" students to play defense only. Again, Taylor questioned the logic of concluding that Tennessee had no clumsy teenaged boys and a state full of clumsy girls, and he found the classification overbroad. Fourth, the TSSAA wanted to provide a "faster" and "more interesting" game for fans, and, fifth, it feared that changing the rules would reduce attendance rates. Taylor addressed goals four and five simultaneously, arguing that mere speculation about a decrease in fan interest was insufficient justification for a gender-based classification. To support his position he described the testimony of one coach who believed that girls' basketball in Tennessee was popular not because of its rules but because of "good coaches, good athletes, citizens in the State who support their young female athletes, and the considerable tradition of high quality, competitive, interscholastic girls' basketball."[16] Taylor completely rejected the TSSAA's argument that girls were just not good enough athletes to play full-court basketball.

After concluding that separate rules based on gender did not rationally relate to any goals the TSSAA articulated, Judge Taylor asked if Victoria Cape had actually suffered a legal injury. The TSSAA claimed that any injury she might have suffered by playing girls' rules was minimal and that court interference would be unnecessary. Taylor, after weighing the testimony of the coaches, concluded that Victoria had, in fact, suffered injuries that deserved judicial response. She was deprived of the health benefits the full-court game afforded boys, and, more important to him, she was likely to be deprived of college scholarships solely because her gender forced her to play by different rules. Therefore, Judge Taylor ordered the TSSAA to delete the six-on-six game from its official girls' rules.[17]

In 1977, after Judge Taylor's decision in Tennessee, Cheryl Lynn Jones, a junior guard in Oklahoma, sued the Oklahoma Secondary School Athletics Association (OSSAA) on the same grounds as Victoria Cape, and her lawyers' briefs relied heavily on the *Cape v. TSSAA* decision. Judge Ralph Thompson of the Western District of Oklahoma, however, came to a radically different decision than his Tennessee counterpart. The only point that Thompson and Taylor agreed upon was that Title IX did not protect the plaintiff. Both concluded that the language of Title IX did not provide individuals a clear right to sue and that even if individuals did have that right, they must have first explored administrative remedies. On every other point, however, the Oklahoma judge reached a different conclusion. Judge Thompson noted that Cheryl's basic argument was that she was being deprived of benefits from interscholastic competition available to Oklahoma boys. He also pointed out that she admitted having no constitutional right to play basketball, no right to complain that Oklahoma girls were treated differently than girls in other states, and no right to complain about the difference between guards and forwards. Therefore, Thompson concluded, Cheryl's complaint did not actually state a constitutional violation. He also believed her claims of having limited opportunities to play basketball beyond high school and being deprived of collegiate scholarship opportunities were insignificant. Cheryl, Thompson argued, was competing not with Oklahoma boys for those scholarships but with girls who, in Oklahoma high schools, all played by the same rules. Thompson encouraged Cheryl to learn to play forward to resolve her frustrations and lack of knowledge about offensive strategy and shooting skills.[18]

At the end of his decision Judge Thompson acknowledged that his reasoning differed from Judge Taylor's in *Cape* and quoted Taylor's comments about how the courts should not intervene in a matter where injury to the plaintiff is minimal. Thompson then said that Taylor was wrong, both with regard to the claims rising to the level of an equal protection violation and the injury being more than minimal. Because both courts were at an equal level (federal district courts), Taylor's decision in Tennessee could be persuasive for Thompson, but the decision was not binding. Thompson was not required to follow this legal precedent or the other sport and gender cases in baseball and football that suggested girls had a right to play contact sports under the equal protection clause. Thompson, though, did not find Taylor's or any other judge's reasoning persuasive, and he was, without binding legal precedent, able to rely on his own reading of the evidence and the arguments, a reading that could be influenced by his personal beliefs and swayed by the influence of a community deeply attached to half-court basketball.

At the conclusion of his decision, however, Thompson noted that girls' rules basketball might "well be out of step with other states' rules and may not be in the best interests of the high school girls who play basketball in Oklahoma," and those comments suggest that personally he was not a huge fan of separate rules for girls' and boys' basketball. But he believed that the issue did not rise to the level of a constitutional violation and that a policy decision should be made by the players, coaches, and administrators of the game and not by federal courts.[19]

Thompson's decision seemed to return girls' rules basketball to six-on-six. And the next month, when the Sixth Circuit of the U.S. Court of Appeals shared Thompson's opinion of Taylor's decision and overruled the *Cape* decision, it seemed unlikely that six-on-six basketball would end because of judicial intervention.

After losing in the district court to Victoria Cape, the Tennessee Secondary Athletic Association appealed. On October 3, 1977, the Sixth Circuit reversed the lower court decision, ruled in favor of the TSSAA, and ordered girls' rules reinstated. The appellate court's analysis, however, had nothing to do with Taylor's reasoning regarding the rational relationship of the classification and the TSSAA's objectives. The court noted that Victoria Cape had not sued as part of a class action and there was "no indication that the other members of her sex . . . share[d] in any way plaintiff's views. Nevertheless, she has succeeded in . . . impos[ing] her own personal notions as to how the game of basketball should be played not only on the high school which plaintiff attends, but upon the approximately 526 junior and senior high schools . . . in the State of Tennessee."[20]

The court then argued that because gender classifications were acceptable in separating boys' and girls' basketball leagues, gender must be a valid classification, and tailoring the rules of a game for different genders is not problematic under equal protection. Gender was especially appropriate for athletic activities, the court noted using a biological definition of the idea of gender, because of the "distinct differences in physical characteristics and capabilities between the sexes." Further, if no separation existed between leagues, girls would be driven out of basketball, presumably because of boys' superior athletic abilities. Finally, the court encouraged Cape to pursue change through the TSSAA itself.[21]

The appellate court's decision was interesting because of things the court failed to address and assumptions that underlined those omissions. The court never discussed Judge Taylor's conclusions that the TSSAA assumed girls as a class were too frail to play full-court basketball, but it expressed at least a similar assumption in repeated references to the "differences in physical characteristics and capabilities" of boys and girls. The

Court of Appeals did not need to address the issue of lost scholarships because there was no constitutional violation; whether an injury was minimal was irrelevant. Further, although the court never directly cited the *Jones* decision in Oklahoma (nor would it have been expected to because the *Jones* court was a district court), the Sixth Circuit did seem to have been aware of that decision. It voiced concern that one individual would change the game for all girls in the state. Moreover, 1,209 high school girls who played basketball in Oklahoma intervened (voluntarily joined the lawsuit) as defendants with the OSSAA because they wanted girls' rules maintained. Many others in Oklahoma also expressed solidarity with the OSSAA and the half-court game, so many that the *Jones* court rejected attempts by the Oklahoma High School Girls' Basketball Coaches Association and the Oklahoma Association of School Administrators to intervene on behalf of the defendants. The court decided that the OSSAA and the intervening girls adequately represented all of their interests.[22] The Sixth Circuit ignored the fact that all discrimination lawsuits brought by individuals affect the rules or status quo of an entire society, many of whom may support the rule. The American court system is not intended to protect the interests of the majority, but in this case that seemed to be a primary intention of the Sixth Circuit.

The Sixth Circuit decision in *Cape,* however, would be the highest court ever to address girls' rules basketball. One might have reasonably assumed that any future change in the game's rules would come, as the Sixth Circuit and Judge Thompson in Oklahoma had advised, from within the sport's administrative structure rather than from the courts. Some girls, however, were undeterred by the final decisions in *Jones* and *Cape.* They used the Fourteenth Amendment and refused to accept the courts' unanimous conclusions that Title IX would not give them access to the full-court game and continued to try to use the legislation as a legal tool. Even after the Department of Heath, Education and Welfare (which had propagated Title IX's enforcement regulations), after lobbying by members of Congress from Iowa, Tennessee, Arkansas, and Oklahoma, announced that the government had never intended Title IX to tell schools what basketball rules to use or ban six-on-six basketball, girls and their attorneys remained convinced it would help, underscoring yet again the power mistakenly being conferred on Title IX.[23]

The final, pivotal case involving girls' rules basketball was decided in 1977 when a fourteen-year-old basketball player in Arkansas, Diana Dodson, filed suit against the Arkansas Activities Association (AAA) to change the game to full court. The trial lasted for two years, and by 1979 only Iowa, Oklahoma, Tennessee, and Arkansas still had girls' rules basketball, Texas having voluntarily shifted to the full-court game. Federal District Court Judge Richard Arnold rendered his verdict in 1979 and ordered the AAA to open the full-court game to girls. Diana made the same claims as Victoria Cape in Tennessee and Cheryl Jones in Oklahoma, maintaining that her rights under Title IX and the equal protection clause were violated. Like the other courts and for the same reasons, Arnold flatly rejected her Title IX claim. He decided, however, that her equal protection rights had been violated. Relying primarily on the evidence of several female physical education professors, Arnold reached a series of conclusions. Girls did not get the full advantage of the game by playing half-court because they were deprived of the physical benefits of the full-court game and the challenge of learning offensive strategies. Girls were also hindered in their quest for basketball scholarships in a way that Arkansas boys were not.

The AAA argued that it had four objectives in maintaining girls' rules. First, more girls could play the half-court game; second, more scoring occurred in the half-court game, making it more exciting; third, the half-court game promoted agility by forcing girls to stop at the half-court line; and, fourth, the half-court game was a tradition. Judge Arnold noted that the first three reasons might well be true and legitimate, but they would also be true for boys. "Half-court may in fact be a better game," he stated. "But if it's better for the girls, it's better for the boys as well." He rejected the argument that tradition alone was a reasonable justification for the gender classification, describing the historical evolution of the girls' game and suggesting that its continued evolution would ultimately lead to the girls' half-court rules' extinction.[24]

Perhaps the most interesting component of this case was Arnold's observation that the AAA did not suggest girls were physically or psychologically incapable of playing the full-court game, adding that the evidence was overwhelmingly to the contrary.[25] Thus, because the AAA relied only on tradition as a reason for the classification, Arnold could distinguish this case from *Jones* and the *Cape* appeal. But Judge Arnold went even further. He "respectfully" disagreed with the two other courts, stating that "their reasoning seems, with deference, unpersuasive." He noted that the *Jones* court had suggested that injury to Oklahoma girls was minimal. But, Judge Arnold countered, "It is certainly not *de minimus* [minimal] to people who play basketball and a lot of people do."[26] Arnold's indignation seemed limited not just to that particular example but to the entire set of assumptions about girls and their opportunities that lay behind the other two decisions. Unlike his counterparts, Arnold was not willing to wait and let the games' administrators make eventual changes.

THE SIGNIFICANCE OF THE HALF-COURT CASES

These cases reflect the power with which the public, if not the courts, endowed Title IX. Over and over, courts rejected Title IX as a right of action to change girls' basketball rules, and yet, over and over, lawsuits were filed claiming Title IX as a right of action. Only the half-court basketball lawsuits so consistently attempted to use a tool the courts and the government said was unavailable. Legal scholars recognized that the Fourteenth Amendment would be more effective than a toothless Title IX at changing the half-court rules, but people retained their faith in Title IX.[27] As late as 1983, girls in Iowa filed a lawsuit against the Iowa Girls High School Athletic Union in order to play full-court basketball. Their complaint relied heavily on the *Dodson* decision in Arkansas, but they still claimed a right of action under Title IX.[28] Much of the public believed that Title IX had more power than it did. Perhaps, if courts had dismissed the half-court basketball cases, the public might have pressured Congress to amend enforcement regulations to match their beliefs. Instead, the equal protection clause filled the gaps in Title IX's protection.

Judges in these decisions were forced to confront cultural beliefs about girls and women in sport and regional affection for six-on-six basketball. One underlying theme of each decision involved girls' physical capacity to play the game. The athletic unions of Tennessee and Oklahoma relied on stereotypes of girls being too physically frail to play a strenuous contact sport like full-court basketball, but judges who ruled in favor of the plaintiffs always concluded that girls, as a class, were just as physically capable as boys, as a class, and rejected adages to the contrary. Those judges who decided in favor of defendants either avoided the question of physical capability or acquiesced to old beliefs.[29]

In 1977, after the Tennessee district court decision opening the full-court game to girls, Wayne Cooley, executive secretary of the Iowa Girls High School Athletic Union, commented on the possibility of changing Iowa rules. "My young ladies," he said, "aren't strong enough to play by standard rules. Besides, watching the girls play this way isn't threatening to the male spectators; it's amusing."[30] His comments exemplified the attitude of those who opposed girls playing full-court basketball because of the girls' alleged weakness. They also highlighted fears that girls would somehow diminish the boys' game of full-court basketball by playing it badly, thus offending their male audience. Those who supported girls' rules basketball believed girls were not good enough athletes to play under any other conditions, and judges who ruled against them had to confront that stereotype. Indeed, judges often had to counter old concerns about female frailty and argue that half-court basketball provided insufficient exercise for growing young women.[31]

The tradition of the game's place in the community also played a role in the decision. The Arkansas Athletic Association maintained that because half-court basketball was a tradition in Arkansas it should be protected and even exempted from the nondiscrimination clauses of the Fourteenth Amendment. The tradition of six-on-six basketball was extraordinarily strong in a few states. As a researcher for the Iowa Girls High School Athletic Union said in 1982, "This half-court game has a long tradition in Iowa. It would be nothing less than a gamble to change it now."[32] When the game ultimately did decline and disappear, fans and players in those states mourned its passing.[33] At the time, however, judges had to acknowledge the community's affection for the game while ruling on its legal merits. Judge Arnold rejected the notion that tradition alone was a sufficient legal reason to keep gender segregation in the rules of basketball, but tradition and love of the game had led states to fight to keep half-court basketball.

The half-court basketball cases not only indicate the power of Title IX in the collective imagination but also the willingness of many communities to fight to keep the old game and their beliefs intact. Because no directly parallel case had been decided in any of these jurisdictions, judges had no binding legal precedent. They were allowed to create decisions based in part on personal beliefs and attitudes about sports and women. Female athletes and their advocates, perhaps inspired by a misconception of Title IX's power, harassed the courts and the game's administrators with lawsuits until rules, if not beliefs and attitudes, changed.

Although, ultimately, only Arkansas was ordered by a court to change the rules, now every U.S. high school basketball team plays by five-on-five rules. Tennessee finally shifted voluntarily. Iowa girls filed a lawsuit that was dropped after the state athletic union agreed to change to a full-court game. Oklahoma girls threatened another lawsuit after Iowa began its shift, and the OSSAA eventually bowed to social pressure, allowing schools to choose to field a full- or half-court team. The girls and the schools eventually chose the full-court game. The last state-sanctioned, six-on-six game in the United States was played in Oklahoma in 1995.[34]

Playing Basketball with Boys

While girls in Tennessee, Arkansas, and Oklahoma filed lawsuits in order to run the full length of the floor, some girls in other states wanted to play with male classmates. Unlike half-court cases, coed basketball cases did not usually name Title IX as a cause of action, although it was ever-present in court analysis of the cases. In the end, as with every other sport, the courts used the Fourteenth Amendment to make decisions. Unlike half-court cases, which took place over a brief timeframe (1977–79), coed basketball cases dragged out much longer (1975–83), perhaps in part because of important legal developments. In 1980 the equal rights amendment to the U.S. Constitution died because not enough states ratified it by the deadline. Title IX was left as the primary legislative tool for gender rights in education. By 1981 the Supreme Court had reiterated its gender classification test for the equal protection clause. The Court had finally established that intermediate scrutiny would be the appropriate test for gender classifications.

The only decision involving soccer was decided in a Colorado district court in 1977, also the timeframe of the coed basketball cases. In that case the judge first articulated a separate but equal doctrine for gender and sports: Establishing separate teams for girls and providing those teams with comparable support would alleviate a school of its obligation to allow a girl to try out for a boys' team.[35] Basketball cases involving playing on boys' teams fell into two categories. In most cases, girls wanted a chance to play basketball with boys because no girls' team existed. In one long, often-appealed case, however, a girl wanted to play on a boys' team rather than the girls' because she believed the boys' team was better. The latter case unsuccessfully challenged the idea that a girls' team was equal to a boys' team. The others provided more case law to establish that the Fourteenth Amendment would prohibit girls' wholesale exclusion from contact sports.

COED BASKETBALL CASES: WHEN ONLY A BOYS' TEAM EXISTS

The first coed basketball case was brought to give girls access to the game when no team but a boys' basketball team existed. In the fall of 1973, Rachel Lavin and Patricia Giannis, seniors, decided to try out for the all-male varsity basketball team at Mather High School in Chicago. After open tryouts, certain selected players were invited to attend preliminaries, from which the varsity squad would be chosen. After neither girl was asked to return to preliminaries Rachel asked Coach Donald Fontana why they did not make the initial cut, and he told her that the Illinois High School Association (IHSA) prohibited all coed interscholastic athletics. In response, Rachel filed a class-action lawsuit against the IHSA for violating the rights of high school girls under the Fourteenth Amendment's equal protection clause.[36] The allegations of discrimination, however, were never heard because the trial court gave the defendants an order of summary judgment based on Coach Fontana's affidavit.[37] After Rachel approached him, Fontana said, he had showed her the IHSA rules barring coed athletic activities, but he never told her "that in the absence of the applicable rule that they would have been called back for the next level of the tryouts, and, in fact, in the absence of such rule they would not have been called back for the next level of tryouts because neither possessed the necessary ability to participate on the school's varsity basketball team." Because Rachel could not counter the coach's statement that she was not varsity material (beyond her own assertions that she was "eligible, ready, willing, and able to participate in high school interscholastic varsity basketball"), the trial judge awarded summary judgment to the IHSA.[38]

Rachel appealed the trial court's decision to the Seventh Circuit of U.S. Court of Appeals, and in April 1975 the court reversed the trial court's decision but still without discussing the constitutional claims.[39] The question, the court concluded, was how to read Coach Fontana's affidavit. Fontana, the court stated, had only said that "in the absence of the rule Lavin would not have been called back. It does not state that his decision not to ask her back was made without consideration of the rule or the fact that she was female." Further, the court noted that Rachel had not had opportunity to respond to Fontana's affidavit. Because of this procedural error, therefore, the court remanded the case back to the trial court level. In order to establish legal authority the court cited several previous Seventh Circuit decisions wherein the importance of allowing each party an opportunity to respond to the other's evidence was critical.[40]

The Seventh Circuit's decision was, like the first baseball case of *Magill v. Avonworth Baseball Conference,* interesting because of the dicta in the decision. The court could have remanded the case to the district court on purely procedural grounds because of that court's failure to give Rachel time to counter the coach's statement that she was not varsity material. Although the Seventh Circuit correctly relied on procedural grounds and did not unnecessarily address her constitutional claims, the court did draft an elaborate, legally unnecessary reading of the affidavit.

On its face, Fontana's affidavit seemed to indicate that he did not believe girls to be talented enough to play varsity basketball at Mather. One could easily conclude that although Fontana cut girls because they lacked talent, he instead chose to blame the regulation. The court of appeals suggested a new reading of the affidavit, however: Fontana never said he was *not* influenced by regulations prohibiting coed basketball. Perhaps, knowing of the regulations, he failed to give girls fair tryouts because he had already, subconsciously, cut them, or perhaps his evaluation was influenced by their gender or knowledge of the regulations.

The fact that the Seventh Circuit discussed the merits of the affidavit in light of gender, as opposed to noting that it was an opinion and thus Rachel should be allowed to provide different opinions, implied that the Seventh Circuit was aware of the importance of the role of gender to the case and wanted to have that significance on record. The Seventh Circuit was not willing to accept the coach's word that Rachel was a sub-par basketball player and gender had nothing to do with his decision. The court of appeals was likely to have been very aware of the tempest over youth baseball in 1974, just a year before this case. The judges knew that Title IX enforcement regulations had been announced three months before the case was argued. Gender and sport were important topics in America, and the judges chose to acknowledge their importance in the dicta.[41]

Although the next case was also about coed basketball, in that instance, unlike most cases where an individual girl filed suit against a state's athletic union, a school district wanted girls to play with boys. In the fall of 1974 Amy Underwood and Leah Wing tried out for and made the previously all-male basketball team at Morgan Middle School in Ohio. The school district, Yellow Springs, believed that boys and girls of middle school age had similar athletic capabilities and hence encouraged coeducational sports teams for that age group. The Ohio High School Athletic Association (OHSAA), however, had a rule that prohibited coeducational interscholastic athletic competition in contact sports, defined as football, wrestling, ice hockey, and basketball.[42] Failure to comply with the rule would result in exclusion of the school district from all interscholastic athletic competition, and therefore, despite its philosophical opposition to the rule, the Yellow Springs School District ordered the girls removed from the team and started a separate girls' basketball team, one that had no competition because no other girls' teams existed. The district also lobbied unsuccessfully within the state to change OHSAA rules and then filed a lawsuit against OHSAA, claiming that the rule was unconstitutional.[43]

U.S. District Court Judge Carl B. Rubin agreed with Yellow Springs and concluded that the OHSAA rule was unconstitutional. Unlike any other contact sport cases ever published, however, Rubin based his decision not on the equal protection clause of the Fourteenth Amendment but upon the due process clause of that amendment: "Nor shall any state deprive any person of life, liberty, or property, without due process of law."[44] Analysis of due process decisions involves similar tests as those under the equal protection clause's strict scrutiny for race. Over the years the U.S. Supreme Court has concluded that certain interests or liberties are fundamental to all citizens, and those fundamental rights can be abridged only if a state can prove it has a compelling objective reached by the rule that impedes the liberty. Marriage, reproductive choices, and child-rearing have been deemed fundamental rights.[45]

Judge Rubin wanted to include interscholastic athletics in that list despite the fact that a number of courts had concluded there was no property interest in interscholastic competition—a property interest is itself a fundamental right.[46] Rubin argued that interscholastic sport is an integral part of education, which is a fundamental liberty; thus, by extension, interscholastic sport is a fundamental liberty. If the OHSAA rule were to stand, Rubin concluded, it would prevent girls and their parents from making personal choices regarding educational opportunities.[47]

Once he established that the liberty was fundamental, Rubin tested it, asking whether the liberty was being deprived for an important governmental objective. The state's objectives, he concluded, were to protect school children from injury and maximize female athletic participation. Rubin conceded that these might be legitimate goals. He argued, however, that such goals were based on the presumption that all girls have less athletic ability than all boys. That presumption was unconstitutional if it could be rebutted with individual examples, and Rubin named an individual example: "Babe Didrikson could have made anybody's team."[48] Mildred "Babe" Didrikson Zaharias, one of the greatest athletes of the twentieth century, male or female, constituted a dramatic rebuttal to the presumption of male athletic superiority.[49] Because Didrikson was a paragon of athleticism, however, girls (and boys as well) who wanted to play basketball in Ohio were unlikely to live up to her standards. Rubin chose not to acknowledge the two girls who had actually made the team in the Yellow Springs School District and instead provided an example whose athletic prowess could not be challenged.

Thus far Rubin's decision was out of the ordinary because he chose to invalidate the rule on due process instead of equal protection grounds, but the decision's most dramatic break with the other contact sport decisions came when he announced that the federal regulations enforcing Title IX, which allowed for separate sports in contact sports, were also unconstitutional. Although Yellow Springs had initially filed suit in 1974 (before release of Title IX's enforcement regulations in 1975), OHSAA changed its rules on coed contact sports in 1976, before the case was argued in front of Judge Rubin in 1978. The new OHSAA rules were intended to comply with the enforcement regulations of Title IX: "In all contact sports (Football, Wrestling, Ice Hockey and Basketball) team members shall be boys only. Girls may play on a boys' team in noncontact sports, if there is no girls' team or if the overall opportunities for interscholastic competition is [*sic*] limited for girls."[50] According to the corresponding Title IX regulation, "A recipient may operate or sponsor separate teams for members of each sex where . . . the activity involved is a contact sport." If no separate teams exist, "Members of the excluded sex must be allowed to try out for the team offered unless the sport involved is a contact sport."[51] Rubin concluded that because OHSAA rules violated the Fourteenth Amendment, Title IX regulations must as well. The Ohio District Court was the only one in the country to conclude that the Title IX enforcement regulations were unconstitutional, and Rubin did so without hearing evidence on the issue or being requested by either party to do so.[52]

Judge Rubin's conclusion did not follow the direct precedent of the Sixth Circuit Court of Appeals, the court that would review decisions from his district. His decision rested on an emotional plea rather than legal justification. The Sixth Circuit had twice before ruled on issues of gender and sport. In 1973 it had concluded that the Fourteenth Amendment's equal protection clause allowed girls to play on a boys' tennis team when no girls' team existed, but the court explicitly stated that the decision was reached because tennis was a noncontact sport.[53] In 1977 the Sixth Circuit had, in *Cape v. TSSAA*, overruled a lower court's decision to allow girls to play full-court basketball because the court was willing to accept that physical differences between boys and girls constituted sufficient justification to segregate the genders in sport. In that case the court had specifically refused to speculate on coed contact sports.[54]

Rubin noted the Sixth Circuit's lack of an explicit decision on coed contact sports and then explained his conclusion that Title IX regulations exempting contact sports were unconstitutional in terms better suited for laypersons than lawyers and judges:

> It has always been traditional that "boys play football and girls are cheerleaders." Why so? Where is it written that girls may not, if suitably qualified, play football? There may be a multitude of reasons why a girl might elect not to do so. Reasons of stature or weight or reasons of temperament, motivation or interest. This is a matter of personal choice. But a prohibition without exception based upon sex is not. It is this that is both unfair and contrary to personal rights contemplated in the Fourteenth Amendment to the United States Constitution.
>
> It may well be that there is a student today in an Ohio high school who lacks only the proper coaching and training to become the greatest quarterback in professional history. Of course the odds are astronomical against her, but isn't she entitled to a fair chance to try? [footnotes omitted][55]

Rubin's argument raises valid philosophical points for those interested in issues of gender and sport and proponents of gender equality. Like Judge Arnold in Arkansas, Rubin rejected the notion that tradition alone was an acceptable reason to continue gender segregation. Moreover, like other judges who supported female access to contact sports, he rejected the idea that no girl could ever be good enough to compete at a "man's" game like football or basketball. It was also unique that Rubin recognized his decision as a cultural marker. Judges often write for laypersons, but rarely do they so explicitly acknowledge that people's lives are affected and that they may want explanations of a decision.

Rubin's tirade about gender, stereotype, and sport did not, however, actually explain to nonlawyers why the Fourteenth Amendment protects future female quarterbacks. On the contrary, his argument appealed to a sense of fairness and equality, concepts that in practice the Fourteenth Amendment sometimes fails to protect. Unfortunately for the Yellow Springs School District, the emotional appeal had little effect on the appellate court that overruled Rubin's decision.

In 1981 the Sixth Circuit of the U.S. Court of Appeals released its decision, which was drafted by Judge Cornelia G. Kennedy. The decision agreed in part with Judge Rubin's conclusion that the OHSSA rules were problematic but disagreed as to why. The Sixth Circuit compared the language of OHSSA rules with the language of the Title IX regulations and concluded that OHSSA rules were not, in fact, parallel. According to OHSAA rules, "In all contact sports (Football, Wrestling, Ice Hockey and Basketball) team members shall be boys only. Girls may play on a boys' team in noncontact sports, if there is no girls' team or if the overall opportunities for interscholastic competition is [sic] limited for girls."[56] The rules prohibited girls from ever participating in designated contact sports. "A recipient may operate or sponsor separate teams for members of each sex where . . . the activity involved is a contact sport," the corresponding Title IX regulation read. If no separate teams existed, "Members of the excluded sex must be allowed to try out for the team offered unless the sport involved is a contact sport."[57] The court concluded that the Title IX regulation, unlike OHSSA rules, allowed for separate teams for contact sports but did not "clearly prohibit" girls from trying out for contact sports teams. Title IX did not proscribe coed contact sports, it simply did not require them. The court held that the Yellow Springs School District could field a coed basketball team if it wanted and ordered the OHSAA rule changed to match Title IX regulations.[58]

The Sixth Circuit then took Judge Rubin to task for holding the Title IX enforcement regulations unconstitutional. First, the court said that even though a program could allow coed contact sports teams under Title IX, that did not mean Title IX regulations were unconstitutional for promoting separate contact sports teams. In fact, the Sixth Circuit majority believed, separate athletic programs would help the development of female athletes. Moreover, if girls were allowed to compete with boys, the most talented girls would do so.[59] That position fit logically with the Sixth Circuit's statements in *Cape v. TSSAA* about males being better athletes than females.[60]

The Sixth Circuit was also confused by Judge Rubin's choice to review the regulations under the due process clause rather than the equal protection clause. Although the appellate court cited the Supreme Court's decisions on gender discrimination generally, it chose not to address other gender and contact sports cases, which by 1981 included cases on football, baseball, basketball, and soccer.[61] The majority of the other decisions had occurred at the district court level, but the Sixth Circuit did not even comment on its own decisions involving equal protection, gender, and sport. In general, the court was confounded as to why Rubin had addressed the issue of constitutionality at all. The Sixth Circuit was convinced that a plain reading indicated that the OHSAA rule and the Title IX regulation were not at all parallel, and therefore the constitutionality of the OHSAA rule was not at issue. More important, however, no one had asked Rubin to address the constitutionality of the Title IX regulations; he heard no arguments on the issue; and the Department of Health, Education, and Welfare, which had promulgated the regulations, had not been asked to testify or become a party to the lawsuit. There was, therefore, absolutely no reason, beyond personal conviction, for Judge Rubin to have commented on the Title IX enforcement regulations. Not surprisingly, the Sixth Circuit completely overruled this part of Rubin's decision.[62]

In the dissenting opinion, however, Judge Nathaniel R. Jones articulated a model argument. His position underlined that reasonable people could disagree on these issues; judges could look at the same facts and reach radically different conclusions based on their own perceptions and experiences. Jones began by reading the OHSSA and Title IX regulations differently than the majority decision did. After describing the legislative history of Title IX, Jones concluded that Congress never intended Title IX to tell the local body what to do about contact sports teams; the local authority could ban or allow coed contact sports teams as it deemed most appropriate. Therefore, Jones argued, the OHSAA rule (prohibiting coed contact teams) was actually compliant with the Title IX regulation (allowing such a prohibition), which meant that the constitutionality of the OHSSA regulations was, as Judge Rubin claimed, the central issue.[63]

Jones, however, based his analysis of the regulations on the equal protection clause instead of the due process clause. He never specified why he made that distinction, but his extensive use of precedents, all of which revolved around equal protection, suggests that he wanted his dissent to have the legal support that Rubin's decision lacked. Jones's argument began with an acknowledgment of two previous Sixth Circuit decisions involving gender and sport, which had allowed a coed tennis team and refused to order a state to play full-court basketball.[64] Because neither case directly addressed the question of whether a girl had a constitutional right to play on a boys' contact sport team when no separate girls' team existed, Jones turned to and evaluated other courts' decisions. He considered a number of cases in which girls successfully argued their way onto boys' teams in baseball, football, and soccer as well as noncontact sports generally.[65]

Jones recognized that the OHSSA had essentially two arguments to exclude girls from basketball. Both ran directly parallel to all the other cases: Girls would get hurt playing a contact sport with boys, and allowing girls to play on boys' teams would undermine separate girls' athletic programs. Like other judges who opened the door of sports to girls, Jones acknowledged that protecting school children is a legitimate goal but one not rationally, let alone substantially, related to excluding all girls from contact sport while having no physical fitness standards for the boys who played. He reiterated the arguments made by judges he cited about how physical difference among genders was greater than that between genders and because tryouts were held, individual judgments could be made about girls' physical capabilities. Jones regarded as speculative theory based on no evidence the OHSAA contention about wanting to strengthen girls' athletic programs generally, a goal that would be undermined should girls play on boys' squads because the best girls would play with boys and boys thus displaced would take over girls' teams. Therefore, Jones concluded that the OHSSA rule violated girls' rights under the equal protection clause.[66]

Like Judge Rubin, Judge Jones was inspired to discuss the case beyond the specific question at issue and consider a broader question. In 1977 a district court judge in Colorado, ruling on a gender and soccer case, had concluded that offering separate but comparable sports teams for boys' and girls' was acceptable under the equal protection clause.[67] Jones disagreed because he began with the premise that the level of competition was "indisputabl[y]" higher among male high school teams than most female high school teams. Therefore, the best female athletes would not reach their potential because they were not playing against the best (male) teams. That meant the best female athletes were not being treated equally with the best male athletes. Further, Jones thought that a stigma did attach itself to female athletes denied the opportunity to play on a male team solely on account of gender; such a denial, by implying that females were weaker or more uncoordinated than boys, would reinforce "archaic and harmful stereotypes." Jones, in fact, emphasized the idea that gender is defined in part by cultural expectations when he maintained that "equal participation in sports by female athletes would be a major step in overcoming the outmoded notions of female roles still prevalent in our society." Therefore, he held the OHSAA rule unconstitutional and concluded that separate but equal in sports was also a violation of the equal protection clause.[68]

Jones ended his dissent with an appendix, a choice intended to disseminate information he considered critical in his decision-making process. He excerpted chapter 1 of the U.S. Commission on Civil Rights, *More Hurdles to Clear* (1980), which described the history of women in sports, summarized the change in women's athletic opportunities in the twentieth century, and countered some of the physiological myths used to exclude women from sport. Judge Jones included the appendix to educate. He may have been trying to instruct the majority or the defendants or even lay readers in much the same way Judge Rubin tried to do with his emotional plea for the right of a girl to try to be the best athlete she could. Inclusion of the appendix, however, is significant because it indicates that Jones felt it necessary to put this single case into a historical context. Although his use of legal precedents placed his reasoning in a legal history, Jones, like Rubin, seemed to recognize that gender and athletics are intertwined socially and that the law cannot pretend to ignore their shared social history.

The two cases were similar to the baseball and football cases in that they all argued about whether girls should be allowed to play on a contact sports team with boys when no comparable girls' team existed. The Ohio case was a bit different. The Yellow Springs School District did, when the OHSSA forced it, create a girls' team, but no other teams existed to form a league. Courts deciding on basketball cases, like baseball cases, were divided on whether girls should play the coed game, but they were contributing to the same discussion of whether the Constitution would allow the exclusion of girls from a contact sport if no girls' team existed. The girls had a choice—play with the boys or not play at all. The next case, however, was unique.

COED BASKETBALL CASES: PLAYING WITH THE BOYS INSTEAD OF THE GIRLS

The final case involved a girl who agreed with the stereotypes about girls not being as athletically talented as boys, but she also believed she was a uniquely gifted athlete and should be able to choose the team, boys' or girls', for which she was best suited. Her fight began in 1980, the year before the Sixth Circuit heard the *Yellow Springs* case, but Karen O'Connor built the foundation for Judge Jones's dissent in *Yellow Springs* (although Jones did not cite the O'Connor case) and argued that separate but equal athletic teams based on gender are inherently unequal because the boys are better athletes.

The Karen O'Connor case was the most appealed and convoluted of the gender and contact sports cases; it was also the only published case that dealt with a girl who specifically wanted to play with boys, not with girls. As Federal District Court Judge Prentice H. Marshall summarized the situation, "Karen O'Connor is an extraordinarily gifted basketball player. She is also female. Therein lies the problem."[69] And that quotation summarizes mainstream America's preoccupation with gender and sport. In the early 1980s, being a talented female athlete was at best problematic and at worst oxymoronic.

The O'Connor case was the first and only contact sports case in which the athleticism of one individual girl was at the heart of the court battle. In a string of cases in which girls struggled to prove that they were as good as the weakest boy, Karen O'Connor announced that she was not only the best female athlete but also the best athlete of her age group. She maintained that individuals should be judged on individual merits, and therefore she should not have to play with the girls' basketball squad, which she considered inferior.

Karen had been playing basketball on boys' teams since the age of seven and had participated in a number of different leagues and camps in which she was always one of the best players. She had accumulated a lifetime record of ninety-seven wins and seventeen losses as well as a collection of awards, playing in a society that assumed male basketball players were superior to female ones. A professional basketball coach rated her, just before she entered the sixth grade, as playing at the level of a tenth-grade girl and an eighth-grade boy.[70] In 1980, at the age of eleven, she entered the sixth grade in Prospect Heights School District no. 23, in a Chicago suburb, and was eager to have her first taste of interscholastic basketball. Assuming that the quality of play would be higher in the boys' league than in the girls', she requested, through her father, an opportunity to try out for the boys' team.[71] Karen's father explained that she was "better than the girls" and needed "the best competition" available to reach her goal of playing in the National Basketball Association. He explained to the *New York Times*, "You've got to start when you're young . . . Bill Russell [one of the greatest centers in the game] could not have walked into professional basketball and been a superstar without playing against the best men in college and in high school. I want Karen to have that chance."[72] Sixth-grade basketball tryouts were scheduled for October 27, 1980, and after the school district refused to let Karen try out, the O'Connors sued under equal protection grounds.

The O'Connors also requested an injunction to allow Karen to try out while the discrimination lawsuit was pending. On October 23, 1980, following an emergency hearing, Judge Marshall granted that injunction and delivered an oral explanation.[73] He explained that the evolution of case law indicated that the equal protection clause would not allow the exclusion of females from "so-called contact sports" like basketball, particularly if no comparable female team existed. Although the school district held that it had a girls' basketball team and the separate-but-equal-teams principle fulfilled Karen's equal protection rights, Marshall doubted that the two teams were in fact equal. He argued that "in any given group today, of women and men, or boys and girls of the same general age and level of experience, the men . . . will dominate or will excel, or will perform at a higher level." That meant the level of competition would be inherently unequal because the competition the boys' team provided would be greater. "The mere fact that they [boys and girls' teams] are coached comparably, have comparable physical plants, comparable schedules, et cetera, does not render them equal," he said. Karen, Marshall observed, would not be able to continue her remarkable development as a basketball player if she did not play against the best competition, boys. Marshall believed that Karen was likely to succeed in her discrimination lawsuit because he thought she had a fundamental right to personal development, which included developing physical talents and skills. Therefore, he granted Karen an injunction and ordered the school district to let her try out for the boys' basketball team.[74]

Marshall's argument was, in fact, grounded in stereotype and prejudice, and his theory of personal development was not deeply grounded in constitutional law. Like Karen and her father, Judge Marshall accepted as fact the idea that the overwhelming majority of boys are better athletes than the overwhelming majority of girls. At this level, everyone seemed to see Karen O'Connor as a Babe Didrikson kind of exception to the throws-like-a-girl stereotype. Judge Marshall's argument was similar to that of Judge Carl B. Rubin in the first stage of *Yellow Springs v. OHSSA* in 1978; both relied on a due process argument based on ideas of fundamental liberties and not on equal protection arguments. Marshall, however, had been presented with an equal protection claim, and his choice to avoid a traditional analysis likely stemmed from the then-chaotic state of gender discrimination law. He held the injunction hearing in 1980 while the Supreme Court was in something of a state of flux in analyzing gender discrimination cases, and he was unsure of what level of scrutiny to apply to this case.[75]

The school district, however, did not give up. First, it asked Judge Marshall to delay, or stay, the injunction until it could appeal. After he refused, the district postponed tryouts until October 28, ostensibly because the gymnasium was no longer available due to a relocated rain-drenched outdoor event. Then the district appealed Judge Marshall's rejection of its request to stay the injunction. Without stating any reasons, a judge of the Seventh Circuit of the U.S. Court of Appeals awarded the stay on October 27. Two days later, at the request of the O'Connors, the entire court affirmed the stay of the injunction, again without stating why.[76]

The O'Connors, in turn, appealed the stay to Justice John Paul Stevens of the U.S. Supreme Court, attempting to allow Karen to try out while the discrimination trial was pending.[77] Justice Stevens produced the first published decision in the O'Connor saga, denying Karen the opportunity to try out before the trial. On November 4, 1980, he affirmed the stay on the injunction, and his written decision set the tone for continuation of the case. Essentially, Justice Stevens said the question concerned whether the defendants had adequate reason to discriminate against Karen because of her gender. Stevens agreed with Marshall that the situation was certainly unfair to Karen as an individual but held that the issue was whether gender segregation in athletics, as a general rule, is constitutional. Stevens agreed with Marshall and the O'Connors that boys are generally much better athletes than girls, but he disagreed as to the best option for the community. Stevens said that separate leagues are fair because "without a gender-based classification in competitive contact sports, there would be a substantial risk that boys would dominate the girls' programs and deny them an equal opportunity to participate in interscholastic events." In other words, boys are better athletes, and unless athletic programs are segregated by gender, fewer girls have a chance to compete. Stevens's ruling suggests that although Karen's rights as an individual might have been impinged, that impingement is necessary to protect the rights of girls as a class—the rights of the collective whole versus the individual. The idea would be critical when boys' tried to use the equal protection clause to gain access to girls' teams. Stevens was also swayed by the fact that the Illinois school district's program was modeled after Title IX and its regulations, and he affirmed the stay because he doubted the O'Connors would be able to prove gender discrimination at the trial.[78]

Justice Stevens's reading of the case should have warned the O'Connors about their likelihood of success in pursuing it. When a liberal member of the Supreme Court writes that a discrimination lawsuit is unlikely to succeed on its merits, lower courts listen. The O'Connors, though, did not quit. After the stay of the injunction was firmly in place and Karen had been prevented from trying out for the boys' team and had refused to try out for the girls' team, the case remained alive and the school board appealed the injunction.[79] The Seventh Circuit Court of Appeals published its decision in 1981, reversing the injunction order. Under the rules of civil procedure, an injunction can only be reversed if an appellate court determines that the lower court abused its discretion and failed to follow the guidelines of issuing preliminary injunctions. The Seventh Circuit held that Marshall had erred in applying the standards he did because he had no evidence of the existence of a fundamental right to personal development. Further, the appellate court concluded, the boys and girls teams were equally supported, and any difference in the quality of play stemmed from individual members of the teams themselves. Relying on Justice Stevens's opinion, this court then added that Karen had failed to show that the separate but equal philosophy harmed girls as a class but had argued only that she personally had suffered because of her unique abilities. Therefore, the preliminary injunction was dissolved, and the case was remanded to the trial court, where the parties were free to participate in a full trial on the issue of discrimination.[80]

For some reason the O'Connors chose to try to go to trial. The school district, recognizing that every court above the district court had already ruled that separate but equal basketball programs were acceptable, asked for a summary judgment order.[81] Judge Marshall, the same district court judge who had originally awarded the injunction to allow Karen to try out, acquiesced to the inevitable and awarded summary judgment. His written decision detailed his reasoning and hinted at his frustration at being forced into reversing his position. The pretrial summary judgment hearing occurred in 1982, after the Supreme Court had finally articulated the intermediate scrutiny test for equal protection cases. Therefore, Marshall this time applied that test instead of his ill-fated fundamental right to personal development. He also cited almost every major Supreme Court decision on gender to back his decision that the school district's gender classification was substantially related to the important governmental purpose of maximizing athletic opportunities for all school children.[82]

Judge Marshall, however, indulged in a bit of judicial subversion. Although his conclusion matched what courts above him had ordered, Marshall noticed a flaw in their reasoning. The school district's separate but equal sport policy was based on a generalization that boys are better athletes and therefore provide greater competition than girls. Ordinarily, Marshall noted, the Supreme Court has been suspicious of broad gender generalizations. In fact, many lower courts have rejected the specific generalization that girls are not talented enough to play with boys. As a reminder, Marshall cited almost every gender and sport case published that allowed girls to play on teams with boys when no comparable female team existed. In doing so he highlighted the fact that the O'Connor case was different from the other gender and contact sport cases in that it seemed to support the weaker-female theory. Alas, Marshall said, no one in the case had challenged that generalization. Karen and the school district both agreed that boys are better athletes, and Karen maintained she was an exception. Therefore, Marshall had no choice but to rule in favor of the school district, but he succeeded in making his point that this case started a new branch of case law that differed from the earlier decisions.[83]

The O'Connor saga is impressive in part because of the amount of time and money both sides spent. The school district was remarkably persistent in its refusal to make an exception for the talented (and, to the district, likely annoying) young O'Connor. The O'Connors themselves revealed an astonishing level of obtuseness in not recognizing the futility of their cause after Justice Stevens rejected their claim. The saga also indicated the passion about the subject that led both sides to spend time and money arguing about whether one exceptional girl should be able to play with boys. In addition, the case suggested that the fear articulated in other cases, and by other school districts and athletic organizations, that the best female athletes would not want to play with girls' teams but with boys was perhaps true. Moreover, despite progress in improving the status of women in society and increasing the possibilities for girls in sport, people still agreed with the generalization that girls are lesser athletes than boys.

Concluding Thoughts on Basketball

Title IX triggered lawsuits for those girls who just wanted to play full-court basketball and for those who wanted to play on boys' teams. Girls who wanted out of the six-on-six game relied repeatedly and unsuccessfully on Title IX. Those who wanted to play on boys' teams, however, almost never relied on Title IX, presumably because of the exception to contact sports in the regulations. All these cases, however, came after the enactment of Title IX, indicating the influence of this legislation on the way girls thought about sport and their right to play.

The struggle over basketball (both in terms of rules and composition of teams) was fierce on the local level, but it failed to draw the same kind of national attention as the struggle over youth baseball or extend for as many years as the struggle over football. Media coverage of girls and football and baseball was much more extensive than for girls who tried to play basketball by boys' rules or on boys' teams. Although such national magazines as *Sports Illustrated* and *Newsweek* wrote about girls and Little League, they essentially ignored school-aged girls and basketball. The *New York Times* ran more than a hundred stories detailing the challenges between girls and baseball during the 1970s but included only six stories of girls and basketball in roughly the same period. Two of those described Victoria Cape's struggle to play full-court basketball in Tennessee. The first story after her loss noted that Tennessee coaches were happy, and it reminded readers that New York girls played full court; the second account reported that her appeal to the Supreme Court had been denied.[84] A third human interest story ran during the appeal of the *Yellow Springs* case in Ohio and described how three girls in Dayton made their middle-school basketball team, which had previously been all male. When one girl entered her first game as a substitute, according to the *New York Times* report, the crowd gave her a rousing ovation.[85]

Despite the growing popularity of the women's and girls' game, basketball did not spark the same passions that baseball did. After enactment of Title IX, most school districts created girls' teams, so relatively few tried to attain what Karen O'Connor wanted. Most were willing to play on the girls' teams and not worry about the competition level provided by boys. Typical was the 1983 example from Millstadt, a small southern Illinois town where Georgia Klotz, the mother of twelve-year-old Becky, threatened to sue the school district unless it allowed her daughter to play on the boys' team or created a girls' team.[86] Most schools had separate teams, and the Supreme Court in the person of Justice Stevens had suggested that separate but equal was acceptable in this context, limiting the likelihood of future lawsuits.

Basketball also did not generate the human interest of football. Girls who wanted to play tackle football had no choice but to play with boys because no separate teams existed, and the media was persistently interested in those who wanted to invade the manly game. Because fewer girls attempted to play coed basketball and "manliness" was not quite so emphatic an issue in that sport, fewer media stories appeared.

Although not as tradition-bound as baseball and football, basketball has held, and continues to hold, a prominent role in American sporting culture. Since the 1890s these three sports have been culturally dominant. Young people in the United States are taught to idolize the leaders of these teams and aspire someday to earn a varsity letter in one of the big three. Not surprisingly, sports have generated the most controversy when girls have attempted to cross the gender boundary and play those that are more "manly." Far more lawsuits have been published (and countless more filed and threatened) about baseball, football, and basketball than any other combination of sports, because protecting the masculine integrity of these games has been important to protecting the masculine integrity of America. When girls did attempt to play with or by the same rules as their brothers, the media and the general public engaged in a national debate about what it might mean should a girl try to play first base, wide receiver, or power forward. Inspired by Title IX and empowered by the Fourteenth Amendment, girls fought for—and generally succeeded in gaining—the right to try out for the major American sports.

Merely having a legal right to try out for a sports team, however, has not thrown open the doors to dugouts or provided access to fields and hardwood courts. Girls on high school football teams and in youth baseball leagues are at best a minority. Frequently, they are rarities. The changes in the gendering of sport have been slow, and football and baseball are still largely men's games. The mere participation of a girl in these sports becomes a media event. Basketball has, perhaps, been the success story of female forays into a traditionally male American game. Every girls' high school basketball team in the country plays by almost the same full-court rules as the boys' (the basketball for the girls' game is smaller then that for the boys'), and women's college and professional basketball often receives national media attention, albeit not yet to the same depth and degree as men's basketball. Breaking the gender barrier in the major American sports has been a slow battle, but girls have made substantial progress thanks in part to court decisions.

5 *Soccer*

After the debate over the gender of baseball players had been resolved, but during a time when football and basketball were still being contested, a quiet struggle over a different sport was being waged. If in 1977 baseball, football, and basketball were sports that had strong American traditions, soccer was somewhere at the fringe, a game played predominantly by immigrants and those not skilled enough for traditionally all-American sports. But in that year, the same one in which an Oklahoma judge and the Sixth Circuit Court of Appeals ruled that girls had no constitutional right to play full-court basketball, a Colorado judge was asked to make a ruling on the sport of soccer. He was asked to decide whether soccer is a contact sport and a suitable game for girls. The decision would have a profound impact on future judicial decisions involving girls' access to contact sports and on the popularity of soccer in America.

Soccer in 1977

The status of soccer in the United States has changed dramatically since the 1960s. It has gone from being a very regional sport played primarily by immigrants and young children to a booming sport sufficiently popular that international matches involving the national teams (male and female) are televised. When the one court decision involving gender and soccer was published in 1977, soccer was just beginning its climb into the American consciousness.

In terms of legal history of gender and sport, the conflict over soccer came very early. By 1977, just five years after the enactment of Title IX and the equal rights amendment, the struggle over integrating the gender of sports was occurring only in the major American sports of baseball, football, and basketball. Although several courts excluded girls from baseball, others allowed them to play under the auspices of the equal protection clause, and Little League Baseball, Inc., officially opened its dugouts to any child who wanted to participate. The Washington Supreme Court had announced that girls, under the state's equal rights amendment, could not be banned from football fields, and courts were mixed in their opinions of whether the equal protection cause forced states to offer full-court basketball to girls. No other contact sport would be contested in court for several years because most girls focused on the traditional games their brothers played. Except for soccer. In the middle of the struggle over America's favorite sports came one critically important case that opened soccer to girls under the Fourteenth Amendment. The case came at a time of flux in American society.

In 1977 more and more American women occupied prominent positions in society, and they were calling for equity of access to higher offices in politics and culture. They were also using the law to obtain that access. Parents, often mothers, were demanding that their daughters have opportunities to participate in contact sports that had been closed to them, and, inspired by the enactment of Title IX, they filed lawsuits under the equal protection clause.

As if the new gender equality was not unsettling enough to society, even the games Americans played were changing. Americans were discovering soccer. Although soccer had been popular worldwide, Americans had been slow to show any real attention to the game, but in the 1970s a record number of children and adults were beginning to participate. Soccer seemed to be a sport without cultural baggage or an American past. It was, unlike baseball and football, neither traditionally nor historically gendered in the United States.[1] Soccer and gender equality became legally entangled in a Colorado federal court case in 1977, when U.S. District Court Judge Richard P. Matsch ruled in *Hoover v. Meiklejohn* that Colorado girls had the right to play on boys' teams when no girls' team existed.[2] That case was the only lawsuit in which girls sued to play soccer to be decided in a published decision.[3] The lawsuit came at a time when soccer was just beginning to be socially and culturally reconstructed in America.

Although soccer had been played in the United States since the nineteenth century, it had never been as widely popular in America as in the rest of the world.[4] During the 1960s, however, its American roots began to spread slowly, first among boys and men. In Torrence, California, in 1964, the American Youth Soccer Organization (AYSO) was founded, with approximately a hundred boys registered to play on nine teams.[5] In 1968 two rival—and, ultimately, commercially unsuccessful—professional U.S. soccer leagues, the United Soccer Association and the National Professional Soccer League, merged into the North American Soccer League (NASL) and began with seventeen different teams.[6] By 1977 the two movements, youth and professional soccer, were closely entangled, and both reached new and unexpected levels of popularity.

One of the key components in the success of some franchises in the NASL was the Warner Communications acquisition of the New York Cosmos team. Warner decided that the team had to spend money boldly in order to make money. After several years of negotiation, the team offered enough money to convince the retired Brazilian soccer superstar Pelé to make a comeback in North America, and he signed in 1975 for approximately $4.7 million for three years. Slowly, attendance numbers for the Cosmos improved. In 1976 the team also signed Franz Beckenbauer, who had been captain of the World Cup–winning West German national team in 1974 and Europe's Footballer of the Year in 1971 and 1976. Attendance numbers at Cosmos games jumped dramatically with the two stars' arrival, but almost every contemporary article in the periodical press credited Pelé with the surge in American interest.[7] On August 14, 1977, a sellout crowd of 77,691 attended a match between the Cosmos and the Ft. Lauderdale Strikers. That record number gave the sport an incredible lift.[8] The next week the Cosmos attracted more fans to their home game than the Yankees did to their first place American League battle with the Boston Red Sox.[9]

Although these numbers were not typical of franchises across the country, they were enough to give soccer enthusiasts reason for optimism. They also indicated that Cosmos marketing techniques were working. The NASL was pitching itself to middle-class, white suburbanites. As one writer said, it was "not the predominantly male, immigrant or ethnic crowd you'd expect." Soccer in America had for years been viewed as an "ethnic" sport played primarily by recent immigrants, but the NASL wanted to change that in order to draw a larger, wealthier fan base. As long as the American public envisioned soccer as a foreign sport, the NASL would not find the support it needed to survive. To make the game more palatable to Americans, the league promoted it to segments of the population thought to be excluded in foreign fan bases. Forty-five percent of fans at NASL games were female, and the key audience was composed of young people.[10]

The interweaving of the two levels of sport, youth and professional, was not accidental. The NASL, leery of the failures of all previous professional American soccer leagues, attempted to build success by creating a new, and long-term, audience for the sport. The league assumed that children who became involved in the youth game would pester their parents into taking them to professional games. Therefore, the league required its players to sponsor or attend a certain number of youth soccer camps and clinics in their teams' regions. The league also offered a number of family nights with inexpensive children's tickets. These evenings made soccer even more a family sport. One editorial in the *Wall Street Journal* noted that in Washington, D.C., the Diplomats' professional soccer games were particularly pleasant because crowds consisted of families, not "gamblers, drunks, or violence addicts."[11] It was, presumably, an implied contrast with the fans of professional football and boxing, who also attended sporting events at Robert F. Kennedy Stadium. This description of the fan base further distinguished America's soccer from soccer in the rest of the world, where fans were often characterized as hooligans.[12] In promoting a family event, the league hoped to Americanize fan support and distinguish the U.S. game from more rowdy matches elsewhere.

Individual teams went to great lengths to lure young fans and their parents to games. The New York Cosmos opened its field and gates before each home game at the New Jersey Meadowlands to local youth teams. In order to play on the professional field each team had to sell at least 250 tickets at $4 each (a discounted rate from the usual Cosmos ticket). Those who bought the cheap tickets could stay for the subsequent professional game. Also, before the professional game, usually during the half-time interval of the youth game, gates opened to those who held tickets to the Cosmos game. By the end of their game the youngsters could be playing in front of as many as fifty thousand people.[13]

The NASL numbers were growing, but so were the numbers of young Americans playing soccer. The growth of the sport was evidenced in the sale of soccer equipment. In 1974 approximately five hundred thousand soccer balls were sold, but by 1977 the sporting goods industry anticipated annual sales of 2.5 million balls.[14] An estimated five hundred thousand young people played soccer in 1977.[15] A number of factors contributed to that growth. The primary one seems to have been the parental and societal belief that soccer was a sport that anyone could play. Over and over, contemporary reports of the game emphasized that physically smaller children could play soccer, which "requires none of the size prerequisites that forces many of today's children out of many competitive sports."[16] Typically, articles implied that soccer was a game for those too small for basketball and football—thus preserving it for smaller boys and even for girls.[17]

Athletic directors across America protested the implication that soccer was a game for runts and lesser athletes. One in New York argued that boys did not play soccer just because they failed to make the football team, claiming there was an "increase in the number of good athletes attracted to soccer."[18] Although the stereotype of a soccer player being a football team reject was initially grounded in some truth, that was changing by 1977. One soccer coach told of asking the local grammar school football coach in 1963 to refer boys cut from the squad; fourteen years later, the football coach was asking for referrals from him.[19] The passion with which soccer's leaders emphasized the sport's ability to attract as many talented athletes as traditional American games like football indicated the power of popular stereotypes. The strength of the assertion suggested that they were fighting a deep cultural image of the game as being less masculine than a sport like football.

The game was not only popular among parents because children of all sizes could play, and play cheaply, but also because of parental perception of soccer's relative safety. The Consumer Products Safety Commission equated soccer with tennis and squash because of the low injury rate among its playing population (2 percent) as against football's almost 16 percent injury rate.[20] In addition, athletic coordinators noted that soccer games, unlike football, did not require the presence of ambulances, an absence that encouraged "otherwise non-athletic youngsters to sign up to play" and described as "allaying parental fears."[21] Size and safety are inexorably linked in the American imagination. The game was financially practical as well. Compared to other sports—particularly football—soccer is cheap. Most estimated that soccer in 1977 cost approximately $30 per player to outfit compared to $200 per player in football. Moreover, football requires a larger minimum of players (in part because of the risk of injury), which further increases the cost of equipping and maintaining a team.[22]

Despite the fact that it is relatively inexpensive to play soccer, the game was played predominantly in middle-class, white suburbs. Although sportswriters and soccer league directors agreed it was a shame that more black athletes did not play, the media cited a variety of factors. Noting that most black athletes emerge from inner cities, they blamed a lack of field space. Further, some argued that inner-city black athletes are pushed toward football (making no explanation of how field space for football but not soccer was possible) and basketball, sports with reputations for providing greater mobility out of cities and toward wealth. The lack of television coverage of soccer was also faulted. As one reporter argued, "Many inner city residents see the world beyond their neighborhoods only through television."[23]

That is not to say that organizers and leaders of soccer were not eager to have black players, in part because of their own racial assumptions. The U.S. National men's team coach told the *Chicago Tribune* that the "black athlete is ideally suited to soccer."[24] Another article noted that Brazil's traditional dominance in the sport could be related to the "high proportion of black players, and it looks as though America may be missing out on something."[25] All enthusiasm—and blatant racist stereotyping—aside, inner-city programs were slow to develop and had not done so in 1977.[26] Soccer was, however, becoming solidly entrenched as a suburban white sport.

Youth soccer's combination of high participation and low competitiveness also appealed to parents and young people. The high participation stemmed from an unofficial slogan: "Everyone's a quarterback."[27] Unlike football and baseball, in which only a limited number of players are ever actively involved with the play, anyone in a soccer match can touch the ball at any time and make decisions about how play should go. In addition, the fast-paced fluidity of the game encourages everyone on the field to participate rather than watch. This idea of "highly involved" players inclined some program directors to argue that "even shy and fearful children can join in and not feel conspicuous at a mistake."[28] Again, the cultural image of American soccer was that of a game that encouraged the active participation of children not tough enough, physically or mentally, for other sports yet at the same time more cerebral, able to recognize the flow of the game and decide how to influence it.

Further, active participation in soccer meant just that. The American Youth Soccer Organization had as one of its fundamental rules that every player should play at least half the game—regardless of skill level. If that rule alone did not diminish competition for competition's sake, the other rules did. The AYSO encouraged leagues to balance teams with an equal number of stronger and weaker players so no one team would be dominant. It also suggested that teams rotate players to different positions to develop well-rounded players and avoid lopsided scores. Coaches and league officials reflected this low-competition attitude. "A win is a win," said a New York coach. "Who needs to pile on goals?"[29] Other programs rotated players from team to team each season to prevent the formation of cliques because, as the director said, "We'd like the kids to learn that the opposition is not necessarily the enemy."[30] Bob Cousey, the former Boston Celtic basketball star and then commissioner of the American Soccer League (a minor-league program started in 1974), spoke at a youth league banquet in Connecticut in 1977. He encouraged the players not to be domineering and to observe how participation, team-work, sacrifice, and courage could be learned when losing as well as win-ning.[31] The spirit of cooperation extended even to parents. The media noted repeatedly that unlike Little League baseball, there was no real opportunity for parents or coaches to make too many adjustments or criticisms of players during the game itself. A Connecticut coach noted, "It is their [the youngsters'] game and we must not interfere from the sidelines."[32]

Given the reasons for the popularity of the sport (persons of any size could play with relatively low risk of injury, the game was not expensive, and the sport was relatively noncompetitive), it comes as no surprise that girls and young women were allowed, in fact, encouraged, to play. As one journalist wrote, "It can be played by girls, who are happy to discover that soccer is not, like baseball and football, a long-established bastion of mas-culinity, a male secret society where machismo reigns."[33] Most media descriptions of the rise of soccer, particularly youth soccer, included at least one reference to how women and girls could play as well. In an arti-cle describing Connecticut youth leagues, the only reference to females playing was a caption under a photograph of girls in uniform, passing a ball: "It's [soccer] also a game girls can compete in."[34] Another article, calling for more players, quoted a league director as saying, "We need girls to sign up. Maybe we can throw them some bait and get a lady coach."[35]

Even coed teams were supported. The media suggested that soccer was a sport in which women could hold their own: "Both males and fe-males can play it. In fact, women in some cases have been known to kick the pants off men on mixed teams. Even so injuries in the game are sel-dom serious."[36] A *Time* magazine article describing the soccer boom concluded that someday young women might play professional soccer, at least in their own leagues.[37]

Speculation about how far women could go in the sport was ech-oed by Phil Woosnam, commissioner of the North American Soccer League. He argued that women could develop the endurance and ball control necessary to play at any level, suggesting that women could someday play "on the same field" as men on the varsity, college, and professional level.[38] The very notion of soccer as a coed sport distin-guished it from the traditional masculine games of baseball, basketball, and football. No one, after all, had suggested that women could play in Yankee Stadium with men. Soccer was in 1977 being positioned differently, with recurring emphases on equality (in terms of gender, size, and participation) and safety.

Woosnam's enthusiasm for female soccer players may have been part of a continued effort to gain a wider market for the professional league. Just as the number of boys who played had skyrocketed, so had the number of girls. In ten years the Dallas–Fort Worth area went from having no female soccer players to having seven thousand.[39] Two thousand girls registered to play soccer in the New Jersey area in 1977; several years earlier there had been none.[40] These female players would, hopefully, be fans for the NASL.

The media contributed to the buildup of the girls' game with frequent coverage and made explicit the link between the men's and women's game by pairing stories on female leagues with stories on either the game in general or the men's game. In June of 1977, for example, the *Chicago Tribune* ran two articles, one on the relation between recent immigrants to the United States and soccer and the other on the newly founded women's league.[41] In October 1977 the *New York Times* did the same thing, with one article on the rise of suburban soccer generally and the other on the weaknesses of the girls' leagues.[42] Although the stories ostensibly promoted the female game, they also subtly distinguished soccer from other American sports. The *Chicago Tribune* linked the game to immigrants, suggesting that soccer was acceptable for U.S. girls to play because it was not truly an American game. The *New York Times* articles gave the game exposure but primarily described its weaknesses, for example, the lack of uniforms and coaches and the lower skill level of players. These examples suggested that soccer, despite its growing popularity, was still a foreign sport, sufficiently nontraditional and noncompetitive enough to be an acceptable game for American girls.[43] Parents knew their small children could play cheaply and safely in an environment protected from harsh adult criticism and overzealous coaches.

In some ways the "new" sport of soccer seemed ideal for girls. Donna Hoover certainly thought so, but the organization in charge of her state's high school sports programs disagreed both with Donna and the general American perception of soccer. In the fall of 1976, Donna was sixteen and in the eleventh grade at Golden High School in the Jefferson County (Colorado) R-1 School District. She had been playing soccer on the boys' junior varsity team because the school had no girls' team. She was the only girl on the squad. The coach permitted her to practice with the team and play in junior varsity matches not officially sanctioned by the Colorado High School Activities Association (CHSAA, or Colorado). No evidence suggests that anyone—referees, players, or other coaches—

complained about Donna's presence on the junior varsity team or on the field.[44] Several weeks into the season, however, the principal of Golden High School ordered the soccer coach to remove Donna from the team because her presence violated the Activities Association's rules limiting soccer to boys. About two weeks after being removed from the team, Donna, represented by the American Civil Liberties Union, sued the Jefferson County Board of Education and the Colorado High School Activities Association on the grounds that the association's rule prohibiting girls from playing soccer violated her constitutional right of equal protection under the Fourteenth Amendment.[45]

Although Donna could not sue under Title IX, the legislation played a significant, albeit unstated, role in the case. Title IX was not yet available as a legal remedy in 1977 because the 1975 Title IX enforcement regulations gave secondary schools until July 21, 1978—more than a year after this case was decided—to comply.[46] Further, other courts dealing with female access to sport had already questioned the legal power of Title IX, and it was unclear in that year whether an individual could sue under Title IX or whether an athletic department had to receive federal funds before being obligated to provide gender equity. Unlike attorneys in the half-court basketball altercations, Donna's attorneys recognized that Title IX was not going to keep her on the soccer team. They hoped the equal protection clause would accomplish that end.

The Colorado High School Activities Association's rules, however, were modeled after the Title IX regulations. Section 2 of the bylaws, for example, stated that the association "encourages the use of comparable athletic teams for members of each sex where selection for such teams is based upon competitive skills." Title IX regulations said that a school could "sponsor separate teams for members of each sex where selection for such teams is based upon competitive skill."[47] Further, those same Title IX regulations stated that the school need not offer a separate team if the "activity involved is a contact sport" nor allow athletes to try out for the opposite-gendered team (if there was no team for their own gender) if it was for a contact sport. The association's rules stated that "participation in this activity [soccer] shall be limited to members of the male sex." The Colorado rules had appropriated the notion of contact sports from the enforcement regulations and agreed that single-sex contact sports were permissible. In addition, "Because inordinate injury risk jeopardizes the health and safety of the female athlete, participation in this activity [soccer] is limited to members of the male sex."[48] Thus the association assumed that soccer was too physical for girls to play—it was, essentially, deemed a contact sport.

Just as it was for those who wanted to exclude girls from baseball and boys from field hockey, the issue of contact was central to excluding girls from soccer. Although Title IX did not yet apply to high schools (and would not be a legal power for gender and sport until 1988), the imagined power of Title IX had already inspired fear, and hence change, on the part of athletic associations across the country. Noncontact sports were being opened to girls nationwide under the Fourteenth Amendment because everyone, the courts and the girls, believed that Title IX sounded the death-knell for female exclusion from noncontact sports, or at least that it would once it was enforced.[49] Therefore, in order to continue to exclude girls from soccer the CHSAA needed to prove that the soccer is a contact sport. The association hoped that the justification of safety would be rational enough to justify gender segregation under the equal protection clause.

Colorado chose to limit soccer to boys after the Medical Aspects of Sports Committee, a division of the Colorado Medical Society consisting of seven doctors from across the state who practiced pediatrics and orthopedics, determined soccer to be physically dangerous. They testified at trial that the recommendation "to classify soccer as a contact sport and to prohibit mixed-sex play was the result of a perception of physiological differences which would subject the female players to an inordinate risk of injury." The committee was most concerned with the risk of collision during play, which, it believed, put females as a class at higher risk than males.[50] The rationalization that girls were frailer than boys and thus in greater physical danger was the only justification for excluding them that the Colorado Association offered at trial.

Judge Richard P. Matsch made his opinion of the medical reasons for excluding women from sport because of their size apparent in his description of Donna Hoover: "5'4" tall, weighs 120 pounds, and is in excellent physical condition." He added that although she "was stunned on one occasion as a result of a collision with a much larger player, she did not suffer any disabling injury in the games or in any practice sessions."[51] He critiqued the medical committee's conclusion but conceded that males and females after puberty differ physiologically in that males have denser bones, more muscle, and "a natural advantage over females in the mechanics of running."[52] Therefore, Matsch concluded, in the event of a collision a female would be potentially at greater risk for injury. The judge noted, however, that a greater difference in physical size exists, on average, within gender classes—from one male to the next—than between males and females generally. The committee and the association did not have a minimum size requirement for males to play soccer but banned all females regardless of size and strength. That overbroad rule, the judge said, justified Donna's claim that her equal protection rights were violated.[53]

Matsch's conclusion would be reiterated and cited in subsequent gender-access sports cases, but in 1977 his decision was one of the more strongly worded rejections of the size and safety justification. His language fundamentally undermined the traditional notion of protecting women from sports. By suggesting that the physical range within a gender is greater than that between genders, the judge sidestepped the traditional argument that women require greater protection than men. He implicitly suggested that if anyone needs protection from physical sport—and one is left to wonder if he believed anyone did—it would be people who are physically small or weak, something decided on an individual basis.

Like most court decisions examining gender segregation under the Fourteenth Amendment, Judge Matsch relied on a multipronged test to determine the constitutionality of the classification. In 1977 the U.S. Supreme Court was in a state of flux regarding the degree of care with which gender segregation should be scrutinized. A plurality of four members of the Supreme Court had stated in 1973 that gender, like race, is a suspect classification and subject to the strictest scrutiny, but that decision was contrary to almost all previous Court decisions.[54]

Lower courts across America were unsure of how to determine whether a gender-segregation law violated the equal protection clause. Most simply applied the traditional rational relationship test, a classification needed to be rational and related to a reasonable governmental objective. During the mid-1970s, a few courts applied the stricter test of requiring that gender classification be necessary to attaining a compelling governmental interest. Judge Matsch took an entirely different route, and he chose, after discussing the traditional legal methods of testing whether equal protection rights were violated, to create a new test from various dissents and a law review article.[55]

Matsch's test had three parts, each of which he discussed separately. First, the judge evaluated the "importance of the opportunity being unequally burdened or denied." If playing soccer were unimportant, then restrictions on it would more easily survive judicial scrutiny. He believed, however, that the opportunity to play soccer was important. He noted that the school district itself thought soccer an important experience and hence offered it as a program for boys. Also, the judge recognized that soccer affords future possibilities of athletic scholarships to colleges and universities. "Whether it is algebra or athletics," he added, "that which is provided must be open to all." He concluded that playing soccer is an

important educational experience. Second, Matsch looked to the significance of the state interest in denying an opportunity to girls. If the state's
rationale for keeping girls from playing soccer was exceedingly strong,
the rule was more likely to survive. He argued that the state's interest
in banning girls from soccer was based on the misconception that girls
would be injured playing the game. Because the state seemed not to worry
about protecting small males, he dismissed this interest as irrational and
was compelled to comment on the datedness of the state's argument. He
wrote that "any notion that young women are so inherently weak, delicate or physically inadequate that the state must protect them from the
folly of participation in vigorous athletics is a cultural anachronism unrelated to reality." Third, Marsch examined the characteristics of the
group being denied an opportunity and concluded that women and girls,
"to be effective citizens," must be permitted every educational opportunity, athletic and otherwise, because "to deny females equal access to
athletics supported by public funds is to permit manipulation of governmental power for a masculine advantage."[56] Thus he announced that if a
school district offered soccer for boys, it must also offer it for girls.

Matsch's rhetoric indicated that he recognized sports to be a key
component to the national culture—and that important social benefits
stemmed from sport. Excluding women from sports was as problematic
as excluding them from other aspects of culture, including more powerful institutions such as government. At the time, sports were emblem-
atic of an older, patriarchal society being challenged on many fronts.
During the 1970s the second wave of the feminist movement had reached
its peak, and legal barriers to women's equality were crumbling. The equal
rights amendment then seemed likely to be ratified, establishing wom-
en's constitutional right to equal treatment.

The increasing number of female athletes during the 1970s implied
that women were including sports in their quest for equality and challenging male domination in that arena as in all others. The contact sports
language of Title IX's enforcement regulations, however, appeared to preserve at least one last bastion of male power from female intervention.
This need for a "male preserve" of sport may have stemmed from a desire to protect masculine identity and intimacy in a country facing fundamental social change with the rise of women's equality.[57] That was one
of the reasons for the fierce cultural wars in the 1970s over baseball, football, and basketball.

Matsch's third point implicitly recognized this theory and implied
that in order to undermine such hegemony the last bastion of contact
sports as a male preserve must be eliminated or at least justified by some

argument more compelling than protecting the female body. Ironically, given the notion that law is based on precedent and not cultural trends, his language was not supported by law. That is to say he was not quoting other judges and not responding directly to the question of access as raised by the case itself. His language would, however, become precedent for other judges addressing the issue of gender and sport.

After concluding that Donna Hoover's constitutional rights had been violated, Judge Matsch gave the school district three options. First, noting that no one argued that Donna should be allowed to play on the boys' team for any reason other than that there was no girls' team, he told the school district that establishing a separate girls' team would satisfy the equal protection clause. That separate team, however, would have to receive substantially equal support, although Matsch noted that the standard should be comparability and not "absolute equality."[58] Second, the school district could choose to have a mixed-gender team and allow boys and girls to play on one team. Third, the school district could discontinue soccer altogether, given that there was no constitutional obligation to fund any particular sport. The only option not available to the school district, the decision stated, was for it to continue to field a boys' team while prohibiting girls from playing.[59]

Judge Matsch did not determine whether soccer is a contact sport because that determination was unnecessary under the equal protection clause claim that Donna Hoover made. If he had accepted that Donna and other girls were at a greater risk for physical injury from soccer than boys were, then the issue of contact might have been relevant under the constitutional claim, but he did not. Although the Colorado Medical Society had concluded that soccer was a contact sport and the state claimed that was why it excluded girls, the judge did not directly address that aspect of the argument. He merely noted that although "the rules of soccer prohibit body contact (except for a brush-type shoulder block when moving toward the ball); there are frequent instances when players collide in their endeavors to 'head' the ball."[60] Just as other judges had for baseball, Judge Matsch left open the question of whether soccer is a contact sport.[61]

This single decision arose during a time of transition. The role of women in society and in sports was changing. The role of soccer in America was not entirely clear; its identity was still being molded. But as soccer was being defined both by commercial interests and legal decisions, it included females, and Judge Matsch's decision provided a legal precedent to do so. The cultural trends surrounding soccer may have swayed him. Presumably, he was aware that soccer was being promoted as a game for less-athletic children, and he probably knew that soccer was not perceived as a hyper-masculine game like football. He was aware of the inconsistency between the arguments of the Colorado Association and the image that the AYSO was promoting. The judge's unambiguous language in conjunction with the cultural perception of soccer in 1977 might have helped convince the state of Colorado not to appeal his ruling. Matsch was not opening a sport that had long been a traditional American masculine preserve. Rather, he was preventing soccer from becoming such a preserve. His rhetoric, however, would be cited when judges opened other traditionally masculine American sports, including football and wrestling, to girls.

Judge Matsch may have listened to the arguments as a man as well as a judge. Physically, he was unimposing, standing about 5'7" and weighing no more than 150 pounds. Arguments in favor of protecting small women from sports probably would not have swayed his emotions, especially as he had been the smallest member of the Burlington (Iowa) Junior College state champion football team in 1948. Although raised in Iowa, he attended the University of Michigan, where he became a loyal football fan. An avid jogger, he was appointed a federal district court judge by President Richard Nixon in 1974, just two years after Title IX was enacted. Further, his youngest daughter was about nine and attending a Denver-area school when *Hoover v. Meiklejohn* went to trial.[62] His decision would have had an effect on her extracurricular options in high school.

Although the Colorado case did not go so far as to say that girls had a right to play on boys' teams (on the contrary, Matsch ruled that separate teams were permissible under the equal protection clause), the New York State Board of Regents did. The Colorado decision, the only published soccer and gender decision, was released in April 1977. In October 1977 a Westchester County girl threatened to bring another case forward.

Valerie Robbins had been practicing on the freshman boys' team at Horace Greeley High School. The school had a girls' squad, a squad that had no uniforms and no scheduled interscholastic games but a squad nonetheless. Valerie, however, was much better than any of the other girls, and she wanted to improve her skills against better competition. Horace Greeley's principal initially told Valerie that she could not play on the boys' team, but he let her join after her parents contacted the National Organization for Women and the American Civil Liberties Union to investigate a possible Title IX violation (he also received a note from Valerie's pediatrician, indicating her good health). Then, in October, an opposing team walked off the field when Valerie entered a game.

The other school's athletic director and principal said they had to observe the New York State Board of Regents' rule that girls could not play soccer on boys' teams. After the incident the State Educational Department issued a report saying that "girls on the whole are not more susceptible to athletic injuries" than boys. The Board of Regents decided to address the issue at its next meeting.[63]

At that meeting the regents revised their rules in order to comply with their perception of Title IX. As a result, girls would in the future be allowed to compete on boys' soccer and baseball teams but not on basketball, football, or wrestling squads (all defined by Title IX as contact sports). In order to try out for a boys' team in soccer or baseball, however, girls—but not boys—would have to go before a review panel consisting of the school doctor, a physical education teacher, and, at the girl's parents' request, a doctor of their choosing to determine her "fitness to participate with boys." The only medical doctor on the Board of Regents voted against the rule change because he was concerned about "the rash of injuries among females" playing sports.[64]

The rule change that allowed Valerie Robbins to try out for the boys' team reportedly pleased her, although she was less than thrilled at the need for a review panel in addition to her doctor's note. She stated, however, that she wanted to play on the boys' squad only because of the greater level of competition, adding, "Actually I prefer to play with the girls—when the guys on the team start talking about the girls they like, what am I supposed to do?"[65] Her reaction indicated that, for Valerie at least, the non-competitive ideal of soccer was not acceptable. She played in order to improve, not socialize. The social controls used to exclude Valerie despite the board's ruling, however, were successful. During tryouts fans harassed her before and after practice, and her teammates often refused to pass her the ball during practice games. Despite scoring the only goal of the pre-season for her team, Valerie was ultimately cut from the boys' squad.[66]

The situation Valerie Robbins encountered in New York, however, seems to have been relatively rare. Although she faced concerted social opposition to her participation in coed soccer, no other similar stories appeared in the media during the 1970s. The New York City area has strong ethnic communities in which soccer is a popular and masculine game, so the fact that the area was less willing than a more homogeneous Colorado to try to make soccer masculine is not surprising. The New York situation was also about coed soccer with high school students. Valerie's school already had a separate girls' team, suggesting that the community was not concerned so much with the dangers of the sport as with the dangers of coed high school teams.

At a time when Title IX inspired women and girls to try to gain access to various sports, soccer was only a minor skirmish compared to conflicts over other, more culturally significant sports where dozens of lawsuits were filed in dozens of jurisdictions. For soccer, only *Hoover v. Meiklejohn* had a written decision, while other communities, like New York state, acquiesced before the matter went to trial. Even the Colorado Activities Association accepted Judge Matsch's decision and did not appeal. Why American males did not fight harder to make soccer a masculine preserve stemmed in part from the nature of the game.

Although America was embracing it as a new national game, soccer had a vaguely un-American reputation as being almost a kinder, gentler sport than football, baseball, and basketball. These were by definition manly sports, requiring size and speed and allowing for intense parental and coaching involvement. Soccer opened its doors to smaller players, fearful players, players who did not want to be yelled at during the game, and children of fearful parents who did not want their child yelled at. By transforming soccer into a less competitive sport, American society deemed it acceptable for girls to join teams, form leagues of their own, and even, on occasion, play with their brothers. That was the case because most Americans knew little about the sport and had no emotional attachment to it.

Soccer at the Turn of the Twenty-first Century

After Judge Matsch's decision, women and girls' participation in soccer grew exponentially. In 1999 the Soccer Industry Council estimated that approximately 7.4 million American females played, most of them girls.[67] The number of girls who play soccer is almost impossible to count when factoring in school, community, and church leagues that do not register with national soccer organizations, but, clearly, many girls do play soccer in the twenty-first century.

Girls and women have continued to participate in soccer on an international level as well, gaining greater international success faster then their American brothers, who have yet to win a World Cup. In 1991 the U.S. women's national soccer team won the inaugural World Cup in China, but no one in their own country paid much attention. No games were televised, and almost no one knew of their feat. In fact, when the team arrived home they were met by four people at the airport.[68] In 1995 the women made it to the semifinals of the second World Cup in Sweden, but again their country failed to notice their achievements.

All that would change in 1996 at the Olympic Games held in Atlanta. In their own country, and in a full University of Georgia football stadium, the national team won a gold medal. National interest was at last piqued. After their Olympic success, the Women's World Cup Organizing Committee of the 1999 World Cup began to rethink its strategy for marketing the games, which would be held for the first time in the United States. Like their NASL predecessors, the committee focused on marketing to young people, especially girls who played soccer. They decided to hold the games in large venues, even though the semifinals of the previous World Cup had drawn only three thousand spectators, gambling that Americans would be more excited about large spectacles. Each game was televised and heavily marketed.[69]

The commercial success of the World Cup exceeded all expectation. More than ninety thousand people (including a large number of young white girls) attended the finals between the U.S. and China in the Rose Bowl on July 10, 1999, and 2.9 million American households watched it on television, more than watched game seven of the National Hockey League's Stanley Cup Finals. Ticket sales generated almost $23 million, and nineteen companies paid $6 million each for sponsorship rights.[70] The event proved that people would watch women's sports and that it could be a lucrative business.

The U.S. National Team is in some ways a microcosm of the youth version of the game. Its members in 1999 were overwhelmingly white, middle-class, and suburban-bred, and youth soccer is one team sport in America filled with white, suburban, pony-tailed girls who compete ferociously on coed and single-sex teams. Despite its competitiveness, in some ways the sport has become perceived as a preserve for attractive, heterosexual (usually white) female athletes. Late-night talk-show host/ comedian David Letterman, for example, repeatedly referred to the 1999 National Team as "Soccer Mamas" who were "hot." *Sports Illustrated* columnist Rick Reilly wrote that year that when he first saw the team he expected "Joe Torre in heels" but instead found, "They've got ponytails! They've got kids! They've got (gulp) curves!" The ponytail, in fact, would be incorporated into the World Cup logo, a signal that organizers wanted to emphasize the femininity (and hence implicit heterosexuality) of the team and sport.[71] The players' ponytails, race, and socioeconomic class, along with the perception that this game would be good for girls, have resulted in a thriving youth game. Much of its popularity among girls at the turn of the twenty-first century had roots of 1977, when soccer in America did not have the chance to became a masculine preserve.

Concluding Thoughts of Soccer

Chronologically, soccer was alone in the midst of a national debate about whether girls should participate in contact sports. The *Hoover* decision in 1977 was earlier than one might have expected, given that soccer was a marginalized sport in America. In 1977 the baseball conflicts had just ended and the struggles over the gender of football and basketball were only beginning, so the timing of *Hoover* was unexpected, but its ramifications would be great. Judge Matsch would be the first to articulate the separate but comparable standard for gender and sports and to indicate that this would be a constitutionally acceptable solution to the situation. Almost every subsequent court would echo his words. Soccer would also be one of the few sports in which public opinion would not oppose female participation after the court-ordered integration of the game.

Another struggle over soccer occurred in 1988. A high school girl in Illinois wanted to play on her school's boys' soccer team because there was no girls' team. She played out the season on a series of temporary restraining orders, and when it concluded her school created a girls' soccer team, at which point her lawsuit was dismissed as moot. In the grand legal history of gender and contact sport the case was much more logically placed than the 1977 decision because it came after the socially important American sports had been gender-integrated. But the 1977 decision likely contributed to the district court's willingness to grant temporary restraining orders and the high school's ultimate willingness to open soccer to girls.[72] The Illinois girl's struggle was not even reported in the Chicago-area newspapers, a suggestion of the degree to which most Americans assumed, just eleven years after Judge Matsch's decision, that a girl had every right to be on a soccer field.

When the U.S. women's national soccer team won the 1999 World Cup, journalists and commentators alike suggested that the victory was proof that Title IX had been successful. Former Congress member Pat Schroeder observed that it was "a dream come true for a Title IX pioneer."[73] *Newsweek* reported that "World Cup Fever seemed to signal that twenty-seven years after Title IX legislation mandated equal financing for girls' athletics, women's team sports have truly arrived."[74] *Time* credited the legislation with even broader powers: "Daughters of Title IX, they've [the U.S. women's soccer team] never been told what they cannot do."[75] Donna De Varona, a women's sport activist, wrote for *USA Today* that "our team is made up of Title IX babies. They are the first generation of athletes to benefit from a university and college sports program that supports them."[76] Mary Jo Kane, a sports scholar, said, "It's impossible to talk about the U.S. women's World Cup [team] and not talk about Title IX." The House of Representatives debated whether a congratulatory resolution should refer to Title IX. The Republican version, which made no mention of it, passed, but the Senate resolution credited Title IX with creating the "opportunity for millions of American girls and women to compete in sports."[77]

It was an appropriate moment to reflect on the power of Title IX, and the surrounding hoopla helped to confirm the law's mythical presence in the American imagination. The World Cup team, however, also owed a large debt of gratitude to Judge Richard P. Matsch, Donna Hoover, and the equal protection clause.

6 Wrestling

Wrestling, one of the world's oldest sports, is built on strength and enhanced fighting skills. The ancient Greeks wrestled in their Olympic games, and the sport has survived in various forms ever since. In general the sport in the United States does not have the numbers (excluding professional wrestling), either in terms of participation or revenue production, of football, baseball, or basketball, although in some regions it is exceedingly popular.[1] For example, midwestern members of the Big Ten and Big Twelve collegiate conferences have long been wrestling powerhouses, and wrestling in those states has been and remains a successful sport, drawing large audiences and recruiting young participants. The captains of wrestling teams in small midwestern towns are often the social equals of the captains of football teams.

Wrestling is, even more than football, an intensely physical sport, and those who participate are lauded for their strength and quickness. Perhaps as a result of that physicality and the sport's origins as training for warriors, wrestling has been predominantly male throughout its history. As with baseball, football, and basketball, however, girls ultimately asked for the opportunity to try out for school wrestling teams, and, as was the case in those other sports, some communities refused to give them that opportunity. The girls sued, trying to rely on Title IX and the Fourteenth Amendment of the U.S. Constitution, and yet even when the courts opened the mats to girls, cultural opposition remained strong.[2]

A Social and Legal History of Female Wrestling

Despite the sport's physicality and warrior-training origins, historians have established that a few women and girls wrestled, at least sporadically, from almost the beginning of the sport. Spartan leaders, for example, encouraged girls and young women to wrestle and otherwise participate in physical activities. Why Spartan females were so active has remained a matter of debate. Some scholars have suggested that the Spartan goal was to encourage strong females who would bear strong sons, but others have suggested that their athleticism represented the greater freedom Spartan women enjoyed compared to their Greek counterparts.[3] In addition, several different African tribes allowed young girls to wrestle. In some the girls wrestled against each other as part of initiation into womanhood. Among the Diola of Gambia, for example, girls and boys wrestled among their own gender, and the champions married. In still other tribes, reportedly, boys and girls wrestled against each other for sport.[4]

In Western civilizations, accounts of commercialized and professionalized females wrestling date to the eighteenth century in Europe and the United States. In the second half of the eighteenth century Margaret Evans from North Wales allegedly wrestled into her seventies, even against men much younger than she.[5] Some women in England wrestled in barns, with the winner taking a plateful of coins collected from the spectators; French women wrestled at fairs. In 1893 in America the *Police Gazette* sponsored a women's championship round for which combatants dressed in tights and, to prevent hair pulling, cut their hair short.[6] Thus the history of female wrestling predates 1972 and Title IX, but that long history did not make it easier for girls in America to gain access to the sport.

Unlike any other contact sport, lawsuits regarding access to wrestling were published before Title IX's enactment in 1972. One particular decision, published in 1956, concerned denying female wrestlers professional permits. The decision is worth examining because it foreshadows many arguments that would follow enactment of Title IX.[7] In October 1955 the state of Oregon prosecuted Jerry Hunter for wrestling without a license, which she had been unable to obtain because Oregon state law limited professional wrestling to men. Hunter appealed her conviction on the grounds that the equal protection clause of the Fourteenth Amendment made the Oregon law unconstitutional. The state supreme court in 1956 concluded that a gender-based classification was rationally related to the legitimate state interest in protecting public health, morals, and the safety of the participants. The Oregon Supreme Court added that no one enjoyed a constitutional right to wrestle or otherwise participate in sports. In a caveat, however, the court attempted to analyze why Oregon's legislature might have enacted the prohibition on female wrestlers. Noting that the legislature was overwhelmingly male, the court stated:

> Obviously, [the legislature] intended that there should be at least one island on the sea of life reserved for man that would be impregnable to the assault of woman. It had watched her emerge from long tresses and demure ways to bobbed hair and almost complete sophistication; from a creature needing and depending upon the protection and chivalry of man to one asserting complete independence. She had already invaded practically every activity formerly considered suitable and appropriate for men only. In the field of sports she had taken up, among other games, baseball, basketball, golf, bowling, hockey, long distance swimming, and racing, in all of which she had become more or less proficient, and in some had excelled. In the business and industrial field as an employee or as an executive, in these professions, in politics, as well as in almost every other line of human endeavor, she had matched her wits and prowess with those of mere man, and, we are frank to concede, in many instances had outdone him. In these circumstances, is it any wonder that the legislative assembly took advantage of the police power of the state in its decision to halt this ever-increasing feminine encroachment upon what for ages had been considered strictly as manly arts and privileges?[8]

No, the court announced, women's constitutional rights had not been denied, and wrestling could remain a man's domain. The court's diatribe was so heavy-handed that fifty years later it seems almost tongue-in-cheek, but concluding it was constitutional to exclude women from wrestling indicates that the justices were quite serious. In 1956 their decision was perfectly reasonable and legal in light of the prevailing Supreme Court decision holding that a Michigan state law could prevent women from tending bar unless their husbands or fathers were present.[9] The conviction, however, that some aspects of society needed to be reserved for males alone would resonate throughout the next fifty years as many in society fought to exclude girls from participating in wrestling, just as they had opposed a female presence in every other socially significant sport.

After this case, little on women and wrestling was published, nothing in legal documents and not much more in contemporary media accounts. Even the initial enactment of Title IX in 1972 did not really change the status of wrestling and the role that girls played in it. Women and girls, of course, as they had in the past and as would in the future, did wrestle, but their numbers were few, and public acknowledgment was limited. In 1974 the University of California at Berkeley offered a women's wrestling class through its physical education department, and a number of women enrolled. Public interest outside UC-Berkeley, however, was so low that three women in 1974 competed for an unsanctioned title they had created and called the National Amateur Women's Wrestling Championship.[10]

Unlike baseball, football, basketball, and soccer, wrestling saw no lawsuits filed in the 1970s by girls attempting access to a team. A few areas of the country had responded to Title IX's enactment and its culturally imagined power and threat by opening all school sports to all children despite the fact that Title IX enforcement regulations allowed schools to prohibit girls from participating in contact sports with boys. Maryland, for example, opened all sports to girls in 1977 if no comparable girls' team existed, and the District of Columbia in 1979 allowed girls to try out for boys' football and wrestling teams, at least until separate leagues were formed.[11] Unlike baseball, football, basketball, and even soccer, over which court and cultural battles were openly waged, girls seemed to be creeping into wrestling, and no one, aside from a few newspaper articles, seemed to care much. Two Oregon girls, for example, were allowed to try out for their high school varsity squad in 1981, and the coach, who was initially skeptical, encouraged them once he realized they were serious. The *New York Times* reported the story in just eighty-nine words, never acknowledging and perhaps unaware of the 1956 Oregon decision that had denied women wrestling permits.[12]

In 1985 wrestling and girls stepped into the public media spotlight in part because America Morris of San Diego, a fifteen-year-old sophomore, pinned her male opponent in the 107-pound weight class twenty-one seconds into the second period. She was possibly the first girl in the country to pin a boy in a varsity wrestling match, and she instantly became a star, gaining national media attention and a front-page photograph in San Diego newspapers.[13] At this point in the mid-1980s, courts had clearly ruled that girls could not be denied access to baseball, football, basketball, or soccer because of gender. But the rulings did not mean all Americans were ready to accept the fact the Fourteenth Amendment gave girls a right to try out for all contact sports teams. After America's mat success, their interest in wrestling began to become a more significant topic in the media and courts.

WRESTLING IN NEBRASKA

In 1988 Stephani Saint wanted to wrestle on her high school team in Omaha, Nebraska, a region with a strong wrestling tradition. Her school had no girls' squad, so Stephani wanted to wrestle on the boys' team. The Nebraska School Activities Association (NSAA), however, prohibited coed wrestling. Despite requests by the school's principal and wrestling coach, the NSAA refused to grant Stephani a waiver that would have allowed her to wrestle, so she sued under the equal protection clause. The NSAA claimed to have excluded Stephani for reasons of safety, the dangers of cutting weight, and the fact she had no experience wrestling. The court declined to consider the last two arguments because they applied boys as well as girls, which invalidated their legitimacy as reasons for gender discrimination.

By 1988 the U.S. Supreme Court had clearly established the intermediate scrutiny test to evaluate gender segregation, which meant the NSAA needed to establish that the segregation was substantially related to important state objectives. Just like all the other courts that heard gender and contact sport cases, Federal District Court Judge Lyle Strom was willing to classify safety as an important state objective. The NSAA offered medical testimony that school-aged girls were smaller and weaker than school-aged boys. Even though wrestlers were divided by weight classes, it added, girls were still in danger from boys, who despite weighing the same as girls would be stronger and more muscular. Girls, by contrast, would carry their weight as fat, making them more susceptible to injury.

Judge Strom, like jurists who had considered the football cases, discounted that testimony because it rested on generalizations and said nothing about Stephani's physical abilities. The NSAA's safety argument was further undermined when the court discovered that the association had granted waivers to play football to two girls, and, the NSAA's medical expert testified, football players were six times more likely to be injured than other athletes. The court found that willingness to let some girls play football and yet exclude Stephani from wrestling to be inconsistent with the justification of worrying about safety. Stephani was thus granted a temporary restraining order, allowing her to wrestle on the team.[14]

Why the NSAA would allow girls in 1988 to play football but not wrestle was unclear. Although the border region between Iowa and Nebraska had a strong wrestling tradition, Omaha was a mere ninety miles from the University of Nebraska football powerhouse, giving the region an equally strong football tradition. By 1988, however, federal district courts across America had unanimously concluded that girls had a right to try out for school football teams under the equal protection clause, rejecting arguments that girls would be injured if allowed to play. Presumably, the NSAA allowed girls to play football because lawyers had advised them that the law was fairly clear with regard to that activity.

The NSAA made essentially the same safety argument regarding wrestling that had failed so many in other sports, but courts had not yet addressed the issue of wrestling specifically in the post-Title IX and equal rights amendment era. The only previous Fourteenth Amendment decision in wrestling was the Oregon case in 1956 wherein the court was willing to protect one final male preserve. Judge Strom, however, ignored the Oregon decision entirely, not even footnoting its existence and citing instead the more recent football decisions.

The *Saint* decision was the only published wrestling and gender case for the next eight years, but the media continued to describe skirmishes in various regions over gender and wrestling. In 1994 the Colorado High School Athletic Association abolished its rule prohibiting coed wrestling teams after several girls who wanted to wrestle argued for that opportunity in front of local school boards.[15] The next year, however, a Denver-area school district refused to sanction coed wrestling matches, preferring instead to hold gender-segregated competitions.[16] Other districts and leagues, such as those in Arizona, refused to allow girls to wrestle; if any lawsuits were filed, they were settled before a published judicial decision.[17] No additional court decisions were published until 1996, when Tiffany Adams sued the Valley Center School Board in Kansas for the right to try out for her school's wrestling squad.[18]

KANSAS WRESTLING

Tiffany Adams was a fifteen-year-old high school freshman who had wrestled the previous season in the eighth grade. Although she had a five-and-three record, three of those wins had come in the form of forfeits from boys who refused to compete against her. One loss had come against a female opponent. Her eighth-grade coach, who was also the ninth-grade coach, testified that Tiffany had not advanced as quickly as her eighth-grade teammates. When Tiffany asked to try out for the ninth-grade squad, the local school board held a meeting on the subject. After listening to numerous parental comments the board voted whether to limit the wrestling teams to boys, but it was equally divided and failed to reach a decision. After the meeting, however, Bob Neel the district superintendent, concluded that girls should not wrestle and accordingly informed Tiffany's high school. Tiffany filed suit under both Title IX and the equal protection clause.

At both the school board meeting and the trial, numerous reasons were cited for excluding girls from wrestling, most of which centered around the physicality of the sport. First and foremost, Neel claimed to be concerned about the physical safety of girls wrestling boys, particularly because of boys' greater size and strength. At the trial, the wrestling coach worried that Tiffany was not as strong as her teammates; she bench-pressed 120 pounds, and other boys in her weight class benched two hundred. He then admitted that he had no baseline strength requirement for boys who wanted to wrestle.

Because of the size and strength differential, some parents feared that coed wrestling would teach boys that they could physically dominate women, an attitude parents did not want to foster, even inadvertently (ignoring the fact that Tiffany had beaten two boys and therefore at least two had learned they could not always physically dominate a girl). Other parents considered coed wrestling morally wrong, suspecting that the "improper touching" of a coed wrestling match would have sexual overtones. The dangers of contact, Bob Neel anticipated, also included the danger of litigation from sexual harassment suits because of the amount of contact between coaches and wrestlers. The coach testified at trial that he never demonstrated holds on young Tiffany when she was on his team, initially implying that he worried about touching her. On cross-examination, however, he admitted he could not demonstrate holds on any wrestler because of a knee injury. The school district also had him testify that, as part of his coaching duties, it was often necessary for him to touch injured arms and chests.[19]

The fears about contact between coaches and female participants were reminiscent of concerns that Little League officials had raised twenty years earlier when baseball officials worried about how to treat girls who might have been struck in their chests or groins by balls. At that time Little League officials said, "Suppose a girl gets hurt on the legs? Why that's not going to go over—some grown man rubbing a little girl's leg."[20] One youth baseball league in 1974 required that female players' parents or guardians be in the stands so the coaches, if a girl was injured, would not have to be "embarrass[ed]" about touching or seeing her body.[21] Wrestling officials had the same concerns, but after many changes in the status of women in society over the previous twenty years they could couch those concerns in the language of sexual harassment rather than speaking in code.

In addition to the concerns about contact, the school district acknowledged other anxieties about implications of coed wrestling. Some parents, like those who had opposed coed Little League more than twenty years earlier, feared that boys would quit the squad or be psychologically damaged if they lost to a girl. Implicit in that argument was the fear that Tiffany's presence on the mat would diminish the sport. When the boys quit, the sport would be ruined, and if boys did choose to stay on the team they no doubt would not want to practice against a girl. If boys were forced to practice with a weaker, less-skilled girl, their skills would deteriorate. The facts at the trial, however, undermined this argument. The coach also testified that several boys had threatened to quit the team because of Tiffany, but none had actually done so; moreover, some had not volunteered to practice against her, but others had. On a practical note, the board also argued that coed teams would disrupt the school setting by complicating locker-room usage and undermining the psychological well-being of boys on the team.[22]

In the published decision, Federal District Court Judge Frank G. Theis considered a few of the district's arguments under Tiffany's equal protection clause claims. The judge immediately dismissed her Title IX claims because the enforcement regulations excluded contact sports like wrestling. First, Theis concluded that the district's arguments based on "moral beliefs and a variety of inconveniences" were not viable reasons for gender segregation because they did not constitute important governmental interests. He noted that school districts did not indulge every "parental complaint or whim" and added that it was "not the duty of the school to shield students" from situations students might find "objectionable or embarrassing due to their own prejudices." Administrative complexities of locker rooms and coaching techniques, the judge added, were "trivial problems" and not "important governmental objectives" because they could be overcome with "minimal effort." Next, Judge Theis acknowledged that the district had named important governmental interests when it worried about safety, sexual harassment, and disruption of the school setting. Just like the *Saint* decision in Nebraska and the football decisions, however, Judge Theis rejected the safety claim as being an overbroad and patronizing generalization about gender size and strength. The judge also considered the danger of sexual harassment litigation, noting that avoiding litigation was an important governmental interest, but then he rejected it as not substantially related to gender segregation. "Wrestling is an athletic activity," Theis wrote, "and not a sexual activity." Girls on the squad, he added, would know the difference. A school district, he concluded, "best avoids sexual harassment litigation by acting to prevent sexual harassment rather than excluding females." The judge also rejected the district's theory that boys on the team, should Tiffany wrestle, would be psychologically damaged because they would feel badly about themselves or perhaps quit the team, disrupting the school's environment. Theis saw no evidence that boys would be damaged, and, he added, the school would not be disrupted if a few boys quit the team. Keeping Tiffany out of wrestling, he observed, was not necessary to keeping the school "running smoothly."[23] Judge Theis allowed Tiffany the opportunity to wrestle.

Perhaps the most significant element of the Nebraska *Saint* case and the Kansas *Adams* case was timing. By 1988 when Stephani Saint sued Nebraska, the majority of the federal district courts had decided that the Fourteenth Amendment gave girls the right to try out for contact sports, yet Nebraska, despite precedent, fought all the way to a trial. The Kansas school district's decision to fight coed wrestling was unusual because of the *Saint* decision eight years earlier. By 1996 it seemed unlikely, given the legal history of gender and contact sports, that courts would allow a school district to bar girls from a school-sponsored boys' team without a comparable girls' team, and yet the Kansas school district did just that regardless of the Nebraska precedent. Both district courts concluded that the law was clear and decided in favor of female wrestlers with a minimum of fuss and a few quick citations to the many contact sports decisions that allowed girls to try out.

Tiffany Adams's choice to use Title IX to gain access to a contact sport was equally unusual, given that every court since the half-court basketball cases twenty years earlier had unanimously rejected such attempts. Her efforts suggested the continuing power that people imagined Title IX carried even twenty-four years after enactment. The athletic association's attempts to exclude girls from wrestling suggested, in turn, strong cultural antagonism to coed wrestling in regions where the sport was popular. The courts, however, did not allow public sentiment to stand in the way of the equal protection clause. Forty years after the *Hunter* decision in Oregon, federal district courts in the Midwest clearly stated that the Fourteenth Amendment prohibited gender discrimination in wrestling.

THE TEXAS BATTLE

Although the two midwestern district courts unambiguously ruled that the equal protection clause allowed girls the opportunity to wrestle, the dispute over coed wrestling was not finished elsewhere in the United States. Around the same time as the *Adams* decision in Kansas, the state of Texas was engulfed in a debate over girls and wrestling. Wrestling had not been a traditionally popular sport in Texas. In fact, the state-run high school athletic association, the University Interscholastic League (UIL) that oversaw sports like baseball, football, and basketball, did not sanction interscholastic varsity wrestling. Therefore, the Texas Interscholastic Wrestling Association (TIWA) was established in 1966 to promote the sport. The TIWA, funded by dues from public schools, wrote all rules for wrestling—including one banning girls. Perhaps cognizant of Texas's youth football leagues' successful arguments in the 1970s about being private groups and not sufficiently involved with the state to be state actors, the TIWA considered itself a private organization as well and as such claimed immunity from Title IX and the Fourteenth Amendment.[24]

The struggle over gender and wrestling began in January 1996, when five girls in the Dallas region joined their high school wrestling teams. The girls were allowed to practice with the school teams, and they wrestled against each other in exhibition duels when their teams had matches against each other. The TIWA had planned to allow two female regional qualifiers to wrestle each other at the boys' state finals in February 1996. Just before the event, however, league officials announced that the two would not be allowed to wrestle because, given the small number of girls in the league, they had not yet "earned the right" to do so. The decision was made after the TIWA faxed a survey to member schools, asking whether the proposed girls' exhibition match should be allowed to proceed at state finals. A coach in Houston replied, "These girls have no right to be allowed to wrestle in the finals when the boys have infinately [*sic*] more hoops to go through to attain this honor. I feel this would greatly take away from the boy's [*sic*] accomplishments in attaining the finals. . . . Please do not detract from what our boys have accomplished!"[25]

Ultimately, the girls were allowed an exhibition match during the event, but immediately afterward the TIWA prohibited female matches, both single-sex and coed, entirely.[26] The following season a few more girls signed up to wrestle, including Courtney Barnett, a nationally ranked judo competitor and junior in high school. As in the previous season, Courtney and the other girls were allowed to wrestle only at the whim of others. The referee could refuse to officiate, the opposing coach could refuse her a match, and the opposing wrestler could refuse to compete. As a result, the girls never knew when or if they would be allowed to wrestle in competition.[27]

The situation came to a head in December 1996. The Barnett family and the American Civil Liberties Union (ACLU) filed a gender-discrimination suit against the TIWA alleging violations of the Fourteenth Amendment and Title IX. Within days the Texas Wrestling Officials Association, which had officially boycotted all coed matches in 1996, disbanded in an unsuccessful attempt to avoid being named in the lawsuit. Officials also announced that they opposed coed wrestling for moral reasons, safety concerns, and issues of liability. In their response to the lawsuit, however, the officials focused on issues of safety and liability.

Like most opponents to coed contact sports, referees were convinced that girls who wrestled against boys would be physically injured. "Hell will freeze over," the organization's former president declared, "before I officiate girls being brutalized by guys."[28] Another referee said, "There's one guy I call the Punisher. If a girl fought him, I'd tell them to call an ambulance—she's going to the hospital."[29] The referee had given the boy that nickname after seeing him wrestle other boys but gave no indication he would refuse to referee an obvious mismatch between the Punisher and another boy.

Referees also claimed to fear being named in sexual harassment suits. The former president explained that "many times we have to grab wrestlers when they fall off the mat, or things are too physical. We have no protection against sexual harassment charges if some girl is offended by the way we touch her."[30] No evidence in the mainstream press suggested that referees had ever worried about being sued by boys offended by how they were touched during a match. The referees reformed their organization at the end of January 1997 in order to preserve the integrity of state championships.[31]

The story became even more complicated when Tom Harrison, state director of the training organization for Olympic wrestlers, announced on December 23, 1996, that he would form the Texas Interscholastic Girls Wrestling Association (TIGWA). The organization would be modeled after TIWA and would provide a separate league in which girls could wrestle. Perhaps not coincidentally, Harrison's son wrestled on the same team and in the same weight division as Courtney Barnett. Although the younger Harrison was an outstanding wrestler whose position on the team was not at all threatened by Courtney, the elder Harrison was opposed on principle to coed wrestling because of "the differences" between boys and girls.[32] Harrison neglected, however, to invite Courtney or any other girl attempting to wrestle in the Dallas region to participate in TIGWA, and the league seemed to disappear after sponsoring the February 1997 girls-only state wrestling championship.[33] Practically, the matter of Texas girls' wrestling was resolved when the state-run University Interscholastic League (which oversaw other high school sports) added wrestling as one of its sanctioned sports for the 1998–99 season and immediately created a separate girls' wrestling league.[34]

Court proceedings continued independently as Courtney Barnett and the ACLU carried their case to the federal district court. At the end of December 1996, Judge Joe E. Fish refused to grant Barnett and the ACLU a preliminary injunction that would have forced TIWA and officials to allow girls to compete against each other and against boys until a trial could be held. Although TIWA had argued that it was not a state actor and hence immune to both Title IX and the Fourteenth Amendment, Judge Fish focused instead on a different procedural argument to deny the injunction. The girls' attorneys, Fish said, had not established that their clients would suffer "irreparable injury" from not being allowed to wrestle.[35]

In August 1998, after Courtney and the other girls had graduated, the case finally reached a conclusion of sorts. TIWA had asked for a summary judgment, arguing that the case should not go to trial for a number of reasons, including the fact that TIWA had been a private organization. Courtney and the ACLU had asked for compensatory damages and an injunction to allow girls to wrestle under Title IX and the Fourteenth Amendment. Judge Fish dismissed the Title IX claims because enforcement regulations exempted contact sport.

With regard to the Fourteenth Amendment, however, the judge expressed frustration that TIWA had raised no defense but "no state action." Fish believed that "it [was] far from clear that the refusal to sanction a mixed-gender contact sport violates the Fourteenth Amendment." He then cited the 1981 *O'Connor v. Board of Education* case from Illinois in which the girl was denied the opportunity to play on a boys' basketball team rather than a girls' basketball team.[36] He also cited several cases in which boys had been denied the opportunity to play on girls' teams.[37] Because TIWA had not addressed the merits of the question, however, Fish awarded damages to Courtney Barnett and the ACLU. The injunction, the court held, was moot because Courtney had graduated and the UIL was running a separate girls' wrestling league.[38]

The controversy in Texas over wrestling was reminiscent of that over football in Texas. The state has seemed particularly reluctant to allow girls into contact sports. Arguments used in Texas to exclude girls were similar to those used elsewhere that focused on safety, litigation, and morals. The major difference was that Judge Fish did not respond as decisively as the federal district court judges in Nebraska and Kansas, instead denying the injunction that would have allowed girls to wrestle. The only element of law on which Judge Fish and his colleagues across the nation agreed was that Title IX did not apply to contact sports. His award of damages seemed to come reluctantly after he expressed regret that TIWA had not addressed the constitutional issues of the case even after he had expressly asked the organization for a brief on the issue.[39] The Texas case is a reminder that female wrestling was still suspect in America and at odds with cultural values and assumptions about gender.

Sex and the Wrestler

Concern about sex and the almost every conceivable way in which it could relate to wrestling was a new element in legal and cultural discourses concerning girls and the sport. Unlike the debates over baseball, basketball, football, and soccer, those who were against girls in wrestling concerned themselves with the sexual side-effects of contact, worries that stemmed in part from the sport itself. From the perspective of the audience, the physicality of participants was outlined by skin-tight tunics that left little about wrestlers' bodies to the imagination. Further, participants' close, full-body contact, grappling, clutching, and throwing, can have sexual overtones, and the language of the sport is filled with sexual innuendoe referring to moves like "high crotch take-downs" and "butt drags."[40] The discussion surrounding girls' wrestling would be marked by sexual considerations that were not as public in debates over sports like basketball, which lack wrestling's extremely physical, skin-to-skin contact.

Some of the more open, public debate about the sexual implications of coed contact sports may have begun during the social changes of the late 1980s and 1990s. Although only about twenty-five years had passed between the struggle to integrate baseball and efforts to integrate wrestling, America had changed a great deal. The fight over integrating Little League occurred in the 1970s before phrases like "sexual harassment" and "sexual orientation" fell as easily from the collective American tongue. By the 1990s, for instance, people had grown accustomed to television talk shows devoted to unusual sexual behavior. That is not to say such discussions or behaviors did not occur during the 1970s, but two decades later they were more public and prevalent in the mainstream press. Just as arguments for gender-segregation in sports had not changed significantly between baseball and wrestling, it is likely that concerns about sexual implications had not changed much either. The issues were not different, but the historical and social contexts were.[41] As a result, sex held a much more prominent position in public cultural discourse during the dispute over gender and wrestling in the 1990s.

Another component of the debate over sex and wrestling was that it deflected sexual suspicion from "our boys" to "these girls."[42] People who had never given much critical thought to scantily clad young men rolling around together on a mat suddenly had a means of deflecting concerns of male sexuality and homoeroticism. They could blame "those girls" for eliciting heterosexual thoughts in "their boys" while ignoring fears about what the boys thought when they touched each others' bodies. The primary focus of the media and opponents of girls' wrestling was heterosexual contact.

The potential for "improper touching" in coed wrestling, which so bothered some parents in the *Adams v. Baker* case in Kansas, was a common theme, and media accounts were rife with fears of the contact having sexual connotations. Generally, the concern was that boys, when wrestling girls, would suddenly realize what exactly they were touching in the midst of a practice or match, and their thoughts would shift from wrestling to sex. Examples ranged over both time and geography. A newspaper began a report about a Michigan girl who wanted to try out in 1986 suggestively: "Every wrestler in the 120-pound weight class wanted to be work-out partners with Stephanie Koets." The coach added, "I could see some problems coming. . . . She's attractive and wrestling is a contact sport."[43] A 1993 editorial in Chicago warned, "Anyone who tells you that such contact [as in wrestling] is completely asexual is either fooling themselves or has never been a teen-age boy."[44] A Florida priest wrote in 1995 to one girl's wrestling coach and asked that she be removed from the team because coed wrestling was an "avenue that might entice improper behavior or erotic feelings."[45]

If the dangers of coed contact were not enough to undermine the moral purity of young men, then contact, it was suggested, might undermine the integrity of the sport itself. A *Los Angeles Times* article, for example, implied that America Morris, the first girl to pin a boy, beat her opponent after he inadvertently touched her breast during the match. The young man was so seemingly disconcerted by this contact that he was unable to concentrate on and thus he failed to wrestle to his potential.[46]

Public discourse centered solely on heterosexual contact and heterosexual desires. No one in the mainstream media suggested that young men might be aroused or even bewildered by any inadvertent contact with male genitalia while wrestling other males. Scholars had long recognized the homoerotic implications of the sport, but the topic, at least judging from its absence in the mainstream media, was not an issue wrestling fans were willing to discuss openly.[47] In that much discussion of heterosexual desire was initiated by wrestling fans who had been (or were at present) actively involved, it is not surprising that they would not want to talk about the homoeroticism of a sport that they, their sons, and their husbands loved—given society's lack of tolerance of homosexuality. Such a discussion might somehow imply something about their own sexual orientation or that of family members. Moreover, social tolerance for a public discussion of heterosexuality was much greater during the 1990s than social tolerance for public discussion of male homosexuality.

Female homosexuality, however, was fair game. Opponents of wrestling worried about the possibility of heterosexual contact between the boys and girls and that perhaps the contact might arouse boys, but many suggested that girls who wrestled were lesbians. For the first time in the debate over gender and contact sport, the sexuality of girls who wanted to compete was openly questioned in the media. Courtney Barnett, a female wrestler in Texas, said that the first question media interviewers usually asked was whether she was a lesbian, and she learned to begin interviews with an announcement that she liked boys and went on dates.[48]

When not overtly inquiring about sexual orientation, people seemed to assume a would-be female wrestler was gay. When a Grand Rapids, Michigan, girl wanted to wrestle in 1986, for example, the coach said he had seen her name on the sign-up sheet and "had thoughts that maybe it was some strong little girl with a butch hair cut that wanted to wrestle. . . . Then [he] met Stephanie [the would-be wrestler] and was very surprised. She [was] a very sincere and attractive girl."[49] The cultural suspicion that female athletes are homosexual is not new.[50] Perhaps because most of the struggle to gender-integrate wrestling occurred during the 1990s—relatively late in the gender and contact sports wars and when society was more willing to discuss sexuality—participants were asked openly about their sexuality. It was the first time the media had felt free to do so.

The threat of lesbians in wrestling served several purposes. It discouraged female participation in the sport because few teenaged girls (regardless of sexual orientation) are eager to be perceived as gay. It worked well in conjunction with the fear of heterosexual contact because it meant that every girl who wrestled was either a slut who wanted to press up against a boy or a dyke who supposedly would not be interested in doing so. Both categorizations kept the discussion away from male homosexuality in wrestling and emphasized instead boys' heterosexuality. They could not help being sexually tempted by sluts, while girls who failed to find their touch sexual must be dykes. The categories were also a form of social control that excluded girls from wrestling. At no point in the public discourse did anyone attempt to reconcile, or even seem to recognize, the contradictory depictions of female wrestlers.

Alongside the specter of lesbian wrestlers was an emphasis in many media articles on the femininity and heterosexuality of girls who wanted to wrestle.[51] Article after article focused on the feminine appearance and girlish hobbies of would-be wrestlers even more so than articles on girls in football focused on their size. A female wrestler in Washington described herself as "girlie" and admitted to spending time shopping and styling her hair; she also planned to go out for cheerleading.[52] Parents of female wrestlers often declared their daughters' more conventionally feminine pursuits, such as ballet, figure skating, and operatic voice training.[53] The title of a *Los Angeles Times* article about America Morris mentioned her femininity and attractiveness, topics reinforced by seven more references in the body of the article. Readers learned everything about Morris—from her hair color (blonde) to her weight (108 pounds) to her embarrassment at once being caught naked at a weigh-in—in addition to information about her boyfriend (Derek) and makeup (used after matches).[54] No media account actually reported a self-identified lesbian in stories about female wrestlers.

Enthusiasm was not universal for girls wrestling in a single-sex setting instead of in a coed setting. Opposition stemmed in part from the notion that female wrestling was entertainment rather than sport, an idea that predated Title IX by at least a century. During the eighteenth and nineteenth centuries, enthusiastic and mixed-gender crowds gathered to watch women wrestle, occasionally even in the nude, foreshadowing the tawdry underside of sport that would be prevalent in boxing.[55] Concerns about audience morality were offered as reasons to deny women professional wrestling permits in Oregon in the 1950s.[56] A sports columnist in a 1993 Chicago editorial updated the argument that female wrestling was just a step away from mud and Jell-O wrestling: "I'm not saying girls should be banned from wrestling—I'm saying it should be restricted along gender lines. That's right—if there's enough of a demand for it, we should institute the sport of girls' wrestling. Hey, I guarantee you it would be popular with spectators, especially the boys. Why, entire entertainment districts in Spring Break college towns have been built on the concept."[57]

That attitude was also present among those prominent in boys' wrestling. A Texas Interscholastic Wrestling Association leader wrote before the 1996 state finals (at which girls were supposed to have an exhibition match) that if girls did wrestle, they should do so "between midnight and 2 A.M., in case they have live t.v. . . . I am strongly opposed to female wrestling. It seems to categorize us with 'W.W.F. RASSLIN.'"[58] In categorizing female wrestling with World Wrestling Entertainment (WWE) and other professional leagues, the official emphasized that girls' wrestling would be for audience titillation and entertainment rather than the athletic capabilities of girls who wrestled. A match might not be fixed, but the audience, he suggested, would not care.

Concluding Thoughts on Wrestling

The struggle to end gender segregation in wrestling has been fierce-ly contested, both legally and culturally, in regions and by those devoted to the sport. Like the major sports of baseball, football, and basketball, the Fourteenth Amendment's equal protection clause and federal courts forced a sometimes reluctant public to open wrestling to girls. The cul-tural discourse on wrestling, like football, remained poised to exclude girls through social control mechanisms by raising fears the girls would be hurt and their weakness would undermine the integrity of the sport, that competing against girls would psychologically damage boys, and, finally, that coed or even female wrestling is about sex, power, and en-tertainment rather than sport.

Courts in the late twentieth century rejected the safety argument along with the implicit contention that weak females would hurt wres-tling as well as themselves, and anecdotal success stories of girls in wres-tling supported those conclusions. Although some who wrestled in coed situations have had matches in which male opponents forfeited rather than compete with them, others have successfully progressed through the ranks and gotten as far as state individual wrestling finals.[59] Their achieve-ments undermine the theory that girls are physically incapable of wres-tling. In fact, some boys who have wrestled against girls suggest that girls have a physical advantage. They tend to be lighter than boys and so do not have to lose as much weight and can train without cutting calories. These boys also claimed girls tended to be more flexible, making it eas-ier to wriggle out of holds.[60]

In addition to individual success, girls' wrestling programs have grown quickly. In 1997 there were 116 girls who competed in Michigan's first girls' state tournament, and organizers and participants were pleased with the event's attendance and level of competition.[61] In 2003 and 2004 the U.S. Girls Wrestling Association reported that almost five thousand high school girls wrestled.[62] At least two high schools have separate boys' and girls' wrestling teams, and at least two states, Texas and Hawaii, have separate leagues. The coach at one school compared the rise in girls' wrestling to that of girls' ice hockey and noted that, ultimately, U.S. women won Olympic gold in ice hockey in 1988 and would someday do that in wrestling as well.[63] Women's wrestling was an Olympic sport in the 2004 games in Athens, Greece.

Contradicting the arguments that smaller, weaker girls would be unable to compete with boys, people worried about how a wrestling loss to a girl would affect a boy's psyche, a concern expressed during the baseball struggles. As one coach said about boys wrestling against girls, "These boys have nothing to gain. If they win, it's expected. If they lose, they're wimps."[64] The first boy to be pinned in America had to meet with his principal to discuss how he felt about the loss.[65] Those who have been most concerned with boys losing against girls have not been the boys who actually compete with girls but the adults involved in the sport. Although a number of boys have chosen to forfeit rather than take the risk and wrestle against a girl, many male wrestlers have not considered competition against girls to be significantly different than competition against boys. The first boy pinned in 1986 admitted that he had been teased by friends and teammates, but he said his psyche and morale were fine and those who teased him were "male chauvinist pigs." He planned to continue wrestling and improve at it.[66] A team member in Texas said of his female counterpart, she "works hard. She's on our team. I don't think of her any differently than anyone else." Another said that the greatest problem was that boys were afraid to lose to girls. "But," he added, "nobody wants to lose. If it's a fair match, you know, it shouldn't matter."[67] Just as they did for baseball, adults worried more about the effect of coed competition than youths who participated. "It's the adults who are running scared," a Texas writer explained.[68]

The most pervasive arguments against coed and even female wrestling, particularly in cultural discourse, have concerned sex, power, and domination. Some have worried that boys who learn to wrestle women will become domestic batterers. A Massachusetts wrestling coach who created a separate girls' team at his school argued that "boys are brought up to respect girls, to never hit them, then all of a sudden they're fourteen or fifteen and you're saying 'Nail her!'"[69] The assumption is that boys cannot distinguish what happens on the mat from what happens in the rest of their lives and do not understand that sports have their own boundaries and rules. The argument fails because boys quickly learn that certain behaviors are acceptable in sports but not in the general society. In sports, they can slap each other's backsides, they can cry, they can hug, and they can show emotions not generally acceptable for men in American society. Moreover, the ranks of professional and collegiate athletes who have been arrested for domestic battery are filled with men who play such sports as football and basketball, where they have infrequently—if ever—encountered women. These men prove that keeping boys and girls from contact in sports will not prevent domestic abuse. Further, the argument assumes that a boy will learn it is acceptable to manhandle a girl, whereas a girl will, apparently, learn nothing about protecting herself from her wrestling experience. It also assumes that boys will always dominate girls on the mat. Those assumptions undermine the strength and power of female athletes.

People have argued that girls will complain about being groped by other wrestlers, by coaches in practice, and by referees in matches and will, therefore, lodge sexual harassment suits. Despite more than two thousand female wrestlers nationwide, however, no complaints have been raised about "immoral touching" by participants, referees, or coaches.[70] The concerns of those who suspect that boys will become sexually aroused when grappling girls have been dismissed by the participants themselves. One girl's practice partner dismissed the groping issues by saying that wrestlers, when out on the wrestling mat, do not worry about whom they are wrestling but about how to win.[71] Whatever sin may be present in female wrestling seems to be in the eye of the beholder, and courts have refused to define wrestling as a sexual activity, thus allowing girls equal access to the sport.

Title IX's role in the sport of wrestling has been convoluted. Ironically, despite the fact that through its enforcement regulations it specifically excludes wrestling, many in the sport blame Title IX for the diminishing numbers of college teams. In 2002 several wrestling organizations, including the National Wrestling Coaches Association, filed a lawsuit against the Department of Education. Enforcement regulations of Title IX and the Office of Civil Rights interpretation of the law, they argued, were unconstitutional.[72]

At least one college wrestling coach, however, has added female wrestlers to his squad in order to meet Title IX requirements that more women participate in sport. Doug Reese, coach at the University of Minnesota–Morris, started a women's wrestling club in 1993, and the team became a varsity sport in 1994. Reese maintains that women's and girls' participation is vital to the survival of wrestling. Wrestling supporters, he says, "can't just fight in courts and in Congress. In the amount of time we've been complaining and petitioning about losing our programs, very quietly women's hockey has gotten in as an Olympic sport and as an NCAA sport." Reese and some others believe that wrestling should follow ice hockey's example and promote female participation in the sport.[73]

7 Boxing

The role of boxing in American culture has been similar to that of wrestling. Like wrestling, boxing is an extremely physical sport historically designed to promote warrior skills, and as such it is and has been male-dominated. Joyce Carol Oates in a cultural consideration of boxing writes that women's role in the sport, according to traditional gender roles, must be marginal, whether as card girls and singers of the national anthem, because female boxers so obviously reverse the gender norm: "raw aggression is thought to be the peculiar province of men, as nurturing is the peculiar province of women. (The female boxer violates this stereotype and cannot be taken seriously—she is parody, she is cartoon, she is monstrous.)"[1] Historically, however, a few women have participated in boxing matches, and thus a rare feminine presence has lurked in the background—although the sport has prided itself as being one of the manly arts. Until relatively recently, however, most Americans have ignored those females in boxing and focused on the masculine aspect of the sport.

The relationship between Americans and boxing has been a complicated mixture of enthusiasm and revulsion. At times prizefighting in any form has been officially banned, but the lure of the ring has remained sufficiently strong to maintain at least minimal interest in the sport, and boxing's popularity and legality have always reemerged. Boxers, especially professional fighters and Olympic champions, have been public figures who perform and live under intense media scrutiny. Even when the scrutiny has been negative, such as that Jack Johnson and Mike Tyson endured, the spotlight on fighters remains bright. The connection between boxing and American culture is a popular subject among intellectuals, cultural critics, and scholars, as in the work of Jeffrey T. Sammons, Gerald Early, and Joyce Carol Oates.[2] Its appeal is largely based on the insight it provides into American society more generally. The role of race and ethnicity in boxing as a microcosm of societal attitudes toward these subjects, for example, has been well documented and critiqued.[3]

Scholars have not been the only Americans intrigued by the sport. The presence of boxing has been pervasive in mainstream American culture, and almost everyone can name at least one boxer, living or dead, either cultural icon or cultural villain. Muhammad Ali, for example, was on almost every all-century athlete list in 1999, even being named ESPN's athlete of the century, and Mike Tyson's multiple criminal convictions have been equally well documented. Love it or hate it, boxing has been and remains an integral part of American culture.

Boxing's negative side, which generates recurrent efforts to ban the sport, has tainted it sufficiently to prevent its rise to the levels of cultural acceptance and approval enjoyed by baseball, football, and basketball. Almost no one has argued that boxing is America's pastime as they have for the big three American sports. In contrast to baseball, football, and basketball, America has no special claim on boxing, given its ancient roots and significance in Western culture dating back to Homer. Although boxing in the late nineteenth century was a popular Ivy League sport practiced by such wealthy blue bloods as Theodore Roosevelt, its link to educational institutions—colleges and high schools—collapsed as the twentieth century progressed.[4] Boxing became a victim of rising insurance costs and fears of litigation. Few high schools or collegiate boxing teams survived the decades beyond World War II. The failure of the connection between education and boxing contributed to a sense that the sport had a different kind of cultural significance than the big three and added to the conviction that boxing was more corrupt and corrupting. The broken link also rendered the structure and hierarchy of the sport complex and confusing.

Amateur boxing is regulated primarily by the Golden Gloves organization, the United States Amateur Boxing Federation (USABF), and USA Boxing, and several different organizations sponsor title fights at the professional level. The organizational structure has never been particularly clear for either amateurs or professionals, and the lack of structure for the pros has led to continuous allegations of thrown fights and bought judges.

The paradoxical nature of the sport has added to its puzzling role in American society. Boxing is a brutal activity of carefully defined and enforced rules. Its role as a warrior art in a civilized world has been further discomfiting. Elliott J. Gorn has argued that the pre-match stripping of clothes represents a stripping away of civilization as well.[5] The result is a sport that enjoys moments of great popularity but also suffers troughs during which Americans question whether boxing should be legal.

Although Title IX regulations explicitly list boxing as a contact sport, very few, if any, colleges or high schools currently offer it at the varsity or even club level, rendering the regulation moot. This is not to imply, however, that Title IX has had no impact on boxing. On the contrary, the wave of increased female participation in athletics that typically has been credited to Title IX crashed into boxing as well as other sports. The numbers of female boxers increased after enactment of the legislation in 1972, and those involved in the sport equated that growth with the legislation. Because of the separation between boxing and education (not to mention the contact sport issue), however, the significance of Title IX for boxing has not been asserted in the courts so much as in the press.[6] Instead, like every other contact sport, the Fourteenth Amendment—specifically, the equal protection clause—would ultimately open amateur boxing to women and girls.

A Brief History of Boxing

Boxing's origins in the Western world, like those of wrestling, lie with the ancient Greeks, who used the sport to train their young men to be warriors. For Americans, boxing first gained popularity in the antebellum South, allegedly among slaveowners who pitted their slaves against each other and gambled on the outcome.[7] After the Civil War, boxing's popularity declined, and in some states prizefighting was banned because of its inconsistency with civilized behavior and values.[8] The sport reemerged in the 1880s, when sparring (boxing with gloves) became popular among elite white Americans who endorsed muscular Christianity.[9] During this period Theodore Roosevelt took up the sport, explaining that civilized men needed to have the physical skills to protect the weak from those who would bully them: "Every good boy should have it in him to thrash the objectionable boy when the need arises."[10] These upper-class men believed they were civilized enough to work with the rough tools of boxing and use them to promote civilized behavior, not behave as brutes who brawled in the streets.[11]

Bare-knuckle boxing was the less civilized counterpart in the nineteenth century to sparring, and bare-knuckle prizefighting occurred in ethnic athletic clubs where drinking and gambling provided profit incentives for promoters. Women were discouraged from attending matches, which were extremely violent and bloody. The only women present were servers and prostitutes. As would-be fight promoters around the turn of the twentieth century attempted to increase boxing's fan base and confront its image as a corrupt, underworld sport, women were encouraged to become spectators but not participants. Their presence, as always in the American mythic view, was thought to make the sport more civilized and respectable.[12] Women occasionally violated the social norms and boxed, but they did so in part for the titillation of male spectators. In 1876 a New York City theater hosted a boxing match between women in which the victor won a silver butter dish.[13]

The twentieth century marked another rehabilitation and resurgence of boxing. It was taught in the armed forces during World War I as a method of preparing for hand-to-hand combat. The military also promoted boxing matches as a way to reduce tension among squads and entertain the troops generally by letting those angry with their mates fight it out in the ring. Returning soldiers, having watched government-sanctioned bouts in the army, and immigrants from Europe, where boxing enjoyed continued popularity, increased the fan base for the sport.[14] Gambling and alcohol were closely linked to boxing, and once gambling and drinking were made illegal during the 1920s the sport and its culture moved closer to the underworld. Boxing remained popular, however, and even more women appeared at matches as spectators.[15] Its popularity in American culture had peaks and valleys, depending in part on the character, ethnicity, and color of the heavyweight professional champion. Throughout most of the twentieth century, women and girls usually stayed on the outskirts as spectators and occasionally journalists watching men hone the manly art.

Still, despite social pressure to stay in the audience at boxing matches, some women and girls did box. When the Dallas Junior Gloves Club was created in 1958 to teach boys to box, a number of girls also asked to participate. In 1966, long before enactment of Title IX and the surge in female athletes, the club went coed. So many girls were boxing two years later that the separate Dallas Missy Junior Gloves was founded. Its founder, Doyle Weaver, insisted that boys and girls should be treated equally and banned phrases like "boys should not hit girls" and "girls should go first" from the club. He rejected the cultural belief that girls should be treated "like they were breakable pieces of glass" while boys were treated "like they were a Roman gladiator." Despite his egalitarian attitude, many gyms refused to let the club use their spaces, refusing to allow girls to box on their premises.[16] Notwithstanding such logistical problems, more than three hundred girls boxed with the Missy Junior Gloves at its peak.[17]

Other females attempted to box in professional arenas. In 1975 Jackie Tonawanda filed suit when the New York state athletic commissioner rejected her request to be a licensed professional boxer. The commissioner said that female boxers would ruin the "manly art of self-defense" and bring the sport into disrepute. Further, he worried that women would be injured if they boxed.[18] Eventually, to avoid going to court the commission relented and licensed Tonawanda, and later that year she fought, knocking out a male karate expert in the first minute of the second round.[19] In 1976 two women boxed professionally in Nevada, where the state's boxing commissioner said he had sanctioned the fight because he feared being sued for discrimination but dismissed female boxers as "curiosities."[20]

The rise in the number of female boxers, both amateur and professional, began during the 1960s and 1970s when violence was generally perceived to be on the rise and "crime in the streets" became a catchphrase. It was also a time when women could no longer pretend to count on men to defend them. Self-defense needed to be a practical skill rather than a manly art. The women's liberation movement had helped highlight the abuses women suffered, usually at the hands of men. Although the actual numbers may not have changed significantly, the reported number of rapes and assaults against women increased during this period. Shelters were built, and women filled them, trying to escape violence from husbands or boyfriends. Boxing seemed one way of combating attacks on women and forcing men to keep their distance.[21]

Legal History

In 1982 the first and only published court decision regarding female access to boxing was released.[22] Jill Ann Lafler was a nineteen-year-old from Lansing, Michigan, who wanted to box as an amateur in the local Golden Gloves competition, a competition limited to males. She had received a temporary restraining order from a state court allowing her to participate, pending the results of a trial, but the Athletic Board of Control of the Golden Gloves organization removed the decision to the federal district court because Lafler's discrimination claim was based on the equal protection clause of the Fourteenth Amendment.

The federal district court analyzed requirements for issuing a temporary restraining order and concluded that Lafler had failed to meet three of the four components. To begin, Lafler needed to prove that she had a reasonable chance of succeeding in trial on the merits of her case. The district court doubted that she could prove the Athletic Board of Control was closely related enough to the state of Michigan for the equal protection clause to apply to the board's rulings. To cover all options, however, the court considered the Fourteenth Amendment claims, assuming for argument's sake that state action was involved. The court, using the newly installed intermediate scrutiny test from the Supreme Court, concluded that gender segregation in boxing was substantially related to the important issue of safety. The Athletic Board of Control maintained that the sport was designed for men and that coed boxing would cause injury to females because of the difference in muscle mass. The court acknowledged that previous cases involving football, baseball, and soccer had rejected this argument as patronizing but differentiated boxing because it used "body weight as a proxy for strength in an attempt to equalize the relative physical capabilities of opposing boxers."[23] The court did note that a separate competition for women would satisfy the equal protection clause and encouraged the Golden Gloves to arrange one to avoid future lawsuits. The court concluded that Lafler would not be irreparably harmed if she missed that year's competition; she was only nineteen and a boxing novice and could box in future competitions. Further, public interest in safe boxing tournaments would not be served by issuing a temporary restraining order, which would have allowed Lafler to box before all the pertinent issues were raised at trial.[24]

The significance of the decision lies in its acknowledgment that Lafler's boxing case had to be viewed in the context of other contact sport decisions. The district court recognized that courts considering other contact sport cases had rejected safety and size arguments as being overbroad and making gender generalizations about size and strength. The judge, however, chose to accept weight as a proxy for strength, defying the other courts. The decision was reached in 1982 before any court had considered the case for girls in wrestling and dismissed the proxy as being unconstitutional. Further, the court acknowledged that other courts had accepted separate but equal athletic programs as fulfilling equal protection rights for gender. It also strongly suggested that the Golden Gloves consider this option to avoid violating the Constitution. In doing so the court protected boxing from the potential disruption of coed competition, and in refusing to issue a preliminary injunction it bought amateur boxing more time to adjust to the idea of sanctioning female fighters. The decision also reemphasized what the courts in *O'Connor v. Board of Education* had said when they refused to allow a girl to compete on a boys' basketball team due to the existence of a female team: Coed contact sports were to be a last resort. Permitting females to box with each other was one thing, but permitting them to box with males was another thing entirely.

In 1993 the USABF dropped its prohibition against female competitors after a sixteen-year-old girl in Seattle won a preliminary injunction against the organization. Jennifer McCleery (who boxed under the name Dallas Malloy) wanted to box in a match and aspired to fight at some future Olympics, and she asked only to box other girls, not boys, in her weight division. Federal District Court Judge Barbara Rothstein concluded that the USABF ban violated antidiscrimination laws and ordered the organization to allow the girl to compete until a full trial could be held.[25] The USABF did not fight the injunction and instead opened its doors to girls. Dallas Malloy won the first USABF-sanctioned female fight in a split decision in 1993.[26]

The original preliminary injunction decision was never published, but it seemed that Judge Rothstein ordered the USABF to do what the *Lafler* judge had suggested eleven years before. By 1993 several wrestling cases had addressed the weight-as-proxy-for-strength argument as overbroad and rejected it, making its use more difficult for the USABF. In fact, the decision to open the sport to girls, and their official entrance into the boxing ring, caused little stir at all. The only major newspaper to announce the McCleery decision was the local one in Seattle.

The minimal interest may have been a matter of timing. By 1993 the law had been fairly well established. The Fourteenth Amendment prohibited excluding girls from contact sports simply on the basis of gender. They had participated in contact sports for any number of years, and boxing was just one more. The success of female athletes was increasing in 1993 as record numbers of women and girls participated in sports. At the same time, boxing was sliding into another trough of disrepute. Mike Tyson, the heavyweight champion until 1990, had the reputation of being a brawler inside as well as outside the ring. His first wife left him among publicized accusations of domestic violence, and in 1991 Tyson was arrested for raping nineteen-year-old Desiree Washington, a Miss Black Teenage America beauty pageant contestant. He was convicted and sentenced to jail in 1992.[27] With Tyson as champion it was difficult to maintain the pretense of boxing being a skill used to protect females. Women and girls in the 1990s, even more than in the 1970s, needed the self-defense skills that boxing had always claimed to provide in order to protect themselves from men—even boxers like Tyson.

Boxing Today

During the 1990s, interest in female boxing increased dramatically, and large numbers of women and girls fought as amateurs and professionals. Tension between the reputations and representations of the two increased, however, and professionals were frequently criticized. The pro bouts have been described as "circuslike."[28] One boxing coach, Jake Magellenez, who was also head of the Arizona amateur boxing association, said, "I wouldn't put them [amateur females] in the ring if this was going to be a clown deal like in the pros."[29] Some professionals contributed to that image. In 1999, for example, Mia St. John, one of the more famous female boxers, was featured on the cover of *Playboy*, cupping her bare breasts with a pair of boxing gloves. An executive with HBO Sports commented that female boxing had a "long way to go before it's considered a world-class sport."[30]

Although male boxing (especially at the professional level) has always been a somewhat tainted sport and there have been periodic allegations of thrown fights, the status of male boxers as athletes has not been questioned, nor has the fact that boxing is an athletic event. The distinction between male and female boxers as athletes was highlighted in a 2000 episode of the HBO series *REAL Sports* in which Frank Deford interviewed Laila Ali (Muhammad Ali's daughter) and then Bryant Gumbel talked with Deford about the interview. Deford asked Ali about a recent bout in which she fought an overweight, forty-eight-year-old woman who had just turned pro. Although Ali scored a knockout in the first round, Deford suggested that she let down the sport of boxing by fighting the woman at all and not insisting on a higher-caliber opponent. Ali and her manager pointed out that the match had been originally scheduled against a more qualified opponent who pulled out the day before due to injury. Moreover, the promoter had located the "bum" (as they described Ali's opponent); Ali had nothing to do with selecting the replacement fighter. When Deford insisted that the mismatch diminished the sport of boxing and that not enough quality female fighters existed to schedule legitimate boxing matches, Ali's manager took offense, pointing out that male fighters often fought "bums" after regularly scheduled opponents withdrew and the best one could hope for was a quick knockout, which Ali had done. Ali noted that she trained more than four hours a day and considered herself a serious boxer. After the interview Bryant Gumbel commented that Laila Ali did not seem as graceful in or out of the ring as her father had been.[31] Presumably, he did not consider grace as a conventionally feminine attribute in this context. Female pro boxers seemed, at least in this representation, held to a higher standard than male pro fighters.

The most coverage of any female boxer, although Ali comes a close second, occurred when Margaret MacGregor, a professional, fought Loi Chow, a male part-time jockey, in 1999. MacGregor won, but press coverage was less than flattering before and after the bout. "Freak show" was the most common description.[32] Before the fight, boxing officials condemned the match and ridiculed those involved, questioning their gender and again alluding to the perceived power of Title IX. One promoter said, "If [the man] beats the crap out of her to teach her a lesson, I'm all for it. But if she wins . . . they should put him in a dress and buy him a ticket out of town, never to show his face again." The president of the Association of Boxing Commissions found "no reason to mingle the sexes in this sport. This isn't about Title IX, and this isn't tennis." An executive with HBO Sports announced that the match was "pure exploitation, and we will never air mixed-gender fighting." Concerns about the match went beyond it undermining the legitimacy of the sport. Echoing the parents of male wrestlers, a worker in a shelter for battered women warned that the mixed-gender boxing event would "perpetuate society's acceptance of violence against women."[33] Even the woman's victory did nothing to legitimize female professional boxing or mixed-gender boxing matches.

In contrast to the negative attitude toward female pro boxers, the attitude toward female amateurs has been surprisingly positive, the difference seemingly based on the amateurs' allegedly purer motives for pursing the sport. The head of the Arizona amateur association said that girls who compete in his tournament "know how to fight" and "have learned the athletic skills."[34] Those who fight in amateur tournaments are reported to "put many of the novice male fighters to shame."[35] One amateur boxer maintained that "the hostility toward women's boxing will go away as the skill level continues to rise . . . I don't want to look like a catfight, I want to look like a boxer."[36] Perhaps the positive image comes from the motives attributed to girls who want to learn to box. Some say they want to do so for reasons of self-defense and to stay out of trouble. Still others say they are interested in the sport because it builds fitness and self-confidence.[37] One coach claimed that boxing made girls "productive members of society" because the discipline of the sport kept them away from gangs and drugs.[38] Other coaches suspect that girls who want to learn boxing are victims of sexual or physical abuse and seek tools to protect themselves.[39] Many of these media accounts attributed similar motivations to boys who wanted to box.

The complexity of America's relationship to boxing in general, and female boxers in particular, stems in part from the paradoxes of boxing as being, historically, a racial battlefield. The Caucasian majority has looked for "Great White Hopes" to "rescue" championships away from boxers of color. Although the early advocates of sparring in the 1880s were elite white males, most boxers in the twentieth century have come from poorer minority homes and entered boxing for self-protection, the possibility of profit, and something to do.

There are similarities and differences between the roles of race and that of gender in boxing. The modern media represents boys who box as disadvantaged youngsters of color who have learned to fight in order to give their lives discipline, learn self-defense, and build self-esteem—all things that girls who wanted to box emphasized. Fighters of both genders often share similar socioeconomic roots, although the most famous modern exceptions to that stereotype are the daughters of Muhammad Ali and George Foreman, who grew up in wealthy households. Race and gender also parallel each other in the ring, a stage upon which the subjugated either perform for the powerful (when, for example, minorities or women fight each other) or they challenge the powerful (when black fights white or female fights male). An all-female bout, however, is titillating, and mixed-gender fights challenge gender roles regarding issues of strength and morality differently than do racially mixed fights.

Complications continue in the image of the sport itself. The purpose of boxing, especially at the professional level, seems to be to beat an opponent to a bloody pulp, to subjugate and dominate the opponent into submission. At the same time, a complicated set of rules prohibits low blows and late hits and gives complete control to a referee who is often significantly smaller and weaker than either participant. Boxing has been envisioned as both saving masculinity (as Teddy Roosevelt imagined) and destroying civilization (as courts in the 1860s feared). Gender roles are carefully divided. Women as spectators validate the sport, women in the gym sap the energy of male boxers, and women as sexual partners destroy a boxer's focus.[40] The careful gender segregation contributes to the homoeroticism of a sport consisting of two nearly naked men grappling and hugging in front of a predominantly male audience, as both Oates and Early assert.[41]

Adding female boxers to the mix only increases the paradox. Women are not supposed to have the same masculine inclinations toward violence and rage that men have. Women are supposed to be the civilizing influence on society, and a conundrum results when they box. Fort Worth columnist Bill Thompson summarized the complication well. After watching eight-year-old girls fight for the Female Pee Wee Novice title in the Texas Golden Gloves regional tournament he observed, "When the bell sounded and the girls charged to the center of the ring to begin pummeling each other, I couldn't quite decide if I was witnessing a great step forward for the female gender or the end of civilization as we know it."[42]

In 1999 more than 1,300 females boxed as amateurs, and four hundred women fought professionally.[43] In 2002 more than two thousand females were registered as amateur boxers with USA Boxing, the national governing body for Olympic boxing.[44] The amateur sport, according to USA Boxing, is growing mainly because of increased female participation. Although those in boxing are often impressed with the caliber of female amateurs, the reputation of professionals continues to lag. Regardless of the growth and questions about the legitimacy of the female pros, female boxing has not been the lighting rod of controversy that baseball, basketball, and football were. Court decisions about boxing received far less media coverage than those dealing with girls' participation in wrestling and the big three sports. Part of the lack of public reaction stems from how late in the battle women and girls tried to enter the sport. By the time Jennifer McCleery received her injunction in 1993, courts had already opened baseball, football, basketball, soccer, and wrestling. Some of the minimal reaction stems from boxing itself. America's relationship with boxing has always been complicated, mixing varying portions of love and hate. Adding gender to the stew was not enough for the pot to boil over into greater public controversy.

8   Boys on Girls' Field Hockey Teams

Most lawsuits involving gender and contact sports, which are traditionally male, focused on girls trying to gain access to boys' teams. Before enactment of Title IX the original lawsuits, quite reasonably, concerned girls who wished to try out for boys' teams. The sport of field hockey, however, holds a unique spot in American sporting history. It is arguably a contact sport, and in the United States it is played almost exclusively by girls. Inevitably in the war over gender and sports some boys have asked for the opportunity to try out for girls' field hockey teams.

Although field hockey has been extremely popular in certain regions of the United States, especially the Northeast, the country as a whole has not been enamored by the sport or in some regions even aware of it. Part of the ambivalence has been that field hockey in the United States has been socially constructed as a feminine sport despite the fact that many men in other parts of the world play the game at the international level. As a result of this feminine construction in America, however, the status of field hockey as a contact sport has been unclear. The struggle boys have waged in order to gain access to the sport has centered around the "gendered" aspects of the game and questions such as whether girls' sports can be contact and participating in them affects a boy's masculinity.

All of the sports specifically listed as contact sports (rugby, ice hockey, football, basketball, boxing, and wrestling) have been traditionally dominated by men and boys.[1] The law, perhaps reflecting societal beliefs, seemed to hold that manly combat sports were contact sports, but feminine pursuits like field hockey could by nature and definition only be noncontact. At issue is whether field hockey is in fact a contact sport.

Although players' femininity has been emphasized by skirted uniforms, those who have seen or played the game know it involves contact and even potential violence. It is a sport played with sticks and a hard rubber ball, and participants must be outfitted in shin guards, mouth guards, and other protective gear. A field hockey goalie wears gear similar to that of an ice hockey goalie, with full body padding and a face mask.

Yet field hockey, unlike ice hockey, is not a designated contact sports under Title IX regulations, although they contain one last caveat after the defining list of contact sports: "Other sports the purpose or major activity of which involved bodily contact" might also be considered contact sports under Title IX and its regulations.[2] Many who opposed boys' presence on girls' field hockey teams argued that field hockey should be defined as a contact sport because of that caveat.

The status of field hockey was important legally as well as socially. If it were a contact sport under Title IX, then it would be exempt from gender equity demanded by the legislation. Like football and other contact sports, it would be removed from Title IX. If the sport was determined to be noncontact, however, then boys could argue that they had a right to play under Title IX. Contact and its role in cultural assumptions about sport and gender would be the linchpins of all coed field hockey debates.

Regardless of whether Title IX allowed access to a sport, however, the equal rights amendments (ERA) as enacted by various state legislators and the equal protection clause of the Fourteenth Amendment of the U.S. Constitution might fill that gap. Several boys maintained that these constitutional rights should have given them access to any sport offered only for girls. Those arguments had been tried in another traditionally female sport in America, volleyball, long before the field hockey cases arose. The Illinois Supreme Court ruled in 1979 that boys could be excluded from the sport because of the physiological differences between them and girls and because girls had been discriminated against in the past in athletics. Thus, the court concluded, banning boys from girls' volleyball teams would not violate boys' Fourteenth Amendment protections. Moreover, even though the state's equal rights amendment imposed a "stiffer test" than the Fourteenth Amendment, the Illinois Supreme Court believed that the purpose of the law was to promote "equalization of general athletic opportunities," and it held the opinion that promoting girls' sports achieved that end.[3] The Ninth Circuit Court of Appeals agreed with the Illinois Supreme Court in 1989 when Wade Clark sued to play on a girls' volleyball team in Phoenix, Arizona. The appellate court added that athletic opportunities for boys in Arizona still exceeded those for girls, because male athletes outnumbered female athletes by a two-to-one ratio.[4] Boys interested in field hockey, however, would try these arguments, with mixed results.

The effort to limit field hockey to girls came relatively late in the controversy over gender and contact sports. Although girls by the mid-1980s had generally established their right to try out for any sport offered by a school or community, boys only began to try to edge into field hockey—the only alleged contact sport in which they would try to gain access to girls' teams—during the late 1980s. With the exception of a 1979 Massachusetts case, all field hockey cases arose after 1987, and by then the courts had opened baseball, football, basketball, and soccer to girls. In 1988 the first of the modern wrestling cases was decided, again allowing girls as well as boys to participate, but the debate over field hockey was just beginning.

Legal Cases

When the issue of allowing boys to play on girls' teams was first addressed in the courts, the question was extremely broad: Was it legal to permit girls to play on boys' teams but prohibit boys from playing on girls' teams? After Title IX enforcement regulations were enacted in 1975, and in the enthusiasm created by adoption of the equal rights amendment, the Massachusetts Interscholastic Athletic Association (MIAA) announced that any child could play on any sports team so long as no separate-gender team existed. That ruling allowed girls to play football and boys to play field hockey, softball, and volleyball.

In 1978 the Newton South High School softball team seemed likely to win the state softball championship, concluding a successful season that many in the state credited to the presence of two boys on the team. The Massachusetts Division of Girls and Women's Sports filed suit against the MIAA to change the rule and keep boys off girls' teams in order to protect athletic programs for females. The next year the MIAA bowed to social pressure and excluded male players from female teams (although female players could still play on male teams) in order to have the lawsuit dropped. Three schools, however, had already placed boys on volleyball teams before the rule change, and the MIAA refused to grant them waivers to allow them to compete. Frustrated, the schools asked the state attorney general to examine the MIAA's rule.[5] He believed it to be a violation of the state's equal rights amendment and filed suit to change the rule. The state's highest court agreed with the attorney general and ordered the rule removed from the books, which allowed boys to play on girls' teams if no comparable boys' team existed.[6]

The Massachusetts Supreme Judicial Court's analysis of this decision was remarkably similar to analyses from a majority of courts that considered girls' access to traditionally male contact sports. The court dealt with the same arguments used for exclusion and rejected most of them as being overbroad. Justice Benjamin Kaplan, who wrote the opinion, acknowledged that the court had already rejected attempts to exclude females from football and wrestling under the equal rights amendment in 1977.[7] He relied in part on that decision to nullify the rule excluding boys from girls' teams. Kaplan wrote that "equal rights provisions . . . tend to protect men as well. . . . Although women have been the usual victims of sex discrimination, there are significant exceptions to this generality." He also cited several mandated criminal sentences that were harsher for men than women.

Further, the justice acknowledged that in that year of 1979 they were unsure which test the Supreme Court would apply to gender-based classifications. After summarizing some of the tests Justice Kaplan concluded that the matter of which was applicable was a moot point because the three MIAA rationalizations for gender segregation could not pass any test. First, the MIAA had argued that "sex" acted as a "proxy for function" because of the physiological differences between males and females. The court concluded, however, that the MIAA was relying on culturally constructed stereotypes of gender rather than significant biological differences. The court refused to accept the argument that all or even most boys are inherently better athletes than girls. Second, Justice Kaplan rejected the MIAA argument that a boy's presence on a girls' team would injure girls as being based on the same overbroad assumptions that had led the MIAA to try to ban girls from football. Third, the MIAA maintained that allowing boys to play on traditionally female teams would undermine fledgling athletic programs for women by displacing girls. Although lauding the good intention of creating and nurturing girls' athletics, the justice concluded that banning boys from teams was not the best way to promote girls' sports. Kaplan said the fear that boys would overrun girls' athletic teams was mere speculation based on no real evidence. Further, even if large numbers of boys did want to play on girls' sports teams, he and the court found no evidence that they would displace the girls. Such conjecture, Justice Kaplan concluded, was based on unproved assumptions about the superiority of male athletes. If such a large number of boys wanted to play field hockey or volleyball, he added, the school district should start a separate boys' program to accommodate the interest of all children.[8]

This first Massachusetts decision regarding boys and field hockey, published in 1979, reflected the ideology of gender equality and equal rights feminism that had inspired the ERA and Title IX. The court was consistent in refusing to treat boys and girls differently when it came to supporting their athletic aspirations and in rejecting stereotyped assumptions about the children's capabilities. Regardless of whom the MIAA wanted to exclude from which sports (girls from football or boys from field hockey), the MIAA made the same arguments based on the same assumptions: Because boys were bigger, stronger, and faster, girls would be injured and quit playing sports. The court rejected those arguments as being overbroad, paternalistic generalizations and ordered all sports opened to all children, either in the form of separate or coed teams. The court seemed to believe that opening all sports to all children would best protect individuals as well as boys and girls as a class, emphasizing that the purpose of school sports was to maximize participation by all. This sense of openness and equal opportunity, however, would not be the typical field hockey decision.

The issue of boys playing on girls' field hockey teams was next addressed eight years later in 1987. A New Jersey boy, C.C., had played on the Cumberland Regional High School girls' junior varsity field hockey team his freshman year (1984–85) because the school had no boys' team.[9] After that one season the New Jersey State Interscholastic Athletic Association (NJSIAA), which had received numerous complaints about C.C.'s presence on the field, excluded boys from girls' teams until "such time as both sexes are afforded overall equal athletic opportunities."[10]

After C.C. was removed from the team his father sued on his behalf on the grounds that C.C.'s rights had been violated under the New Jersey State Constitution's version of the Fourteenth Amendment equal protection clause. In a hearing before an administrative law judge (ALJ), the judge ruled in favor of the boy, holding that no substantial public interest was served by excluding him from field hockey because of his gender. The ALJ concluded that field hockey is a noncontact sport in which stickwork is more important than size and speed. The school district appealed to the commissioner of education, who disagreed with the ALJ and refused to let C.C. play what the commissioner believed to be a contact sport. The boy and his family appealed the decision in the state court system.[11]

The Superior Court of New Jersey upheld the commissioner's decision and concluded that banning boys from girls' sports was constitutional under the intermediate-scrutiny test as created by the U.S. Supreme Court. Judge Neil F. Deighan, who wrote the decision, decided that whether field hockey is a contact or noncontact sport was irrelevant for the analysis because everyone agreed, at a minimum, that incidental contact during games was likely. The NJSIAA argued that the purpose of the regulation was to redress prior discrimination against girls in athletics, and the court held that to be an important governmental objective. Exclusion of boys from girls' teams, it observed, was "an appropriate and proper means" of achieving that objective. As proof of its purpose the NJSIAA noted that Title IX's enactment had triggered a rule to be instituted about boys on girls' teams. The New Jersey organization argued that gender segregation was needed to protect girls' athletics. Embedded in that argument was the assumption that because males are bigger, stronger, and faster than females they would be better at field hockey and displace girls from teams.

Addressing these subarguments, Judge Deighan concluded, just as in 1982 the court had in the case of boxing, that gender is an acceptable proxy for size and strength, thus accepting both generalizations.[12] Deighan, recognizing that most courts had rejected the size argument as an invalid classification for excluding females from contact sports, was quick to distinguish letting girls try out for football from allowing boys to try out for field hockey. Girls who tried out for football were not endangering any of the boys with whom they might compete, and they and their parents would be aware of any physical dangers they might face. Boys who played field hockey faced no increased dangers, but their teammates and opponents, who could not necessarily anticipate that they would be playing against a boy, might be endangered. The court feared that a male presence on the field would intimidate female players, causing them to play more timidly or even quit the sport entirely.[13]

This decision raised complicated issues of ideology, discrimination, legislation, and contact. The New Jersey decision to exclude boys from field hockey stemmed from a seemingly feminist argument—the need to redress past discrimination against female athletes. Yet underpinning that argument were the same theories of male superiority that other courts had called overbroad, paternalistic generalizations. Thus those who argued in favor of female equality were placed in the paradoxical position of supporting female participation in sports like football regardless of issues of safety and intimidation while accepting the argument that boys should be excluded from girls' sports because of the same issues. By 1987 most American courts had opened contact sports to girls, but the decision implied that the door to field hockey would be closed to boys.

Even though Title IX did not have a direct role in the decision, both the New Jersey athletic group and the court acknowledged its influence in inspiring rules to help fledgling programs for female athletes. Further,

American courts in the second half of the twentieth century allowed classifications to redress prior discrimination, classifications without the remedial affect that would ordinarily have been unallowable. In other words, because most agreed that female athletes had long been subject to discrimination, affirmative action for them was acceptable. Finally, the *B.C.* decision underlined the difficulties of determining what constitutes a contact sport. The ALJ and the commissioner heard the same testimony and reached opposite conclusions, and the state court declined to make a decision at all, deeming the designation irrelevant for an equal protection clause analysis. The issues would arise again, however, as the gender of field hockey continued to be contested.

The next field hockey decision was published in 1991.[14] Brian Kleczek was a sophomore in 1990 when he tried out for his high school's team. He had played the game in gym class, and his sister had been a varsity player for the team. Relatively few players tried out for the team that season, and no one was cut. Based on his skill level, Brian was assigned to the junior varsity team. The Rhode Island Interscholastic League (RIIL) learned of Brian's participation and ordered him removed from the squad because its rules prohibited coed field hockey. Brian served as team manager that season and occasionally practiced with the team while his parents filed suit under Title IX and the equal protection clause of the Fourteenth Amendment. The federal district court denied their request for a preliminary injunction, which would have allowed Brian to play until a trial, on the grounds that the Kleczeks were not likely to prevail in a trial.[15]

Federal District Court Judge Ronald R. Lagueux rejected Brian's Title IX and equal protection claims. The Kleczeks had argued that field hockey is a noncontact sport, and therefore Brian had a right to play on the girls' team under Title IX until a separate boys' team was established. The judge summarily dismissed the Title IX arguments for several reasons. First, he concluded that the RIIL did not receive direct federal funding and thus was likely immune to Title IX. Even if Title IX did apply to the RIIL, Laguex added, it did not apply to this case because past athletic opportunities for boys in Rhode Island had not been limited, and field hockey is a contact sport. He acknowledged that the rules prohibited contact but from witness testimony concluded that incidental contact was extensive, which placed it in the catch-all category of Title IX enforcement regulations—"the purpose or major activity of which involve[d] bodily contact." The judge also rejected Brian's equal protection claims. He noted that to affirm that classification the league must prove it had an important governmental objective, and the classification employed was substantially related to that objective. The league claimed that its reason for gender segregation in field hockey was to redress past discrimination against female athletes, which the judge agreed, as had the New Jersey court, was an important objective, gender classification being the best way to achieve it.[16]

After failing to win a federal court injunction allowing him to play field hockey, Brian and his parents tried again in the Rhode Island state court system. In his first effort in the state superior court Brian won his injunction after arguing that the ban on boys in field hockey was unconstitutional under article one, section two of the Rhode Island state constitution. The article, ratified in 1986, provides "no otherwise qualified person shall, solely by reason of race, gender or handicap be subject to discrimination by the state." RIIL immediately asked the Rhode Island Supreme Court to stay the injunction until the state's highest court could hear the matter. The supreme court gave RIIL that stay and in 1992 overruled the lower court's decision and kept Brian off the field hockey team.[17]

The lower court had analyzed the article under the strict scrutiny test, requiring that gender segregation be necessary to attaining a compelling state interest, and concluded that Rhode Island had no compelling interest in segregating field hockey. The supreme court, however, believed that the lower court had erred in comparing the article to the equal rights amendment. Because Rhode Island had not adopted the ERA, the state supreme court believed article one could best be compared to the equal protection clause of the Fourteenth Amendment of the U.S. Constitution. Therefore, the court said the proper test for gender segregation was intermediate scrutiny as described by the U.S. Supreme Court in the early 1980s. The court also noted that it believed that RIIL's reasons for gender segregation (safety and the promotion of girls' athletic programs) were important governmental interests.[18]

The two published *Kleczek* decisions continued the trend established four years earlier by the *B.C.* decision in New Jersey. The focus of the decisions, however, differed. The federal court reiterated that issues of contact versus noncontact sports were irrelevant for equal protection analysis but extensively addressed whether field hockey is a contact sport under Title IX. Although the Rhode Island federal district court decided that it is, the space given to a description of the testimony indicated the controversy surrounding field hockey's status. The federal *Kleczek* decision did, however, reiterate that contemporary discrimination is an acceptable means of redressing past discrimination. The state supreme court was involved to address a procedural question of how to test a clause in the state constitution. The state court chose, though, to agree with the federal district court that protecting girls' athletics is important.

Although the legal decisions themselves were significant, perhaps the most dramatic point is that the two separate cases exist at all. Brian Kleczek and his parents went through two separate court systems trying to gain access to field hockey. Although both ultimately rejected his arguments, his persistence revealed how important the sport was to him.

The same year that the Rhode Island Supreme Court rejected Brian Kleczek's claim, 1992, a U.S. District Court bucked the national trend and ruled that John Williams could play field hockey in Bethlehem, Pennsylvania.[19] As a freshman, John tried out for his high school field hockey team and was selected as the junior varsity goalie. Before the start of the season, however, the school district informed the coach that boys were not permitted on the field hockey team. He would not even be allowed to practice with the team.

John sued under Title IX, the equal protection clause and the due process clause of the Fourteenth Amendment, and the Pennsylvania state constitution's equal rights amendment. His request for a preliminary injunction that would have allowed him to play until trial was denied on the grounds he would not suffer irreparable harm if not allowed to play. During the discovery phase of the trial the school district compromised and allowed John to practice with the team for the 1991 season but continued to exclude him from interscholastic games. John pursued his lawsuit, however, and asked the federal district court for a summary judgment order that would allow him to play during the 1992 season.

The federal district court concluded that John Williams had a right to play field hockey under Title IX, the Fourteenth Amendment, and the ERA. Judge E. Mac Troutman, who wrote the decision, began his analysis with Title IX. The school district had argued that Title IX did not apply in this situation because field hockey is a contact sport (which would make it exempt under the enforcement regulations) and because athletic opportunities for boys in the Bethlehem school district had not previously been limited. Title IX's enforcement regulations said in part that if a sport is offered for "members of one sex but operates or sponsors no such team for members of the other sex, and athletic opportunities for members of that sex have previously been limited, members of the excluded sex must be allowed to try out for the team offered."[20] Because this clause had opened noncontact sports teams across America to girls, the Bethlehem school district argued that boys were not the legislation's target because they had historically been given many more sporting opportunities than girls.

The district court, however, rejected both theories. First, Judge Troutman examined the conflicting testimony and decided that because the rules of field hockey prohibited contact, the sport must therefore be non-contact regardless of any incidental collisions. He also examined the enforcement regulations of Title IX, which stated that contact sports were those in which "the purpose or major activity of which involve[d] bodily contact" and concluded that contact was neither the purpose of nor a major activity in field hockey.[21] Second, the court disagreed that boys in Bethlehem had a history of greater sporting opportunities than girls, accepting John Williams's theory that the boys had actually been deprived of athletic opportunities in the eighteen years since Title IX's enactment. The school district allowed girls to try out for all twenty-two sports teams it offered; boys, however, could only try out for the twelve sports ostensibly designated for their gender (sports for which girls could also try out). Judge Troutman concluded that eighteen years had been sufficiently long to remedy any past discrimination against female athletes and pronounced that it was now time to open the doors of all sports to all athletes.[22]

Judge Troutman next addressed John Williams's claim that his constitutional rights under the Fourteenth Amendment had been violated. The school district argued that its gender classification was substantially related to several important goals. First, the school district claimed that it wanted to remedy past discrimination against female athletes, an argument the judge, noting that had been accomplished, rejected. Second, the school district argued that it wanted to protect the girls' athletic program and maintained that gender segregation was necessary because boys, bigger, stronger, and faster than girls, would, if allowed, dominate the girls' program. Troutman agreed that physiological differences exist between teen-aged boys and girls but did not agree that gender segregation is substantially related to protecting the program. The district court believed that a blanket rule such as Bethlehem's actually perpetuated stereotypes and generalizations about the two genders. Further, the judge found the theory that boys would flood girls' sports if John was allowed to play field hockey to be mere speculation.

Because Judge Troutman had found that John's equal protection rights had been violated, he concluded that his ERA rights had also been violated because the ERA provided even greater protection than the equal protection clause. Judge Troutman awarded John summary judgment and the right to play on the field hockey team.[23] He played goalie for his high school team in the 1992 season.[24]

The Bethlehem, Pennsylvania, school district, however, appealed the district court decision, and in 1993 the Third Circuit of the U.S. Court of Appeals overruled every aspect of the lower court's decision.[25] First, the Third Circuit in the majority decision drafted by Judge Delores K.

Sloviter rejected the district court's Title IX analysis. Judge Sloviter said that Judge Troutman was wrong to conclude that field hockey was, as a matter of law, a noncontact sport. She noted that John Williams produced four witnesses who argued that field hockey, based on its rules, is a non-contact sport, while the Bethlehem school district produced two witnesses who said that contact routinely occurs during play regardless of the rules. Judge Sloviter considered the issue of contact a matter of fact for a jury to decide rather than a matter of law for a judge to decide. Further, she said that the lower court had erred in assuming that Title IX regulations required contact to be a "purpose or major activity of field hockey" when, actually, regulations defined a contact sport as one "which involve[d] bodily contact."[26] Sloviter maintained that the question of whether field hockey involves body contact during the "realities" of a game should be considered at trial because, based on conflicting testimony, reasonable people disagree on that issue. Therefore, the lower court was wrong to grant John Williams a summary judgment order rather than holding a trial.[27]

Second, the court of appeals added that the district court's analysis of how boys' opportunities over the previous eighteen years in this school district had been limited was short-sighted and flawed. Judge Sloviter said that the opportunity to try out for a team did not compensate for previous discrimination and that athletic opportunities meant "real opportunities, not illusory ones."[28] Therefore, the court concluded that the question of physiological differences between boys and girls is relevant to the discussion because physiology affects athletic opportunities in many sports. If, as many have argued, boys are bigger, quicker, and stronger, then more boys than girls would make teams like football and wrestling that favored such skills. The result would be fewer female athletes. Further, Judge Sloviter characterized the lower court's analysis as being "sport-specific" in questioning whether boys had limited opportunities in Bethlehem field hockey. The court of appeals concluded that Congress never intended Title IX to integrate specific sports but rather to increase female participation in athletics generally.[29]

Next, Judge Sloviter and the court of appeals rejected John Williams's arguments under the state ERA. The court said the question was whether the gender-based classification used by the school district was based on "genuine physical differences" between boys and girls or on "unwarranted and stereotyped assumptions" about the sexes. Judge Sloviter also suggested that testimony was needed to determine whether boys would take over the girls' athletic program if allowed to compete on girls' teams. The appellate court decided the question was a matter of fact that a jury needed to determine and opened the possibility for the Williamses to continue their struggle under state ERA protection.[30] After the Supreme Court refused to hear the Williamses' appeal, however, the family chose not to pursue the case, in part because John had already graduated.[31]

The *Williams* case, at both district court and appellate court level, signified the complexity of what is understood as a contact sport and how to deal with reverse discrimination. Judge Troutman of the district court wanted a sport's rules to define its status and believed that enough time had passed for girls to have gained sporting equality. Judge Sloviter, however, believed that the conflicting statements of field hockey experts indicated that no one, not even those involved in the sport, were quite sure how to categorize the game, and thus the matter should be explored in depth during a trial. One of her fellow judges, however, argued in his concurrence that Troutman was in error and that the testimony indicated that field hockey, like basketball, is theoretically a noncontact sport but in practice involves contact.[32] Further, the court of appeals did not believe that eighteen years of Title IX was enough to make up for decades, if not centuries, of discrimination against female athletes. The Third Circuit, the highest court to consider the issue of boys and field hockey, implied that it would be difficult if not impossible for them to prove they had a right to play under Title IX.

The *Williams* case, although the last published decision, was not the last courtroom confrontation over whether boys could be excluded from field hockey. A more recent struggle over coed field hockey began in Maine in 1996 and lasted for three years. Jeremy Ellis, a freshman, had asked to be allowed to play for Portland High School, but the request was denied by the Maine Principals Association (MPA), which oversees high school sports. The MPA argued that allowing boys to play would limit girls' athletic opportunities because the boys, bigger, stronger, and faster, would take girls' spots on teams. As Richard Tyler, a member of the MPA told the press, "Opening field hockey to boys will significantly decrease the already limited athletic opportunities for girls."[33]

Jeremy had the support of his local school district, but the MPA was not swayed. His fight began before the Maine Human Rights Commission, which agreed that the boy's state ERA rights were being violated and ordered the MPA to open field hockey to boys. As a compromise while the MPA filed suit against the state, Jeremy was allowed to practice with the junior varsity team but not to compete in games. Witnesses at the state court trial in 1998 testified that even a few boys would dominate the game and that, ultimately, to remain competitive schools would recruit boys to play. Eventually the MPA won, and boys continued to be excluded from field hockey in Maine. The judge ruled in an unpublished decision that the ban was needed to preserve equal athletic opportunities for girls.[34]

These five different cases, from 1979 to 1999, failed to establish a cohesive position on whether boys should be allowed to play on girls' field hockey teams. Only the earliest case in Massachusetts under the state ERA in 1979 unconditionally opened field hockey to boys. In the later cases attitudes were mixed. Lower courts and commissions believed that field hockey was noncontact and should therefore be open to any student under Title IX, but those arguments were overturned by higher courts on appeal. The two most significant concerns were whether field hockey is a contact sport under Title IX enforcement regulations and whether it is constitutional to limit boys' access to certain teams as a way of compensating for past discrimination against girls. Generally, higher courts suggest that although the matter is still open for a state-by-state battle, field hockey is a contact sport and girls have not yet gained athletic equality. Although the courts seem tentatively sure about this, the public has not reached the same conclusions. The debate over whether boys should play field hockey reverberated throughout regions that valued the sport.

Cultural Rhetoric Regarding Field Hockey and Masculinity

In essence, the courts addressed two basic issues, whether field hockey is a contact sport and whether allowing boys to play undermines girls' athletic programs. Public discourse added one other question: Does the presence of boys in field hockey undermine their masculinity? Even the question of contact was most culturally relevant in relation to questions about physical differences between boys and girls and issues of safety.

These debates were similar to those raised in all contact sports cases. Questions of the legitimacy of the sport itself, of participants' safety, and of what it means to be gendered in sports in America were recast in the battle over field hockey. Now, however, the liberal feminist argument of inclusion—that supporting separate athletic programs for girls is imperative to achieving gender equality—resulted in exclusion. The noble goal of saving girls' sports was premised on the previously villainized paternalistic assumptions that boys are essentially better athletes; that boys are bigger, stronger, and faster than girls; that girls will be injured playing with boys; and that girls will be intimidated by male players and quit the sport. Media reports on coed field hockey were filled with arguments for both sides, and opponents tried an added element of social control by shaming boys away from a sport in which participants wear skirts.

It is worth noting that all published decisions, and the overwhelming amount of press coverage of the debate, occurred in the northeastern region of the United States. That is not surprising because most field hockey programs, both high school and collegiate, are based in that area. A survey of midwestern newspapers revealed only five stories about boys on field hockey teams since the 1980s—several of which had picked up stories of the struggle on the East Coast.[35] Regardless of the location of the debate, however, the focal points remained the same.

In field hockey cultures, most people seemed to agree that protecting girls' athletic programs is a laudable goal. Although the issue of whether field hockey is a contact sport was relevant to legal arguments surrounding the applicability of Title IX, socially the problem of contact was more connected to protecting girls' sports. Questions about physical differences between boys and girls, safety, and intimidation became particularly relevant. Noncontact sports are by nature less dangerous than contact sports. Fewer catastrophic injuries, for example, occur in tennis than in football. Size and strength are less of an issue because a larger player cannot intentionally use that size and strength to physically harm an opponent. Therefore, the public is less concerned with coed noncontact sports; no one, for example, worries about the physical dangers of coed golf teams. Contact sports, however, do raise the collective eyebrow when teams are coed, in part because size and strength and gender become factors during a game and in terms of safety. Therefore, the struggle over field hockey, both in the courtroom and American societies, began with the question of contact.

The issue of whether field hockey is a contact sport has been highly subjective. Even courts in the same jurisdiction have disagreed on the matter. In the New Jersey case, for example, the administrative law judge and the New Jersey court looked at the same witness testimony and reached opposite conclusions. The ALJ concluded that contact is incidental in field hockey, and the court concluded it is a major part of the game. The ALJ let the boy play, and the court did not.[36] The debate stemmed from the inherent contradiction between the rules of field hockey and the realities of the way the game has been played.

Those who have concluded that field hockey is a noncontact sport focus on the literal language of the rules prohibiting contact.[37] Those with the opposing view have cited the course of play itself. Elizabeth Beglin, a former Olympic field hockey player and former coach of the University of Iowa team, has suggested that field hockey is parallel to basketball. Contact has been against the rules, but it has occurred constantly and has only infrequently been penalized. Beglin believes that if basketball is considered a contact sport then field hockey should be as well.[38] Other coaches have submitted affidavits in different cases and used the same analogy, also made by a concurring judge in the Pennsylvania case.[39] Similarly, in exculding boys the judge in the Rhode Island federal court case relied heavily on the testimony of a high school coach who stated that contact does occur despite the rules against it, especially among novice players or with poor officiating. Further, the coach suggested that contact from sticks and flying balls is frequent. She emphasized the required safety features like shin guards and mouth guards to support her argument.[40]

If field hockey is a contact sport, that would imply that bigger, stronger, faster players would likely have more success. Because boys have those traits, they would be better field hockey players than girls and would therefore take over a team. To prove that point, opponents of coed field hockey began by emphasizing the size, strength, and speed of boys. C.C.'s coach in New Jersey testified that C.C., although only a freshman, was already faster and stronger and had more endurance than anyone on the squad except for two or three juniors and seniors, and C.C. was denied the opportunity to play field hockey in part because of this testimony.[41] Viola Goodnow, who coached field hockey for forty years but never coached a boy, said, "If you have a male on the team, he's obviously going to get a spot, because he's quicker, faster, and stronger."[42]

In the media, however, the most repeated concern was not that more athletically gifted boys would take over a team. Rather, people opposed to coed field hockey warned that girls would be injured if boys were on the field.[43] People assumed that boys would not just be larger than girls but somehow more predatory than females who played. An athletic director, for example, argued that having boys on a team would be dangerous: "I have a freshman daughter on the team, and [the boy who wanted to try out] weigh[ed] about 175 pounds. As a parent, I don't know if I would want him swinging a stick next to my 130 pound daughter."[44] The director did not specify if he would discourage his daughter from playing with 175-pound females, implying that size alone was not enough to concern him but gendered size—size enhanced by testosterone—would.

Some newspaper articles emphasized the physical danger of the coed game. One began with a graphic description of the injury of a female player who had "underestimated the power of the opposing [male] player" taking a free shot. The female player "limped" off the field after the ball struck her in the knee and sat out the rest of the match.[45] Physical danger from larger male players aside, those opposed to field hockey saw a link between gendered size and intimidation. These opponents argued that not only are boys bigger and stronger but they also use their superior size to intimidate girls in a way, they implied, that large girls do not. In a self-fulfilling prophesy, the injured girl said that before the game she had been "intimidated" by the four boys on the other team, one of whom shot the ball that hit her.[46]

A coach of a single-sex female team that played coed teams pronounced that boys who played field hockey "play on the edge, like they think they're playing street or ice hockey. They throw elbows and push. We're talking about boys that are much bigger than the girls. It isn't fair."[47] No mention was made of the fact that such contact is technically illegal and pushing and elbowing can be penalized by the referees. The concern seemed not so much about the unfairness of the size differential but the unfairness of the difference in perceived attitude between male and female players. Playing a bigger, stronger, faster girl was one thing, but playing a bigger, stronger, faster boy would be another, these coed opponents suggested, because of how the boy would use those physical attributes. The implicit argument was that the aggressive male culture of sport would overwhelm the more supportive female culture of sport.

The result of physical differences and concerns about injury and attitude, those who favored single-sex field hockey maintained, would be that girls would quit the sport or refuse to play with or against boys, hence undermining athletic programs for females. Massachusetts, the one state in the country that mandated the possibility of coed field hockey, was asked at the 1987 New Jersey trial to comment on the results of its experience, which MIAA executive director Richard Neal called a "disaster." He claimed that the presence of twenty to thirty boys in Massachusetts field hockey leagues from 1979 to 1987 had displaced at least some girls from a sport in which they had previously participated. He also testified at trial that an unknown number of girls had quit rather than risk injury of playing against boys and that the same fear of injury had limited the playing opportunities of teams that chose to forfeit rather than play a coed squad. Even girls on the coed team lost playing chances when their opponents forfeited.[48] Because of the perception that boys would hurt or intimidate girls with their superior size, strength, speed, and aggressiveness, many feared that coed field hockey would result in fewer female players.

Inherent in arguments that having boys on a team would hurt girls' athletic opportunities was the unarticulated assumption of male athletic superiority. No one ever argued that having a girl on a football team would take playing time away from a boy or that once a girl wrestled at the 103-pound level other schools would need to recruit girls in order to compete. People seemed to assume that one single boy could dominate a field hockey team and even a league. The director of the NJSIAA, for example, argued in 1987 that having boys play on occasion would be unfair to other teams, because he assumed the coed team would be better than the all-female squad.[49]

Further, pitting boys against girls would only emphasize the difference between the two. A 1991 editorial in the *St. Louis Post-Dispatch* argued that the size differential and physical athleticism of boys would overwhelm girls. The author quoted a college women's basketball coach ("within their context, girls' sports can be just as exciting, as dramatic, as anything as boys' sports") and reemphasized the words "within their context." Readers were reminded that Chris Evert admitted she could not beat her brother, who did not play professional tennis.[50] The editorial exemplified the assumption that males are essentially better athletes and that having coed teams would underline girls' athletic limitations. The assumption of superiority was also evident in the reporting of a fund-raising event in Providence, Rhode Island. When the football team challenged the field hockey team to a field hockey match for a fund-raiser, the local newspaper compared the event to the Billy Jean King–Bobby Riggs match, ignoring the fact that at least King and Riggs both played professional tennis. The implication was that it would be an even contest. The girls, however, emphasized the fact that field hockey is more difficult than it looks.[51] By accentuating the need for separate boys and girls sports, especially in field hockey, these stories highlighted the public perception that girls, try as they might, could not really be competitive with boys.

Whether boys are inherently better field hockey players is mostly a matter of opinion, as indicated by the mixed results of coed field hockey teams. Sometimes female teams have been unable to defeat male teams. The 1998 undefeated Simsbury, Connecticut, High School girls' varsity team, for example, could not beat the fourteen boys against whom they practiced.[52] The assumption of athletic superiority, however, has often been based solely on physical attributes, ignoring the role of skill in the game. One male sophomore who played in Massachusetts was described by his coach as faster and stronger than most of his teammates, but the coach added that the boy lacked stick-handling skills. He was not the best player on the team, but the coach admitted that he was an "impact" player.[53] Further, despite presumed superior size, speed, strength, and aggressive qualities, usually one boy cannot dominate a team or a league. Many coaches who have boys on their squads have emphasized that they are often not the best on the team.[54] After John Williams initially won the right to play in Pennsylvania, his team compiled a 4–11–4 record, indicating that one boy could not carry a field hockey team to a state title.[55] Often boys would not make the varsity squad if allowed to play. Two in Maryland, denied the opportunity to play by the school district, were allowed to practice with the team and serve as its managers. The coach said that even had the district had allowed them to play they were unlikely to make the squad as anything but practice players because one boy lacked stick-handling skills and the other was the slowest person on the field.[56] The evidence, however, did not change the cultural assumptions.

Although courts have generally excluded boys from field hockey teams, the rhetoric around the coed field hockey debate strongly suggests social controls aimed at convincing boys not even to try. Although the traditional field hockey uniform, a skirt, was never mentioned in court cases, the media remarked on it frequently, and many stories about boys who wanted to play mentioned kilts, especially on occasions when a boy chose to wear one. An article about a male field hockey manager in Maryland (the school district would not allow him on the team) focused on the fact that on game days he wore the uniform kilt to school as well as to the event.[57] A headline for one Associated Press story announced that a Connecticut field hockey team practiced with "Kilted Boys."[58] Boys who chose to play in kilts have been mocked by fans at games.[59] In 1986, for example, two who wanted to play in Annapolis, Maryland, warned that "males won't inundate the sport because of all the harassment [about kilts] they have to put up with."[60]

When the social control element failed to convince boys to avoid field hockey voluntarily, a Missouri school district apparently excluded a boy who had qualified for the U.S. men's eighteen-and-under team because of its rules requiring skirts. Presumably, other reasons existed as well, but the school's athletic director referred only to the uniform in explaining why the boy was not playing for his high school team.[61] Similar to press interest in the femininity of the female wrestlers was its interest in boys willing to wear skirts.

Cultural interest in the attire of field hockey reiterated that field hockey, regardless of what the courts might rule, was still considered a feminine game in America and to play it would endanger boys' masculinity. By keeping the traditional kilt, the feminine aspect of the game has been maintained, and athletes have remained "young ladies" despite mouth guards, sticks, and bruising contact.

Regardless of the experiences of those who have played the game, the illusion of a noncontact sport, implied by the rules, has been underlined by the tradition of wearing skirts. If contact sports have been culturally defined as being manly, it would be impossible to define a sport in which participants wear skirts in similar terms. Thus, regardless of how the courts or Title IX defined contact sports, field hockey for many would remain a more feminine, noncontact game. Further, the media, in emphasizing the femininity of the sport, belittled those boys who want to play. Unlike sports such as wrestling and baseball in which those who opposed female participation worried that girls' presence would diminish the masculinity of the activity, the implication in field hockey was that boys who played diminished their masculinity by competing in a feminine game. Because of fans mocking them and media accusations of gender-bending, sections of American society discouraged those boys who might have wanted to cross over to a new sport.

Concluding Thoughts on Field Hockey

The battle over the gender of field hockey was in many ways more complicated than the those over the gender of other contact sports. Five different cases, many of which were repeatedly appealed, went to court. Their number, similar to popular national pastimes like baseball, football, and basketball, reflected the cultural significance that certain regions of America attached to field hockey. On the East Coast in particular, people cared who played the sport and the gender of its players.

The courts' failure to consistently rule one way or another on field hockey only inspired more battles. Despite the fact that upper-level courts usually validated the choice to limit the sport to girls, conflicting lower-court decisions left the door open for lawsuits in other jurisdictions. Although the struggle for boys to gain access to field hockey generally came after most traditionally male contact sports had been opened to girls, the courts' inconsistencies regarding field hockey allowed a multitude of lawsuits that legally could not have happened with wrestling. That is to say, many people in America likely felt very strongly that girls should never be allowed to wrestle, but by the time girls sued for that right the law was fairly clear. Under the equal protection clause they could not be excluded from a sport solely because of gender. Filing more lawsuits on the matter would have been pointless. Not so with field hockey. Because the courts could not consistently decide whether it was a contact sport, whether Title IX applied, or whether boys had some sort of constitutional right to try out for field hockey teams, more lawsuits and appeals were filed.

Ideologically, the issue of boys on girls' field hockey teams has been problematic. On the one hand, the feminist argument concerning traditionally male contact sports was clear and simple: Gender equality demanded that girls have a chance to play, and the equal protection clause and the equal rights amendments guaranteed that right. On the other hand, if the goal was to increase female participation and simultaneously promote gender equality, then the presence of boys in field hockey was a complicating factor. Although promoting and protecting girls' athletic programs was a strong pro-female position, the reasons for excluding boys from field hockey were often based on the same overbroad paternalistic generalizations that had been used to exclude girls from contact sports. People argued obliquely that boys are superior athletes because they are bigger, stronger, and faster than girls. Girls would be injured playing coed field hockey, boys would intimidate them, and then girls would quit the sport.

Although there may have been a certain practical reality to that argument, philosophically it was inconsistent with everything proponents of female participation in contact sports had argued because it accepted that girls are weak, frail, awkward, and timid athletes who need protection. It accepted the stereotype that boys, as a class, are better athletes than girls. In fact, by excluding all boys from girls' teams it might have promoted that very theory. One court warned that the stereotype might undermine the goal of promoting athletics for females. In 1979 the Massachusetts Supreme Court, ordering that boys not be excluded from girls' teams if no comparable team existed, wrote that "to immunize girls' teams totally from any possible contact with boys might well perpetuate a psychology of 'romantic paternalism' inconsistent with such development [of competitive athletics for girls] and hurtful to it in the long run."[62]

Even if boys are in general better athletes after puberty, excluding them from field hockey to protect girls and their egos is an extreme reaction. The Massachusetts Supreme Court suggested that if girls were in such danger from large boys, then perhaps standards should be adopted limiting participants to a certain size and weight, regardless of gender, to avoid an overbroad generalization that all boys are bigger, stronger, and better athletes than all girls.[63] If excluding girls' from boys' sports to save boys' egos is unacceptable, then so is the converse. Perhaps playing with boys would make girls better athletes, or perhaps it would teach them that they can compete with boys without undue risk of injury or embarrassment.

The most compelling and consistent feminist rationalization for excluding boys from field hockey was not the primary argument but a secondary one mentioned almost in passing in cultural discourses (although featured a bit more prominently in legal decisions). Everyone opposed to the presence of boys on girls' field hockey teams argued that having even one boy on a squad would displace one girl or diminish the playing time of one girl. Even in regions that had no-cut policies or undersized field hockey teams, some worried that having boys on a team would hurt girls by limiting their time with coaches.[64] Those who wanted to exclude girls from baseball and wrestling used the same argument. In those instances, however, opponents worried about the integrity of the game rather than athletic opportunities for girls. In field hockey, the theory was that because girls as a class had been discriminated against in school athletics for decades, it was better to hinder one boy, who had ample other sporting opportunities and whose class had always had more opportunities, than to hurt a girl. Although admittedly unfair to individual boys and their interests, the argument focused on overall gender equality and held hope for a time when individuals would not be discriminated against in order to level the playing field for an entire class.

The argument about the importance of nurturing athletic opportunities for women is similar to the argument Justice John Paul Stevens made in refusing to grant a stay that would have allowed Karen O'Connor a chance to try out for a boys' basketball team instead of a girls' team. Stevens warned that if there were no gender segregation in sport (he was addressing the issue of separate teams for boys and girls), then boys might come to dominate a league to the exclusion of girls. When he refused to force the school district to allow Karen to try out for the boys' team, he acknowledged that he was limiting her rights as an individual in order to protect the rights of girls as a class.[65]

The difference, however, is that Stevens was addressing the issue of separate teams in the same sport. For field hockey, usually, there are no separate teams, and the case is arguably more parallel to a girl who, if not allowed to try out for a boys' football team, will have no opportunity at all to play that sport. To accept the argument that boys should be excluded from field hockey because they have other sporting opportunities might open the door to excluding girls from football, because girls in the twenty-first century have other sporting opportunities.

As a matter of practicality, however, boys in the twenty-first century do have certain advantages in sport, including—on occasion—size and strength. More important, American boys still have certain cultural advantages. As a class, they are encouraged to play sports at an early age and taught early on to be aggressive and physical, whereas girls are still often discouraged from such behavior.[66] Girls do not participate at the same rate as boys, which may indicate that they still do not have the same athletic opportunities as their brothers. Although the goal of the lawsuits is inclusion, boys participation on girls' teams, from a pragmatic perspective, may work to exclude girls. Ideally, if so many athletically gifted boys want to play field hockey or some other "girls' sport" that they take all or many of the slots on a team, then a school or community would provide a second team, perhaps segregated by gender, size, or talent. Again, however, schools do not have the funding to provide athletic opportunities to every child who wishes to participate—most high school varsity teams cut less-talented players. Allowing any child to try out for any sport probably would result in fewer female athletes.

In many ways the battle over field hockey, for youngsters who played and those who wanted to play, was the same as the struggle over other contact sports. Female players were not usually the ones who wanted to keep the sport female. Much like the boys on wrestling teams, girls were not overly upset at the notion of competing with boys. Twelfth-grade girls in Annapolis, Maryland, for example, believed that two boys who wanted to try out deserved a chance, and they said they would not be intimidated playing against boys. The girls' greatest concern was that boys would receive special treatment because they had less experience playing field hockey.[67] Ten years later, girls on another Maryland team still supported the rights of two boys to try out for the squad and, using modern parlance, called for "gender equity."[68] After having multiple teams forfeit to her coed field hockey team rather than play a team that had a male member, the female captain of the Chatham, Massachusetts, high school team said, "It just seems like the adults are getting in the way of our fun."[69]

Boys who fought to play field hockey seem to have done so for the same reason girls struggled to gain access to traditionally male contact sports. They just wanted to play. Being on a girls' squad has usually been their only opportunity to play regularly. To indicate that their intentions were serious, many boys said they played on a girls' team because doing so was their only option if they wanted someday to make the U.S. National Men's team or play on a college club team.[70] John Williams, who sued for the chance to play field hockey, insisted that he was serious about the sport and wanted to play collegiate field hockey—and perhaps ultimately play for the men's Olympic field hockey squad. The only chance he had to play with a team composed solely of men, however, was once a month at Drew University in New Jersey, a sixty-five-mile trip from his home.[71] Emphasizing their ambitions in the sport allowed the boys to establish that they did not want to play field hockey merely because it was a girls' game but because of its value as a sport. In the United States, however, field hockey is a girls' game, and because of complexities of politics, budgets, and gender equality it is likely to stay a girls' game.

9   *Wrapping Up Contact Sports*

Title IX triggered numerous lawsuits, and the equal protection clause often was the deciding factor in the most of these cases. There were, however, contact sports in America into which girls and women seemed to slip almost unnoticed without lawsuits being filed to keep the sports female-free. An examination of the sports helps explain the discord between law and society over those that were more fiercely contested and how Americans have come to accept the notion of separate but equal for gender and sport.

Nonlitigated Sports

Legally contested contact sports arose in part from the Title IX enforcement regulations that introduced the legal distinction between contact and noncontact sports but failed to define contact sports precisely, saying only that they included "boxing, wrestling, rugby, ice hockey, football, basketball, and other sports the purpose or major activity of which involve[d] bodily contact."[1] The vagueness of the final clause allowed leagues to argue that baseball, soccer, and field hockey were contact sports and therefore exempt from Title IX. Of the designated contact sports, however, only rugby and ice hockey were not litigated.[2] Not one single decision regarding an attempt by girls to be allowed to try out for these sports was published, and no public record exists of any lawsuit being filed.

The sports were likely not contested in the courts because they are less culturally noteworthy in the United States and because the law had been settled by the time they gained popularity. American girls demanded access to the most popular and culturally significant sports before going after any others. With the exception of soccer, the first challenges were over baseball, football, and basketball—sports that play significant roles in the nation's culture and identity. Because one of those roles was teaching masculinity to American boys, the conflict between a society that wanted to keep its national games masculine and girls who wanted access to all that was American resulted in the series of lawsuits that began in the 1970s. Other popular sports such as wrestling, boxing, and field hockey, not as closely linked with America's national identity, were contested later, beginning in the 1980s after the fight over baseball, basketball, and football.

Ice hockey and rugby were even less culturally important to the United States in the 1970s, when the dispute began over gender and sport. Few youth leagues existed for ice hockey, and those that did were not as extensive as Little League Baseball, Inc., or pee-wee football organizations. There is no evidence of any youth rugby leagues during the 1970s.[3] Although both sports have grown in popularity, especially ice hockey, the games still do not carry the kind of cultural history that more traditionally American pastimes do. Further, by the time the sports became popular enough to have widespread youth organizations, the law had been fairly firmly established: The equal protection clause and state ERAs allowed girls to try out for any sport offered. Separating leagues by gender was acceptable; separating sports by gender was not.[4]

ICE HOCKEY IN THE UNITED STATES

In North America, ice hockey has traditionally been the national pastime of Canada and not the United States. Customarily, the best North American players have come from north of the border, where geography and climate have spurred the popularity of the sport. For much of the year a large number of lakes and ponds in Canada are frozen over, allowing far greater access to the sport than one would find in the southern United States. Although many people in the northern tier of the United States also played hockey, the sport does not have the same role in defining national identity as it does in Canada.[5] In terms of popular culture, for example, the national broadcast of *Hockey Night in Canada* was a popular showcase for one significant game a week in 2000.[6] In the United States, however, most televised professional matches have been relegated to cable stations and local broadcasts.[7] Historically, even one of the earliest professional leagues in the United States from 1904 to 1907 relied on Canadian players to form the bulk of participants.[8]

Most scholarly articles on ice hockey have been based on the Canadian experience. Unlike boxing, which drew attention from writers like Joyce Carol Oates and Gerald Early, and baseball, which drew odes from A. Bartlett Giamati and George F. Will, cultural commentators in the United States have left ice hockey's role in American culture unexplored.[9] Furthermore, issues of masculinity have also been examined primarily in a Canadian context. The most extensive work on gender and hockey, that of Nancy Theberge, is based on observations of a Canadian women's team.[10] The limited American academic interest in hockey reflects the limited cultural interest in the sport more generally.

American boys, however, especially those on the Canadian border, have long played ice hockey. Girls played alongside their brothers, but, unlike the national media coverage of girls in the 1970s who tried to play baseball, female hockey players received little attention from the popular media. Only one national article in a 1973 issue of *Sportswoman* described the foundation of a girls' ice hockey league. Tony Marmo established the American Girls Hockey Association in the northeastern part of the United States because he felt his four sisters had been "deprived" and that "the boys got everything." As an adult, he founded several hockey teams for girls and claimed that 1,800 of them competed in the region.[11] In another example of the media indifference toward female hockey players, New York state officially opened youth ice hockey to girls in 1978, but there was no media reference to a girl on a boys' hockey team in that state until 1987.[12] At the same time that the controversy over gender and baseball was publicly raging, girls who were playing ice hockey did so outside the gaze of the national media.

During the mid-1980s the media began to pay a bit more attention to girls who played on boys' teams; in 1985, for example, the *San Diego Union Tribune* reported on three who played in a San Diego league.[13] The *New York Times* noted in a small story in 1987 that a girl played in a suburban New York City youth league.[14] Coverage, however, was minimal. The media also paid little attention to the fact that the National Collegiate Athletics Association (NCAA) had recognized women's ice hockey and a small number of schools were fielding women's varsity ice hockey teams. Again, the lack of coverage suggests the limited role the sport has been assigned in American culture.

After the first women's international ice hockey championship in 1990, however, media interest as well as girls' general participation boomed. Relatively few articles on girls' ice hockey were published before 1990, but the numbers increased dramatically after that date.[15] Although many of the stories were about girls who played on boys' teams, a large number reported an ever-increasing number of girls' teams and all-female leagues. In 1995, for example, girls' ice hockey was the fastest growing sport in Minnesota.[16]

In 1998 USA Hockey, the sport's organizing body, maintained that more than twenty-four thousand females, three-quarters of them under the age of sixteen, played hockey, some in girls' leagues but many in predominantly boys' leagues. In 1998 the U.S. women's national ice hockey team won the gold medal in the Nagano Olympics, and fascination for the game increased for girls and the media. As a coach in Massachusetts said after the Olympic victory, "My phone is ringing off the wall. It seems that girls who were afraid to skate or put on hockey equipment will no longer be afraid." Another coach said that interest in the sport was "exploding."[17]

Despite the dramatic growth of ice hockey among American girls there is no evidence that lawsuits have been filed regarding access to the game. One was threatened in 1999 in Ohio, where a female member of her high school varsity team felt she was not being played because of her gender, but she had, nonetheless, been allowed to try out and made the team. The suit would solely be about playing time.[18]

The lack of conflict about access to the game stemmed in large part from the intersection of the rising popularity of ice hockey with the time-line of legal cases involving gender and contact sport. When the struggle over the gender of contact sport began in the 1970s, ice hockey was not a significant sport in American culture, and as a result the media and the general public paid little attention to the girls who played. Excluding girls, however, was no longer an option as ice hockey grew in popularity in the United States, gaining greater social prominence in the 1990s. They had (under the equal protection clause and states' equal rights amendments) successfully gained the right to try out for every contact sport. Arguing from a legal standpoint in the late 1990s that ice hockey was too dangerous for girls, particularly after the success of the women's national ice hockey team, would have been very difficult if not impossible.

RUGBY

Rugby, the final enumerated contact sport under Title IX enforcement regulations, has been even more tangential and peripheral than ice hockey in American society and to American identity. Professional and collegiate ice hockey leagues have guaranteed that most Americans know at least something about that sport. Rugby in America, however, has been a club sport, and often struggled for survival. Although rugby has a long history in England, the last bright spot in its history for American men came in 1924 when the men's U.S. national team beat France—in Paris—to win an Olympic gold medal.[19] The athletes, most of them from California, had not played since winning the 1920 Olympic gold but came out of retirement when France invited the U.S. team to play.[20] The field was small—only France, the United States, and an undermanned Romanian team—but the U.S. team dominated the event and won the last Olympic gold medal offered in rugby.[21] That was also the end of the U.S. national men's team's international success. The nineteenth-century conversion of rugby to American football doomed the sport to the fringes of the nation's culture.

Women, however, began to play the sport during the 1970s. They started slowly; only five American women's teams existed in 1974.[22] The women's game, however, built a more solid base over time, and by 1981 the media reported that enough women were playing to hold tournaments.[23] In 1990 the U.S. women's national team won the Rugby World Cup, and as was the case in ice hockey, international success spurred girls' participation. In the mid-1990s the number of girls playing rugby was increasing, and an all-girls' team, possibly the first in the country, was formed in Kansas City, Kansas, in 1995.[24] By 2000, thirty-eight of the 278 youth programs registered with the national organizing body, USA Rugby Football Union (USARFU), were girls' teams.[25] This was an increase of twenty new clubs from 1999 and twenty-six from 1998.[26] But rugby still remained only a very minor sport compared to soccer and softball.

The presence of American women and girls notwithstanding, rugby has a reputation of being an intensely masculine sport, in large part due to the extreme degree of physical contact it requires and the absence of padding. Most scholarly work on rugby and masculinity has focused on Europe and Australasia.[27] Studies of the sport in America agree that it has been a site for reproducing masculine identity.[28]

The intersection of American females and a masculine sport usually generates lawsuits, but not in the case of rugby. Just as in ice hockey, the lack of legal action stems from the growing popularity of the sport and other legal decisions regarding gender and contact sports.

During the 1970s, at the beginning of the conflict over contact sports, very few children, let alone girls, played rugby, and no record exists of organized youth teams in America before the 1990s. Fewer youth teams meant fewer opportunities for conflict over who played, and the lack of cultural interest in the sport allowed the quiet growth of the American women's game. Alison Carle and John Nauright's work supports this theory, suggesting that the development of women's rugby was much slower in regions where rugby was extremely popular, in part because rugby was "man's stuff."[29]

As rugby's popularity increased in the 1980s the organized sport (controlled by U.S.A. Rugby Football Union) focused on increasing adult participation. By the time children began playing on organized teams (both single-sex and coed) in the 1990s the courts had already opened baseball, football, basketball, boxing, and wrestling to girls under the Fourteenth Amendment. Nothing suggests that rulings would have been different for rugby. Nor is there evidence that enough people cared passionately enough about the sport to litigate participation. Rugby's inclusion as an enumerated contact sport is surprising (in that it was such a minor, peripheral sport in the United States) and can only be explained by its violent reputation.

When Law and Culture Clash

The dispute over the gender of contact sports has lasted since enactment of Title IX. The length of the struggle signifies how important it is to many Americans to protect the American identity. In the United States, sports have been one way of creating a masculine identity, and masculinity, especially in this arena, has required the absence of females. Sports provide opportunity to bond with other males without female interference or distraction. Sportswriter Maury Allen recalled during the 1970s that going to baseball games with his father "was very special to me. It was something that separated me from my mother."[30] For Allen, learning to be a man apparently meant spending time with his father, away from his mother. By creating female-free spaces in which to learn to be men, American men are also free to create and perpetuate myths about those missing females. Even though a boy cannot be a man in the presence of women, he needs to define himself against the stereotype of a woman. All-male sporting venues provide the opportunity to bond and learn to be American men in opposition to missing American females.

In the space of contact sports males learn combat skills and chivalry as well as stereotypes. Games promote talents necessary to warfare. Contact sports teach boys to tolerate a certain amount of pain and discomfort for the good of the team and to continue to do their job until relief comes. Boys in sports learn the kind of sacrifice required in war. In football, for example, they use their bodies to protect the ball-carrier, and the line must give everything it has to protect the quarterback as he surveys the entire field, looking to advance the ball. These talents, however, are significant not only because they teach males to protect themselves and their countries but also because they teach boys to protect those who are weaker and more vulnerable—traditionally, women. Boys have learned that they, as men, are physically bigger, stronger, and faster than girls but can only be those things when compared to someone else. The stereotype requires that women provide smaller, weaker, and slower points of comparison. If that is the case, then women need men to protect them. To learn to guard frail females, men and boys practice combat sports. At one point historically, boys learned to box and wrestle in order, theoretically, to protect their gender opposites from other, presumably strong but less scrupulous, men who might harm weaker members of family and society.

Warrior games also allow men to avoid the homosexual implications of homosocial sports. Although the games involve touching, grappling, pushing, and hugging, such contact is not acknowledged as sexual because it still occurs in a context that will develop skills that will make the boys better men and better protectors of women. Even smaller boys, not big or strong enough to participate in mock-combat sports like football and wrestling, have the opportunity to learn warrior skills in baseball. Smaller boys cannot compete on the gridiron, but they can play shortstop and left field, learning strategy, sportsmanship, and chivalry in a sport with suicide squeeze plays and sacrifice flies. Although they may not be learning the infantry-type skills of hand-to-hand combat as linemen do, they are learning to be officers in a thinking-man's game. Because contact sports are so clearly marked as manly, warrior spaces, even an activity like patting backsides is an integral part of conveying approval and congratulations rather then evidence of homosexuality, which might be the case outside the sporting venue.

Contact sports are also linked to America's sense of national values, reflecting belief that the United States is a just and civilized society that will protect its weaker members and, more recently, those of the world community. The clarity of the rules in contact sports parallel how Americans like to imagine the clarity of their laws. As in sport, law is designed to bring order to chaos and provide rules for controlling the anarchy of the natural state. Law often borrows the metaphors of the sports world, promising to level the playing field and demand fair play. The equal protection clause, Title IX, and the ERA were all intended to treat people equally and keep things fair. Sports, especially combat sports, have historically been intended to teach toughness and other skills necessary to protect civilization and restore order when the rule of law fails. Wrestling and boxing foster particularly violent and aggressive behaviors generally associated with men. Women and girls were traditionally thought disinclined to such conduct and thus dependent on men (whose nature was violent and aggressive), who controlled and exercised these tendencies for the protection of the weak (i.e., women and children) against the barbaric and uncivilized among men. Men would keep the barbarians and chaos at bay while women stayed at home.

Cultural tensions arose when two different worldviews confronted each other. In the old view, men ruled society, men protected women, and men played contact sports. In the new world women wanted access to political power, women did not want to rely on men's protection, and women wanted access to contact sports and all the skills and privileges associated with those games. The exclusion of females from contact sports was symbolic of the exclusion of females from power. By 1973 even *Sports Illustrated* acknowledged that the reason for gender discrimination in sports was because women in sport posed "a formidable threat to male pride and power." Further, if women played sports they would take a greater, more prominent stand in society and demand equality, leading to a "democratic balance."[31] This, the authors suggested, was the real reason men wanted to exclude women from sport, especially contact sports.

American females began to demand access to contact sports as their roles in American society began to change. By the second half of the twentieth century they were unwilling even to pretend they were going to remain in the domestic sphere. If they were going out into the world then they needed the skills to protect themselves and succeed, skills contact sports might help develop. As society changed and women's unrest manifested itself in protests and the second wave of the women's movement, the landmark legislation of 1972, Title IX and the ERA, was enacted.

Despite the legal limitations of these laws, many Americans seemed to believe that new times required new laws, and most were unwilling to admit that the hundred-year-old equal protection clause afforded far greater protection than Title IX, perhaps because such an admission would indicate that the country and the courts had been violating the Constitution for more than a century. In the final analysis, however, Title IX gave women no new rights, but it inspired them to take advantage of those they already had.

When faced with the conflict between the old, sexist society and the (theoretically more equal) new one, courts sided with the new equality. Judges once again found themselves on the cutting edge of social equality, just as they had been with matters of racial desegregation. Most Americans were no more eager in 1954 to embrace racial integration in schools than they were in 1973 to embrace gender integration in dugouts, but the courts acted as agents of social change in both instances—long before many in society were ready. Despite some social pressure to keep sport gender-segregated, courts responded quickly and ultimately chose to simplify the law by applying it evenly to all citizens.

The persistent resistance to gender equality in contact sports reflects anxiety about whether the presence of women and girls would complicate a simple, gender-stereotyped system and the values it was thought to serve. When a society defines masculinity in opposition to an absent female, the presence of females disturbs the entire equation. If women really are so weak and frail, then men should have nothing to fear when women try to play contact sports because women will be injured, frightened, and discouraged.

The fear, however, is not that females are inferior to males but that they may be equal if not superior. If a girl can play shortstop better than a small boy, what does that boy learn? The myth of masculine superiority is destroyed, and the boy need not protect a girl who has demonstrated some degree of physical superiority over him and has learned the skills needed to protect herself. Once traditional stereotypes are undermined and rationalizations for gender-segregated sports are undone, the question arises about who and what sport leagues want to protect. Leagues claimed their efforts to separate boys and girls reflected a desire to protect the female body. When that concept was deflated by medical testimony about physical similarities between prepubescent boys and girls, leagues had to admit they sought to keep genders separate in order to protect boys' psyches. Little League baseball did not want small, male shortstops to learn that girls were better athletes and/or better strategists.

When the law failed to protect America's cultural identity, the culture moved to protect itself. The first step was the struggle over the definition of Title IX regulations. When people realized that the law might be so interpreted as to allow girls to play football, Congress tried repeatedly to water down the law and limit its scope. The result was an artificial distinction between contact and noncontact sports. In making that distinction, those who drafted the regulations acquiesced to what they sensed was cultural opposition to all coeducational sports. If they could not stop the progress of female athletes, they could slow it and limit women's athletic options to noncontact sports.

Unfortunately for these opponents, they forgot about the power of the equal protection clause. When the law failed them again, they resisted first in the form of lawsuits, which (even though the opponents knew they were probably going to lose eventually) at least allowed them to delay the inevitability by littering the paths of female athletes with obstacles. Their willingness to go to court demonstrated the depth of the commitment to excluding girls from the significant "manly" sports, and it probably stopped some from even trying to play.

As soon as courts would open a sport to girls, opponents would devise new methods of social control to close it again. When girls were allowed to wrestle legally, for example, they were suddenly redefined not as athletes but as sexual predators. People who never openly considered or discussed the homosexual implications of a high-crotch takedown when two boys in tight uniforms performed that maneuver were suddenly certain the touching was immoral when one of the participants was female. Quite illogically, the threat of lesbianism in sport reemerged in the popular press when girls asked to wrestle and once again was used as a means to keep them off the mat. The comparatively small number of female athletes versus male athletes in contact sports suggests that these social controls have had at least some measure of success.

The lawsuits involving children who sued to gain access highlight the distinction between contact and noncontact sports in America. It is a distinction that was strategically invoked when it seemed women would gain the legal opportunity to enter traditionally masculine preserves. The stories of the lawsuits prove that not only is the personal political but also that the law is personal. Despite best intentions to be impartial and consistent, legal decisions are determined as much, if not more, by people involved than by legal precedents. The judges who excluded girls from baseball and football did so not because of any binding legal precedent but because they believed what their culture had taught them: Girls are too frail to play, and to let them do so not only puts them at significant risk but also somehow undercuts the fabric of American masculinity and hence American identity.

Culture and law are too closely interwoven to be mutually exclusive. The suits were intensely personal to the girls and families who filed them as well as to the leagues that opposed them. Volunteers who coached the teams in Little League Baseball, Inc., believed their rights were being infringed upon when courts told them they must allow girls to participate, that the decision was about them rather than the girls who sought to be included. The powerful emotions and passion that surrounded these cases must not be lost over time and retelling.

Separate but Equal

Most Americans are more concerned about boys and girls participating in coed contact sports than they are about single-sex contact sports events. Opponents of wrestling were usually more opposed to coed wresting than to single-sex wrestling. As a society, Americans find single-sex sport less threatening and less dangerous to participants, the sport, and the social structure. The language of Title IX and the written decisions of numerous judges suggest that separate but comparable or separate but equal sports teams for boys and girls are both reasonable and constitutional. Given the cultural advantages and the more than occasional physical advantages that American males enjoy in sports, it seems likely that coed teams, especially among postpubescent players, would be dominated by men. Without separate teams, the fear that female participation in sports will dwindle seems well-founded. The problem, however, is the issue young Karen O'Connor raised when she wanted to try out for a boys' basketball team rather than a girls' basketball team, When is separate unequal or incomparable? Courts have not yet addressed that question for gender and sports.

The Supreme Court has addressed separate but equal first with regard to racial segregation. In the infamous *Plessy v. Ferguson* decision in 1896, the Court concluded that separate but equal did not violate the equal protection clause of the Fourteenth Amendment. In upholding the Louisiana state law requiring separate but equal accommodations for black and white railway passengers, the Court concluded that separate did not suggest "inferiority," and that any such feeling was "solely because the colored race chooses to put that construction on it."[32] In 1954 the Supreme Court overturned separate but equal with regard to race and education in *Brown v. Board of Education.* In a series of cases, the Court found a variety of separate educational systems unequal in terms of tangible factors.[33] The Court concluded in *Brown* that even if all those tangible factors (including funding, facilities, and quality of teachers) were equal in racially segregated schools, the intangible factors generating feelings of inferiority in black students made "separate educational facilities . . . inherently unequal."[34]

The Supreme Court has addressed gender segregation in education on three occasions. The first time, an equally divided court affirmed without comment an appellate court decision that separate but equal honors schools in Philadelphia were constitutional. The lower court had concluded that all-male and all-female magnet high schools that admitted students who had exceptionally strong academic records were constitutional largely because the two facilities were equal in tangible as well as intangible aspects. They were of a similar age and had similar rates of alumni enrollment in Ivy League schools and similar funding and facilities. In addition, the lower court saw no stigma attached to segregation in this situation. The Supreme Court barely agreed with a 4–4 decision, and no one wrote an opinion.[35]

On the second occasion, just two years after Justice John Paul Stevens had denied the request of Karen O'Connor to be allowed to try out for the boys' basketball team because of the need to protect the sporting opportunities of girls as a class, the Court ruled in 1982 on *Mississippi University for Women v. Hogan.* The school was the oldest state-supported women's college in the country, and Joe Hogan wanted to attend its nursing school. After being rejected because of his gender, he sued. The Court upheld his admission after concluding that Mississippi's argument about excluding men from the program to make up for past discrimination against women merely furthered the stereotype that nursing is "a woman's job" and failed to compensate for a history of discrimination.[36]

The Supreme Court would return to the consideration of separate but equal in gender and education for the third time in *U.S. v. Virginia* (1996, the VMI case).[37] The Virginia Military Institute was a public school historically devoted to training male citizen-soldiers. Despite being state-funded, it had never admitted women and even insisted that the presence of female cadets would destroy the institution's system of building character. The "adversative method" to which VMI subscribed and which it practiced was based on British public schools, which used systematic psychological and physical abuse to instill discipline in cadets.

In 1990, after the Virginia attorney general received complaints about VMI's refusal to admit women, the United States filed an equal protection suit against the state of Virginia for funding VMI. The Fourth Circuit Court of Appeals ruled that the existence of VMI caused the state to violate the Fourteenth Amendment and gave Virginia three options: admit women to VMI, discontinue state support of the institution, or establish a separate, parallel institution for women. The options were parallel to those a judge gave the state of Colorado in 1977 when ordering that it could not exclude girls from soccer. As a result, Virginia established the Virginia Women's Institute for Leadership (VWIL) and housed it at Mary Baldwin College (a private liberal arts school for women). The VWIL, however, did not follow the adversative method, its students did not live a militaristic lifestyle, and the institute did not have anything close to the funding that VMI enjoyed. Six years later the United States renewed its suit, contending that the VWIL was not a parallel institution to VMI and hence Virginia was still violating the equal protection rights of its female citizens.

The Supreme Court heard the case in 1996, and Justice Ruth Bader

Ginsberg wrote the majority decision, holding that the admissions policies of VMI did violate the Fourteenth Amendment. The majority relied
on the intermediate level of scrutiny but emphasized *Mississippi University for Women v. Hogan*'s demand for an exceedingly persuasive
justification for gender segregation.

The state of Virginia made several arguments justifying the exclusion of women from VMI. It maintained that VMI existed in order to
provide diverse educational experiences for its citizens, that the presence
of women at VMI would destroy the program, and that the VWIL was a
parallel program for women. The Court rejected the diversity argument
because the history of VMI suggested that excluding women for reasons
of diversity had no grounding in the history of the school or in the state's
educational system in general, which had for years denied women entrance into a number of colleges and universities. The Court also disagreed that the presence of women would destroy the adversative method, arguing that although some aspects of the system might need to
change (such as allowing privacy in the showers), some women might
prefer the adversative method and be well served by it. The Court also
concluded that the quality of a VWIL education was nothing like a VMI
education. There were differences in the number of doctorates held by
the faculties in the two different programs, in endowments, in degree
programs offered, and in experiences within the programs themselves. In
short, the VWIL was not equal to VMI, and the Court maintained it never would be. Admission of women into VMI was ordered or there would
be an end to state funding.

Justice Antonin Scalia argued in his dissent, however, that the majority had ratcheted up the requirements for gender segregation beyond
intermediate scrutiny and closer to strict scrutiny. Although the majority did not argue that single-sex public education could never be constitutional, Justice Scalia contended that the Court, as a practical matter,
had done just that. The issue was "functionally dead" because of the
Court's insistence on using the "exceedingly persuasive" test in addition
to the intermediate scrutiny.[38]

The VMI case has been the Supreme Court's latest word on gender
segregation in education. If gender segregation in sports was challenged
now, the state would need to prove that the classification was substantially related to an important governmental objective and that the justification for segregation was exceedingly persuasive. Given the legal history, it seems likely that a court would find the need to promote and protect
athletic programs for women and the need to rectify past discrimination

to be important governmental objectives. It is also likely that gender segregation would be found to be substantially related to those objectives, just as the Rhode Island Supreme Court did with field hockey.[39]

What courts have not fully explored is what constitutes equal or comparable athletic programs. When Karen O'Connor first asked for an injunction allowing her to try out for the boys' basketball team, the district court judge agreed, writing "in any given group today, of women and men, or boys and girls of the same general age and level of experience, . . . the men . . . will dominate or will excel, or will perform at a higher level." He added that for this reason, "The mere fact that they [boys and girls' teams] are coached comparably, have comparable physical plants, comparable schedules, et cetera, does not render them equal." The judge questioned the notion that separate can ever be fully equal, even in sports, and ordered that Karen be allowed to try out.[40] A federal district court judge agreed and argued that excluding boys from girls' sports teams actually perpetuated stereotypes and generalizations about the two genders' athletic capacities.[41] Although both judges were overruled on appeal, the question about whether separate is really comparable remains.

The answer likely lies in individual circumstances and the general attitude of society. So long as the courts, laws, and program administrators keep the tangible factors of separate sports teams comparable, they seem likely to be on solid ground legally. Any unfairness suffered by an individual who believes they would be better off on an opposite-gendered team when a team of their own gender exists is offset, as Justice Stevens told Karen O'Connor, by the state's need to protect the class as a whole. Changing social perceptions of women's athletic abilities is likely to be a slow process and achieved through time and increased numbers of female athletes.

A more complicated issue concerns the fairness of allowing girls to compete on a boys' team when no girls' team exists (like football) while excluding boys from girls' teams when no boys' teams exist (like field hockey). One must acknowledge that stereotypes of males being bigger, faster, and stronger have some grounding in truth. It is also necessary to accept the reality that boys, more than girls, are more consistently encouraged to participate in sports and be aggressive. Boys who play on girls' teams are likely to be taking away sporting experiences from the girls, who as a class have historically been denied sporting opportunities. Although girls who play on boys' teams also take away opportunities for individual boys who may be displaced, boys, as a class, do not have a history of being limited in sporting opportunities. Until girls have viable numbers to support their own separate teams and leagues, for the classes, it is fair to allow them access to all teams while limiting options for boys.[42]

That discussion of fairness and legality, however, is theoretical. The reality of gender and sports at the beginning of the twenty-first century is a bit different. The discrimination and the fierce battle in America over the right of girls to try out for contact sports teams suggest that in the end—and after the promise of 1972 with enactment of Title IX and the ERA and the seeming triumph of liberal feminism—the story of gender and contact sports is as much about failure as success. Liberal feminists were convinced that gender equity would follow legal equity, but that did not happen.

Although the law and the courts opened contact sports to girls, few have entered. Sometimes girls have not made a team, and sometimes girls have not even tried out. Further, many in American society have tried to keep entire sports segregated by gender. Deterred by cultural opposition, girls have chosen to stick with softball rather than play baseball even though courts long ago opened Little League to them. When an Arizona softball team that included five boys won the Little League World Series of Softball in the summer of 2000 their opponents were outraged that boys would invade a girls' sport.[43]

Girls who play on their high school football teams are still newsworthy, and the rare female who appears on a college gridiron receives national media exposure. Girls have won the legal battles to play contact sports, but American society has yet to catch up to the law. Although the equal protection clause added teeth to the paper tiger of Title IX and its enforcement regulations, opponents armed with traditional cultural values have continued to file those teeth. As a result, relatively few girls play contact sports.

APPENDIX:

LAWS AND MAJOR CASES

1868   Fourteenth Amendment to the U.S. Constitution ratified.

1948   U.S. Supreme Court in *Goessaert v. Cleary* concludes that gender classifications are benign and should be tested with the rational relationship test.

1954   U.S. Supreme Court rules in *Brown v. Board of Education* that separate but equal is unconstitutional under the Fourteenth Amendment for racial segregation in education.

1971   U.S. Supreme Court rules in *Reed v. Reed* that gender classifications should be more strenuously examined but still uses rational relationship test.
In *Hollander v. Connecticut Interscholastic Athletic Conference* the court rules girl has no right to run cross-country with boys under the Fourteenth Amendment.

1972   Title IX is enacted by Congress.

Equal rights amendment is ratified by Congress.

1973   The U.S. Supreme Court rules in *Frontiero v. Richardson* that gender is a suspect classification like race.
Pennsylvania district court excludes girls from baseball in *Magill v. Avonworth Baseball Conference*.

1974   New Jersey state court orders girls admitted to baseball in *National Organization for Women v. Little League Baseball*.
Rhodes Island district court excludes girls from baseball in *Fortin v. Darlington Little League*.
Ohio district court orders girls admitted to football in *Clinton v. Nagy*.

1975   Title IX enforcement regulations announced excluding contact sports.
Little League Baseball Inc. opens dugouts to girls.

The Fourth Circuit overrules *Fortin* and orders girls admitted to baseball.

Illinois district court excludes girls from boys' basketball teams. Reversed by the Seventh Circuit in *Lavin v. Illinois High School Association.*

Washington state court orders girls admitted to football in *Darrin v. Gould.*

1976   U.S. Supreme Court in *Craig v. Boren* creates intermediate scrutiny to test gender-based classifications.

Tennessee district court orders girl admitted to high school baseball team in *Carnes v. Tennessee Secondary School Athletic Association.*

Tennessee district court orders state to allow girls to play full-court basketball in *Cape v. TSSAA.*

Texas state court excludes girls from football in *Junior Football Association of Orange County v. Gaudet.*

1977   Colorado district court allows girls to play soccer in *Hoover v. Meiklejohn.*

Oklahoma district court allows state to continue girls' half-court basketball in *Jones v. Oklahoma Secondary School Activities Association.*

The Sixth Circuit overrules *Cape* decision and allows states to continue girls' half-court basketball.

Massachusetts strikes down rule excluding girls from football and wrestling in *Opinion to the House of Representatives.*

1978   Ohio district court says coed basketball constitutional and Title IX enforcement regulations unconstitutional in *Yellow Springs Exempted School District v. Ohio High School Association.*

1979   The U.S. Supreme Court says Title IX has an implied right of action and allows suits under that legislation in *Cannon v. University of Chicago.*

Arkansas district court orders state to allow girls to play full-court basketball in *Dodson v. Arkansas Activities Association.*

Texas state court excludes girls from football in *Lincoln v. Mid-Cities Pee Wee Football Association.*

Massachusetts state court strikes down a rule excluding boys from field hockey in *Attorney General v. Massachusetts Interscholastic Athletic Association.*

1980   Equal rights amendment is not ratified by enough states to amend the U.S. Constitution.

Illinois district court grants injunction to allow girl to try out for boys' basketball team despite existence of girls' team. Injunction is overturned by Seventh Circuit and Justice Stevens in *O'Connor v. Board of Education.*

1981   The U.S. Supreme Court commits to intermediate scrutiny for gender classification in *Michael M. v. Superior Court* and *Rostker v. Goldberg.*
The Sixth Circuit reverses *Yellow Springs* decision and says coed basketball can be prohibited and the Title IX regulations are not unconstitutional.

1982   Michigan woman fails to win preliminary injunction to box in Golden Gloves tournament in *Lafler v. Athletic Board of Control.*

1983   Iowa girls file a suit to play full-court basketball. Suit is later dropped.
Missouri district court allows girl to play football in *Force by Force v. Pierce City R-VI School District.*

1984   The U.S. Supreme Court rules in *Grove City College v. Bell* that unless the specific program at issue receives federal funding, Title IX does not apply to that program.

1985   New York district court allows girl to play football in *Lantz v. Ambach.*

1987   New Jersey state court says it is constitutional to ban boys from girls' field hockey teams in *B.C. v. Cumberland Regional School District.*

1988   Congress enacts the Civil Rights Restoration Act and applies Title IX to athletic programs.
Nebraska district court allows girl to try out for wrestling team in *Saint v. Nebraska School Activities Association.*

1989   West Virginia district court rules that softball is not the same sport as baseball, and thus even if a girls' softball team is offered that does not mean girls can be excluded from the boys' baseball team in *Israel v. West Virginia Secondary School Activities Commission.*

1991   Rhodes Island district court says it is constitutional to ban boys from girls' field hockey teams in *Kleczek v. Rhode Island Interscholastic League.*

1992   Pennsylvania district court rules it unconstitutional to ban boys from girls' field hockey teams in *Williams v. School District.*

1993   The Third Circuit overrules *Williams* and allows state to ban boys from girls' field hockey teams.
Unpublished injunction allows girls to box in Golden Gloves.

1996   Kansas district court allows girls to wrestle on boys' team in *Adams v. Baker.*

1999   The Fourth Circuit rules that if a school allows a female to try out for a contact sport then Title IX prohibits any gender discrimination during that tryout in *Mercer v. Duke University.*

2000   Jury awards female football player $2 million, concluding that Duke University discriminated against her because of her gender during tryouts.

NOTES

Preface

1. U.S. Constitution, amend. 14, sec. 1 (1868).
2. Education Amendments of 1972, Publ. L. No. 92–318, §§ 901–9, 86 Stat. 235, codified at 20 U.S.C. §§ 1681–88 (1990) (hereafter Title IX).
3. 34 C.F.R. § 106.41(b) (1991).
4. Ibid.

Chapter 1: The History of American Women in Sport, Society, and Law

1. Allen Guttmann, *Women's Sport: A History* (New York: Columbia University, 1991) contains a broad overview of the history of women's sport from the Ancient Egyptians to the present.
2. Susan Birrell and Cheryl L. Cole, eds., *Women, Sport, and Culture* (Champaign: Human Kinetics, 1994).
3. Reet Howell, ed., *Her Story in Sport: A Historical Anthology of Women in Sports* (West Point: Leisure Press, 1982), and Nancy Struna, *People of Prowess: Sport, Leisure, and Labor in Early Anglo-America* (Urbana: University of Illinois Press, 1996).
4. Helen Lenskyj, *Out of Bounds: Women, Sport, and Sexuality* (Toronto: Women's Press, 1986).
5. Susan K. Cahn, *Coming on Strong: Gender and Sexuality in Twentieth Century Women's Sport* (New York: Free Press, 1994).
6. Mary Jo Festle, *Playing Nice: Politics and Apologies in Women's Sports* (New York: Columbia University Press, 1996).
7. Paula Welch and D. Margaret Costa, "A Century of Olympic Competition," in *Women and Sport: Interdisciplinary Perspectives,* ed. D. Margaret Costa and Sharon R. Guthrie (Champaign: Human Kinetics, 1994), 126–27.
8. Janice A. Beran, *From Six-on-Six to Full Court Press: A Century of Iowa Girls' Basketball* (Ames: Iowa State University Press, 1993).
9. Bil Gilbert and Nancy Williamson, "Programmed to Be Losers," *Sports Illustrated,* 11 June 1973, 62.
10. See William H. Chafe, *The Unfinished Journey: America since World War II,* 2d ed. (New York: Oxford University Press, 1991) for a thorough analysis of the history of America since the 1950s.
11. See Stephanie Coontz, *The Way We Never Were: American Families and the Nostalgia Trap* (New York: Basic Books, 1992) for a discussion of the role of women and the family in the second half of the century.

12. Mary A. Boutilier and Lucinda F. SanGiovanni, "Politics, Public Policy, and Title IX: Some Limitations of Liberal Feminism," in *Women, Sport, and Culture*, ed. Susan Birrell and Cheryl L. Cole (Champaign: Human Kinetics, 1994), 97–109. They question whether liberal feminism was actually the best approach to equality in sport as it meant accepting the competitive male model of sport as the norm.

13. For an exploration of gender rights legislation with regard to athletes, coaches, and administrators, see Susan B. Craig, "The Law and How to Use It," *The Sportswoman*, July–Aug. 1974, 32–34.

14. In U.S. law, the federal constitution carries the most weight. A law can be declared invalid because it violates the Constitution, but the Constitution can only be changed by an amendment, which is more difficult to pass than a law.

15. See Walter LaFeber, Richard Polenberg, and Nancy Woloch, *The American Century: A History of the United States since the 1890s*, 4th ed. (New York: McGraw-Hill, 1992), 477–80 for a discussion of the ERA.

16. Mark Starr and Martha Brant, "It Went Down to the Wire and Thrilled Us All," *Newsweek*, 19 July 1999, 50.

17. Robert Sullivan, "Good-bye to Heroine Chic," *Time*, 19 July 1999, 62.

18. For example, Boutilier and SanGiovanni, "Politics, Public Policy, and Title IX," explore the philosophical limitations of Title IX but not the legal limitations. Peggy Burke, "The Effect of Current Sports Legislation on Women in Canada and the U.S.A.–Title IX," in *Her Story in Sport: A Historical Anthology of Women in Sport*, ed. Reet Howell (West Point: Leisure Press, 1982) examines the numbers of participants as players, coaches, and administrators as well as the practical application of how to comply with Title IX. Diane Heckman discusses compliance and interpretation of Title IX in "Scoreboard: A Concise Chronological Twenty-Five Year History of Title IX Involving Interscholastic and Intercollegiate Sport," *Seton Hall Journal of Sport Law* 7 (1997): 391–400 and "Women and Athletics: A Twenty Year Retrospective on Title IX," *University of Miami Entertainment and Sports Law Review* 9 (1991): 9–25. Examples of law review articles focusing on the contact sport exception include Suzanne Sangree, "Title IX and the Contact Sports Exemption: Gender Stereotypes in a Civil Rights Statute," *Connecticut Law Review* 32 (2000): 381–447; Kimberly Capadona, comment, "The Scope of Title IX Protection Gains Yardage as Courts Continue to Tackle the Contact Sports Exception," *Seton Hall Journal of Sports Law* 10 (2000): 415–33; and Abigail Crouse, comment, "Equal Athletic Opportunity: An Analysis of *Mercer v. Duke University* and a Proposal to Amend the Contact Sport Exception to Title IX," *University of Minnesota Law Review* 84 (2000): 1655–88.

19. U.S. Constitution, amend. 14, sec. 1 (1868).

20. In fact, no suits were filed regarding school-age girls participating in sports at all until 1970, when two different district courts ruled in unpublished decisions that girls could be excluded from tennis and cross-country. Margo L. Anderson, "A Legal History and Analysis of Sex Discrimination in Athletics: Mixed Gender Competition, 1970–1987," Ph.D. diss., University of Minnesota, 1989, 116–18.

21. Alexander M. Bickel, "The Original Understanding and the Desegregation Decision," *Harvard Law Review* 69 (1955): 1–66.

22. Joseph Tussman and Jacobus tenBroek, "The Equal Protection of the Laws," *California Law Review* 37 (1949): 344.

23. *Goesaert v. Cleary*, 335 U.S. 464 (1948).

24. *Reed v. Reed*, 404 U.S. 71 (1971).

25. *Frontiero v. Richardson*, 411 U.S. 677 (1973). Justices Brennan, Douglas, White, and Marshall joined the plurality opinion. Justices Powell, Burger, Stewart, and Blackmun concurred in the decision, and Justice Rehnquist dissented from the judgment.

26. *Craig v. Boren*, 429 U.S. 190 (1976).

27. See, for example, *Michael M. v. Superior Court*, 450 U.S. 464 (1981) (holding that California could lawfully prosecute men only for statutory rape); *Rostker v. Goldberg*, 453 U.S. 57 (1981) (holding that male only registration for the draft was constitutional); and *Mississippi University for Women v. Hogan*, 458 U.S. 718 (1982) (holding that a policy allowing women only into a state nursing school was unconstitutional and adding that the state must have an "exceedingly persuasive" justification for gender segregation in educational settings).

28. *U.S. v. Virginia*, 518 U.S. 515 (1996).

29. Ginsberg had written several amicus briefs in the earlier gender discrimination decisions. Justices Stevens, O'Connor, Kennedy, Souter, and Breyer joined in the majority decision. Justice Rehnquist concurred in the decision, Justice Scalia dissented, and Justice Thomas took no part in the case because his son was a cadet at VMI.

30. Education Amendments of 1972, Publ. L. No. 92-318, §§ 901-9, 86 Stat. 235, codified at 20 U.S.C. §§ 1681-88 (1990) (hereafter Title IX).

31. 117 Congressional Record 30,407 (1971).

32. Bil Gilbert and Nancy Williamson, "Programmed to Be Losers," *Sports Illustrated*, 11 June 1973, 65.

33. Javits Amendment to Title IX, quoted in Heckman, "Scoreboard," 395.

34. Heckman, "Scoreboard," 393.

35. Anderson, "A Legal History and Analysis of Sex Discrimination in Athletics," 220, quoting a 3 June 1975 press release from HEW.

36. Ibid., 221–23.

37. HEW press release 3 June 1975, quoted in Judith L. Oliphant, comment, "Title IX's Promise of Equality of Opportunity in Athletics: Does it Cover the Bases?" *Kentucky Law Journal* 64 (1975): 435.

38. 34 C.F.R. § 106.41(b) (1991).

39. Ibid.

40. *Cannon v. University of Chicago*, 441 U.S. 677 (1979).

41. *Grove City College v. Bell*, 465 U.S. 555 (1984).

42. 20 U.S. C. § 1687, 102 Stat. 28, Pub. L. 100–259 (1988).

43. Burke, "The Effect of Current Sports Legislation," 338.

44. Bil Gilbert and Nancy Williamson, "Women in Sports: A Progress Report," *Sports Illustrated*, 29 July 1974, 28–31.

45. Burke, "The Effect of Current Sports Legislation," 340.

46. Joan S. Hult, "The Story of Women's Athletics: Manipulation of a Dream, 1890–1985," in *Women and Sport: Interdisciplinary Perspectives*, ed. D. Margaret Costa and Sharon R. Guthrie (Champaign: Human Kinetics, 1994), 95. Sports scholars examining Title IX correctly identified the increase in female athletic participation, and they also recognized the damage that Title IX did to women in sport. As more girls played sports and more schools allocated more money to female teams, coaches and administrators of female teams suddenly had money and power unprecedented in women's athletics. In 1972, before the enactment of Title IX, approximately 90 to 100 percent of women's intercollegiate athletic programs were administrated and coached by women. By 1992 the number of athletic programs for women and administered by women dropped to 17 percent, and the percentage of teams coached by women dropped to 48 percent. R. Vivian Acosta and Linda Jean Carpenter, "The Status of Women in Intercollegiate Athletics," in *Women, Sport, and Culture*, ed. Susan Birrell and Cheryl L. Cole (Champaign: Human Kinetics, 1994), 114–15. Sports scholars like Burke and Hult blamed the declining numbers on Title IX, recognizing the mixed results Title IX would have for women's athletics. Burke, "The Effect of Current Sports Legislation," 340;

Hult, "The Story of Women's Athletics," 95. More girls would play on more teams coached by men in athletic departments headed by men.

47. *Hollander v. Connecticut Interscholastic Athletic Conference No. 12447* (Super. Ct., Conn., New Haven County, 1971) quoted in Anderson, "Sex Discrimination in Athletics," 117.

48. *Magill v. Avonworth Baseball Conference*, 364 F. Supp. 1212 (WD PA, 1973) (holding that a girl could not join the boys' baseball team).

49. *Mercer v. Duke University*, 32 F. Supp. 2d 836 (M.D. N.C. 1998), *reversed* 190 F. 3d 643 (4th Cir. 1999) (holding that Title IX prohibited subsequent gender discrimination against a female the school allowed to try out for the men's football team). This decision holds only in the Fourth Circuit and conflicts with a Third Circuit decision. *Williams v. School District of Bethlehem*, 998 F. 2d 168, 174 (3d Cir. 1993) concluded that a boy who wanted to play field hockey could not rely on Title IX for access because the contact sport exception of the enforcement regulations meant all contact sports were completely exempt from all aspects of Title IX. Unless the Supreme Court rules on this issue, the jurisdictions will remain divided.

In October 2000 a jury awarded Mercer $2 million in punitive damages after concluding that the Duke football staff had discriminated against her because of her gender. "Female Kicker's Suit Is Good," *New York Times*, 13 Oct. 2000, D5. The punitive damages were vacated on appeal, however, because the appellate court concluded that Title IX did not provide for punitive damages. *Mercer v. Duke University*, 50 Fed. Appx. 643 (4th Cir. 2002). Mercer was awarded attorney's fees. *Mercer v. Duke University*, 301 F. Supp. 2d 454 (M.D.N.C. 2004).

Chapter 2: Baseball

1. Horace Trauble, ed., *With Walt Whitman in Camden* (New York: Mitchell Kennerley, 1915), 4:508.

2. Benjamin G. Rader, *American Sports: From the Age of Folk Games to the Age of Televised Sports*, 2d ed. (Englewood Cliffs: Prentice Hall, 1990); Allen Guttmann, *A Whole New Ball Game* (Chapel Hill: University of North Carolina Press, 1988).

3. For a discussion of the conjunction of baseball and American mythology, see John Bowman and Joel Zoss, *Diamonds in the Rough: The Untold History of Baseball* (New York: Macmillen, 1989).

4. Barbara Gregorich, *Women at Play: The Story of Women in Baseball* (New York: Harcourt Brace, 1993).

5. Susan E. Johnson, *When Women Played Hardball* (Seattle: Seal Press, 1994), and W. C. Madden, *The Women of the All-American Girls Professional Baseball League: A Biographical Dictionary* (North Carolina: McFarland, 1997) describe the history of the AAGPBL.

6. Gregorich, *Women at Play*, 4.

7. Judge Kennesaw Mountain Landis was named baseball commissioner after the infamous "Black Sox" scandal in 1919, when members of the Chicago White Sox were accused of throwing the World Series. Landis was charged with cleaning up major league baseball and its image. He was given almost absolute authority over the league.

8. Gregorich, *Women at Play*, 60–65.

9. Ibid., 66–71.

10. Margo L. Anderson, "A Legal History and Analysis of Sex Discrimination in Athletics: Mixed Gender Competition, 1970–1987," Ph.D. diss., University of Minnesota, 1989.

11. For a discussion regarding the link between baseball and masculinity, see Michael S. Kimmel, "Baseball and the Reconstruction of American Masculinity, 1880–1920," in *Sport, Men, and the Gender Order: Critical Feminist Perspectives,* ed. Michael A. Messner and Donald F. Sabo (Champaign: Human Kinetics, 1990), 55–65.

12. Joseph B. Treaster, "Town's Little League Reluctantly Signs Three Girls," *New York Times,* 27 April 1974, 33.

13. Children played baseball long before Little League; Little League was merely a national organization that provided even more structure to the youth game. Robert Pruter, "Youth Baseball in Chicago, 1868–1890: Not Always Sandlot Ball," *Journal of Sport History* 26 (1999): 1–28.

14. Lewis Yablonsky and Jonathan Brower, *The Little League Game: How Kids, Coaches, and Parents Really Play It* (New York: Times Books, 1979), 35.

15. Joseph B. Treaster, "Girls a Hit in Debut on Diamond," *New York Times,* 25 Mar. 1974, 67.

16. Yablonsky and Brower, *The Little League Game,* 4–6.

17. Anderson, "A Legal History," 170–71.

18. 34 C.F.R. § 106.41 (b) (1991).

19. See Helen Lenskyj, *Out of Bounds: Women, Sport and Sexuality* (Toronto: Women's Press, 1986) for an analysis of medical evidence to exclude women from sport.

20. The cases were *Gregorio v. Board of Education of Asbury Park,* in which a 1970 New Jersey state court rejected attempts by a girl to try out for the school's all-male and only tennis team, and *Hollander v. Connecticut Interscholastic Athletic Conference,* in which a 1971 Connecticut state court excluded a girl from her school's all-male and only track team, described in Anderson, "A Legal History," 116–18. District court decisions, especially at the state level, are often given orally. The judge reads or announces the decision in court because of the volume of cases heard and the time and expense of writing and publishing all of them. Oral decisions are not usually published, and thus it is difficult for anyone not otherwise aware of a case to know of its existence. Therefore, this project focuses on published decisions.

21. Two arms of the U.S. court system exist, state and federal. The baseball cases were heard in both arms. State courts hear cases dealing with state law, and federal courts primarily with federal law. State courts, however, often rely on federal courts' interpretations of the federal constitution to interpret their own state constitution. Thus, to interpret the equal protection clause of their own state constitution, state courts rely on the Supreme Court's interpretation of the federal equal protection clause. In federal courts, a case is tried first in a district court. Then the loser can appeal to the court of appeals, and, ultimately, the losing side may be able to appeal to the Supreme Court. Any higher court can let stand a lower-court decision by refusing to hear a case. State courts have a similar hierarchy.

22. Although the Avonworth Baseball Conference was not associated with the official Little League Baseball organization, it was, like most youth baseball in America today, modeled after the Little League organization in terms of structure, rules, and goals.

23. *Magill v. Avonworth Baseball Conference,* 364 F. Supp. 1212 (W.D. Pa. 1973).

24. *Magill,* 1213–16.

25. Other baseball cases were decided on the grounds that no state action was involved, see, for example, *King v. Little League Baseball,* 505 F. 2d 264 (6th Cir. 1974) and *McDonald v. New Palestine Youth Baseball League, Inc.,* 561 F. Supp. 1167 (S.D. Ind. 1983).

26. Dicta is language that is superfluous or unnecessary to the court's actual holding. Judges are supposed to answer only the question asked. This holding was vacated and remanded without opinion by the Third Circuit Court of Appeals, 497 F. 2d 921

(3d Cir. 1974) and was later decided on the grounds that there was no state action. 516 F. 2d 1328 (3d Cir. 1975).

27. *Magill*, 1216.

28. Ibid.

29. Michael J. Yelnosky's "If You Write It, (S)he Will Come: Judicial Decisions, Metaphors, Baseball, and 'the Sex Stuff,'" *Connecticut Law Review* 28 (1996): 813–54 explores whether baseball metaphors in judicial opinions exclude female readers. Yelnosky concludes, in part because of girls' increased participation in baseball in recent years, that they do not.

30. Anderson, "A Legal History," 170.

31. "Cathy at the Bat?" *Newsweek*, 1 April 1974, 53. The New Jersey system required that the first hearing be in front of an examiner from the state's Division of Civil Rights. The decision could then be appealed, as it was, in front of the Superior Court. The examiner's decision was binding as law until the appeal.

32. "Cathy at the Bat?" 53.

33. On appeal, Little League Baseball chose to focus the argument on the theory that a baseball diamond is a place of public accommodation. If deemed a place of public accommodation, then, under New Jersey law, gender discrimination would have been legal. The court, however, said that a ball diamond, unlike a hotel or restaurant, is not a place of public accommodation. *National Organization for Women v. Little League Baseball, Inc.*, 318 A.2d. 33 (N.J. Super. 1974).

34. *NOW v. LLB, Inc.*, 35–36.

35. Ibid., 38–39. The dissenting judge, however, accepted this last argument that girls would waste the coaches' time and that boys who might have a future in baseball would suffer. Ibid., 43.

36. Ibid., 39–41.

37. "Cathy at the Bat?" 53.

38. Frank Deford, "Now Georgy-Porgy Runs Away," *Sports Illustrated*, 22 April 1974, 26.

39. Anderson, "A Legal History," 180–85.

40. Letty Cottin Pogrebin, "Baseball Diamonds Are a Girl's Best Friend," *Ms.* (Sept. 1974): 80.

41. "Say It Ain't So, Flo," *Newsweek*, 24 June 1974, 75; Robert W. Peterson, "'You Really Hit That One, Man!' Said the Little League Boy to the Little League Girl," *New York Times Magazine*, 19 May 1974, 36.

42. Peterson, "'You Really Hit That One, Man!'"

43. Deford, "Georgy-Porgy," 30.

44. *Fortin v. Darlington Little League, Inc. (American Division)*, 376 F. Supp. 473 (D. R.I. 1974).

45. *Fortin v. Darlington Little League, Inc.*, 475–79.

46. *Fortin v. Darlington Little League, Inc. (American Division)*, 514 F. 2d 344, 346 (1st Cir. 1975) (hereafter *Fortin II*). LLB might have given up because of twenty-two class action suits against them throughout the country. After LLB admitted girls, most of these suits were dismissed as moot (e.g., *Rappaport v. Little League Baseball*, 65 F.R.D. 515 [D. Del. 1975]).

47. *Fortin II*, 348–50.

48. Ibid., 351.

49. *Carnes v. Tennessee Secondary School Athletic Association*, 415 F. Supp. 569 (E.D. Tenn. 1976). Carnes was not the first high school girl to threaten a lawsuit, but she was the first one to take the case all the way to trial. In 1973 the American Civil Liberties Union (ACLU) threatened to sue on behalf of a girl who wanted to play catcher

on her New Jersey High School team but was banned because of New Jersey Interscholastic Athletic Association Rules. "Girl Goes to Bat against Ban in Sports," *New York Times*, 11 April 1973, 49. After her local school board ordered the coach to give her a tryout, the player demurred, saying she did not want special treatment. Richard Phalon, "Girl Wins but Rejects the Right to Try Out for Baseball Team," *New York Times*, 27 April 1973, 72.

50. *Carnes*, 572. By the time the order was granted, only one game remained in the regular season. The judge in this decision would, that same year, become the first judge in the country to rule that different rules for girls' basketball violated the Equal Protection Clause. *Cape v. Tennessee Secondary School Athletic Association*, 424 F. Supp. 732 (E.D. Tenn. 1976).

51. David Q. Voight, *A Little League Journal* (Bowling Green: Bowling Green University Popular Press, 1974), 62.

52. Deford, "Georgy-Porgy," 26.

53. Yablonsky and Brower, *The Little League Game*, 159.

54. Murray Chass, "When a Girl Picks Baseball over Ballet, Her Team Gains," *New York Times*, 6 June 1977, 34.

55. Lynne Ames, "Girls Playing Heads Up Ball," *New York Times*, 17 July 1977, xxii.

56. Deford, "Georgy-Porgy," 28.

57. Treaster, "Town's Little League," 33.

58. Deford, "Georgy-Porgy," 29.

59. Melvin L. Thornton, "Healthy Criticism: Little League Baseball: It's Not Good Enough for Girls," *Today's Health* 52 (July 1974): 6. In the author notes, the reader learns that "Mrs. Thornton runs a mile a day. The author himself covers two miles daily, at a brisk pace." Ibid., 72.

60. "People in Sports," *New York Times*, 17 May 1973, 58, 26 May 1973, 22.

61. Treaster, "Town's Little League," 33.

62. Deford, "Georgy-Porgy," 36.

63. Joseph B. Treaster, "Little League Baseball Proving Just a First Step for Girls Athletes," *New York Times*, 23 June 1974, 40.

64. Louise Saul, "Little League Gets a New Umpire: The Courts," *New York Times*, 24 Feb. 1974, 63.

65. Peterson, "'You Really Hit That One, Man!'" 37.

66. Joseph B. Treaster, "Girls a Hit in Debut on Diamond," *New York Times*, 25 Mar. 1974, 67.

67. Deford, "Georgy-Porgy, 26.

68. Ibid., 26–37.

69. Walter B. Waggoner, "Byrne Declares 'Qualified' Girls Should Play Little League Baseball," *New York Times*, 28 Mar. 1974, 81.

70. "Little League Battles," *The Sportswoman* 2 (Mar.–April 1974): 7.

71. "Say It Ain't So, Flo," 75. In 1988 a federal district court in Virginia agreed. Julie Croteau had been cut from her high school baseball team. She sued, claiming her rights under Title IX and the Fourteenth Amendment had been violated. The court, however, concluded that Croteau had not been cut solely because of her gender but because of her lack of skill, adding that Title IX and the Fourteenth Amendment only guarantee the right to a fair try out, not a spot on the team. *Croteau v. Fair*, 686 F. Supp. 552 (E.D. Va. 1988).

72. The numbers of girls in organized youth baseball are estimated at about one girl per league, but those numbers are somewhat misleading because a larger number of girls play in the youngest Little League divisions, whereas almost none play in the older divisions. Amy Ellis Nutt, "Swinging for the Fences," in *Nike Is a God-*

dess: The History of Women in Sports, ed. Lissa Smith (New York: Atlantic Monthly Press, 1998), 50.

73. Gary A. Fine, *With the Boys: Little League Baseball and Pre-Adolescent Culture* (Chicago: University of Chicago Press, 1987), 1.

74. See Matthew J. McPhillips, comment, "'Girls of Summer': A Comprehensive Analysis of the Past, Present, and Future of Women in Baseball and a Roadmap to Litigating a Successful Gender Discrimination Case," *Seton Hall Journal of Sport Law* 6 (1996): 301–39 for a comprehensive history of the Silver Bullets and discussion of women who played ball in college.

75. Not all regions, however, equated softball and baseball. The New York State Board of Regents allowed girls to try out for baseball and soccer in 1977, distinguishing those sports from "more vigorous contact sports" such as enumerated in Title IX regulations. Ari L. Goldman "Regents Let Girls Join Boys' Teams," *New York Times*, 19 Nov. 1977, 1. In 1989 a West Virginia court rejected the West Virginia Secondary School Activities Commission (WVSSAC) theory that softball was substantially equivalent to baseball. The WVSSAC had prevented Erin Israel, who had played Little League ball, from playing on her high school baseball team (even after she made the team after open tryouts); the WVSSAC said she could play on the softball team instead. The court, echoing the attitude of most baseball and softball players, ordered the WVSSAC to allow girls to try out for baseball or create all-girl teams, because the two games were not the same. *Israel v. West Virginia Secondary Schools Activities Commission*, 388 S.E. 2d 480 (W.Va. 1989).

76. From 1974 through 1976, the *New York Times* reported on six occasions that federal courts and the State Division of Civil Rights were threatening Little League teams for noncompliance.

77. Anderson, "A Legal History," 186.

Chapter 3: Football

1. 34 C.F.R. § 106.41(b) (1991).

2. For a history of rugby and soccer's origins, see Eric Dunning and Kenneth Sheard, *Barbarians, Gentlemen and Players: A Sociological Study of the Development of Rugby Football* (New York: New York University Press, 1979).

3. Bruce K. Stewart, "American Football," *American History* 30 (Dec. 1995): 26–30.

4. For a history of the evolution of football in America, see Michael Oriard, *Reading Football: How the Popular Press Created an American Spectacle* (Chapel Hill: University of North Caroline Press, 1993), especially chapter 1, "In the Beginning Was the Rule."

5. Patrick B. Miller, "The Manly, the Moral, and the Proficient: College Sport in the New South," *Journal of Sport History* 24 (Fall 1997): 285–316.

6. Andrew Doyle, "Foolish and Useless Sport: The Southern Evangelical Crusade against Intercollegiate Football," *Journal of Sport History* 24 (Fall 1997): 317–40.

7. Stewart, "American Football," 67–68. For a contemporary account of early football in the United States, see Ronald A. Smith, ed., *Big-Time Football at Harvard, 1905: The Diary of Coach Bill Reid* (Urbana: University of Illinois Press, 1994).

8. Donald F. Sabo and Joe Panepinto, "Football Ritual and the Social Reproduction of Masculinity," in *Sport, Men, and the Gender Order: Critical Feminist Perspectives*, ed. Michael A. Messner and Donald F. Sabo (Champaign: Human Kinetics, 1990), 115.

9. Nancy Gager Clinch, *The Kennedy Neurosis* (New York: Grossett and Dunlop, 1973), 266.

10. Michael A. Messner, *Power at Play: Sports and the Problem of Masculinity* (Boston: Beacon Press, 1992), 168. Mariah Burton Nelson explores the relationship between men and women as mediated by football in *The Stronger Women Get, the More Men Love Football: Sexism and the American Culture of Sports* (New York: Harcourt Brace, 1994), arguing that American men view sports in general, football in particular, as the last masculine domains from which women are excluded. And, men believe, can truly be men in the mythic and stereotypical senses of the gender. Worth noting, however, is that despite opposition to women in football, they have long played the game, especially at the professional level. For pictorial evidence and analysis of early women footballers, see Oriard, *Reading Football*, 250–75. In 1999 the National Women's Football League was founded, and it remained in competition through 2004 (www.womensfootballcentral.com accessed 21 April 2004).

11. *Force by Force v. Pierce City R-VI School District*, 570 F. Supp. 1020 (S.W. Mo. 1983); *Lantz by Lantz v. Ambach*, 620 F. Supp. 663 (D.C. N.Y. 1985).

12. *Clinton v. Nagy*, 411 F. Supp. 1396 (N.D. Ohio 1974), 1396–97.

13. *Clinton v. Nagy*, n.1.

14. The defendants did not maintain that they were not state actors, so the judge did not discuss the matter in any detail.

15. *Clinton v. Nagy*, n.1.

16. Ibid., 1399.

17. *Morris v. Michigan State Board of Education*, 472 F. 2d 1207 (6th Cir. 1973), cited in *Clinton v. Nagy*, 1398.

18. *Darrin v. Gould*, 540 P.2d 882 (Wash. 1975).

19. Ibid., 892.

20. Washington Constitution, Art. 31 quoted in *Darrin v. Gould* at 889.

21. *Darrin v. Gould*, 891–92.

22. *Commonwealth ex rel. Packel v. Pennsylvania Interscholastic Athletic Association*, 334 A.2d 839 (1975).

23. Opinion of the Justices to the House of Representatives, 371 N.E. 2d 426 (Mass., 1977).

24. *Darrin v. Gould*, 884–88.

25. Ibid., 891.

26. Ibid., 893 (Hamilton, concurring).

27. Texas Constitution Art. 1, § 3a, quoted in *Junior Football Association of Orange County v. Gaudet*, 546 S.W.2d 70, (Tex. App. 1976), 70–71.

28. State action is needed for courts to prohibit gender discrimination on the basis of a constitution. Purely private organizations may (at least in theory) limit membership to whomever they choose. State action is determined by the amount of public funding invested, directly or indirectly, in a project or by how much control a branch of government has over the project. No clear formula exists, however, to determine state action. In 1988 the Supreme Court drafted a narrow opinion concluding that the National Collegiate Athletic Association was not a state actor when it ordered a member to fire a coach (*NCAA v. Tarkanian*, 488 U.S. 179 [1988]). The ruling was narrow enough, however, that sports law scholars suggest it does not preclude ever finding the NCAA to be a state actor. Walter T. Champion, Jr., *Sports Law in a Nutshell*, 2d ed. (Minneapolis: West Publishing, 2000). The Texas football cases occurred before 1988.

29. *Lincoln v. Mid-Cities Pee Wee Football Association*, 576 S.W.2d 922 (Tex. App. 1979).

30. Several courts in the baseball cases, however, concluded that no state action existed in suits to allow girls to play. See, for example, *Magill v. Avonworth Baseball Conference*, 364 F. Supp. 1212 (W.D. Pa. 1973); *King v. Little League Baseball*, 505 F.

2d 264 (6th Cir. 1974); and *McDonald v. New Palestine Youth Baseball League, Inc.*, 561 F. Supp. 1167 (S.D. Ind. 1983), emphasizing the power of the individual court in determining state action.

31. *National Organization for Women v. Little League Baseball, Inc.*, 318 A.2d. 33 (N.J. Super. 1974).

32. See H. G. Bissinger, *Friday Night Lights: A Town, a Team, and a Dream* (New York: Harper Perennial, 1990) for an ethnographic account of the 1988 Permian High School Football team in Odessa, Texas.

33. *Force by Force v. Pierce City R-VI School District*, 570 F. Supp. 1020 (S.W. Mo. 1983).

34. *Force* at 1022–23.

35. Ibid., 1024–25.

36. Ibid., 1026–28.

37. Ibid., 1029–31.

38. *Lantz by Lantz v. Ambach*, 620 F. Supp. 663 (D.C. N.Y. 1985), 665.

39. *Lantz*, 665, quoting *Mississippi University for Women v. Hogan*, 458 U.S. 718, 725 (1982).

40. By 2003 American women were allowed in the military but not, theoretically, in the ground-combat infantry. As warfare evolves, however, and moves beyond traditional warfare with well-defined combat zones, American women play a greater role as support troops but are still officially barred from ground combat in the infantry.

41. "Judge Says Girl Can Suit Up for Fall Football Practice," UPI Newswire, 16 Aug. 1983.

42. Andrew Blum, "State May Appeal Girls-in-Football Decision," UPI Newswire, 29 Oct. 1985.

43. Robert Hanley, "Girl Wins Right to a Football Tryout," *New York Times*, 2 Oct. 1985, B2.

44. After winning the case in front of an administrative law judge, the New Jersey State School Board decided not to appeal. Balsey then sued for attorney fees she had incurred in her efforts to gain a tryout with the football team. Although initially denied relief because the lower court concluded it did not have the power to order the board to pay the fees, on appeal the Superior Court of New Jersey reversed the lower court, concluding it did have that power, and ordered the case remanded for a determination of whether Balsey merited the award. *Balsey v. North Hunterdon Regional High School Board of Education*, 542 A.2d 29 (N.J.Super.A.D. 1988).

45. "Girl Seeks Football Tryout," *The Record* (Bergan County, N.J.), 7 June 1985, C2.

46. "Girls and Football: Board Eases Stand," *New York Times*, 28 Aug. 1985, B2.

47. "Girl Football Player Wins Case," UPI Newswire, 13 Sept. 1986.

48. Heather Hafner, "Girls in Football; It Isn't Working Out; They Worry about Broken Bones More Than Broken Fingernails, Not to Mention Coaches and Players with Chips on Their Shoulders; Impressions from a Short Career; Jarring Hit Helped Cyndi Bays Find Place Out of Football," *Los Angeles Times*, 30 Oct. 1986, pt. 3, 16.

49. "A Gridiron Standoff: Judge Demurs on High School Girl's Plea to Play Football," *San Diego Union-Tribune*, 3 Dec. 1998, B13. The article's concern about possible litigation if Kymberly was injured was supported by a 1994 lawsuit in which a girl who had been injured playing football in Maryland sued the school district for failure to warn her of the game's inherent dangers. She lost because the court concluded that she, like all her male teammates and their parents, had been duly forewarned and that the girl had assumed the risk of voluntarily participating. *Hammond v. Board of Education of Carroll County, MD*, 639 A.2d 223 (Md.Ct.Spec.App. 1994).

50. *Mogabgab v. Orleans Parish School Board*, 239 So.2d 456 (La.App., 1970), hold-

ing a coach and school district liable for failure to summon medical aid in a timely fashion when a player showed signs of heat stroke; *Woodson v. Irvington Board of Education* (New Jersey, 1987), an unpublished decision described in Champion, *Sports Law*, 124, holding a coach and school district liable for failing to teach proper tackling techniques to a football player.

51. *Seamons v. Snow*, 206 F. 3d 1021 (10th Cir. 2000), holding that a football player removed from a high school team for failing to apologize for reporting an assault could recover damages under the First Amendment. Coach Bob Davie of Notre Dame University committed age discrimination when he fired a coach for being too old. *Moore v. Notre Dame*, 22 F. Supp. 2d 896 (ND, IN, 1998).

52. *Mercer v. Duke*, 190 F. 3d 643 (4th Cir. 1999) *overruling* 32 F. Supp. 2d 836 (M.D. N.C. 1998).

53. Timothy W. Smith, "A Kicker Sues, Saying She Was Treated Unfairly," *New York Times*, 17 Sept. 1997, C1.

54. *Mercer v. Duke* also opens the door for an appeal to the Supreme Court because the decision conflicts with one made by the Third Circuit: *Williams v. School District of Bethlehem, PA*, 998 F. 2d 168 (3d Cir. 1993).

55. "Female Kicker's Suit Is Good," *New York Times*, 13 Oct. 2000, D5. On November 15, 2002, a three-member panel of the Fourth Circuit U.S. Court of Appeals overturned the award, concluding that punitive damages are not available remedies in private actions under Title IX. "Court Throws Out $2 Million Verdict," *New York Times*, 15 Nov. 2002, accessed at www.nytimes.com.

56. One court, however, has concluded that baseball and softball are two different sports and the mere presence of a softball team is not enough under the Equal Protection Clause to exclude a girl from a school baseball team. *Israel v. West Virginia Secondary School Activities Commission*, 388 S.E.2d 480 (W.Va. 1989). Basketball originally had separate girls' rules, but currently most school provide separate teams that play by the same rules.

57. *Muscave v. O'Malley*, Civil No. 76–C-3729 (ND IL, 1977), described in Karen Tokarz, *Women, Sports, and the Law* (Buffalo: William S. Hein, 1986), 71.

58. Stephanie Desmon, "High School Girls Get Football League of Their Own," *Palm Beach Post*, 8 Mar. 1999, 1A. Scholars have suggested that the answer to equalizing Title IX inequities at football schools might lie in creating women's football programs at the flag-football level. If flag football were added, it would also help racial diversity because it would not necessarily be a predominantly white sport like crew and soccer. Further, the presence of a football team might help overcome the myth of women being physically weak and frail. Rodney K. Smith, "Solving the Title IX Conundrum with Women's Football," *South Texas Law Review* 38 (1997): 1057–80. Smith also suggests that because tackle football is too violent a game to be encouraged at any level, flag football should be offered for men as well.

59. "Texas Forty-second State to Allow Girls to Play Football," *Atlanta Journal and Constitution*, 13 Feb. 1993, D6.

60. "Two Girls Denied Shot at Football," *Chattanooga Times*, 29 Aug. 1996, G7.

Chapter 4: Basketball

1. 34 C.F.R. § 106.41 (1991).

2. *Magill v. Avonworth Baseball Conference*, 364 F. Supp. 1212 (W.D. Pa. 1973), *vacated and remanded* 497 F. 2d 921 (3d Cir. 1974), *affirmed* 516 F. 2d 1328 (3d Cir. 1975) (ultimately excluding girls from baseball); *National Organization for Women v.*

Little League Baseball, Inc., 318 A.2d 33 (N.J. Super. 1974) (including girls in baseball); *Fortin v. Darlington Little League,* 376 F. Supp. 473 (D. R.I., 1974), *reversed* 514 F. 2d 344 (1st Cir. 1975) (ultimately including girls in baseball); *Clinton v. Nagy,* 411 F. Supp. 1396 (N.D. Ohio, 1974) (including girls in football).

3. See Betty Spears, "Senda Berenson Abbott: New Woman, New Sport," and Joanna Davenport, "The Tides of Change in Women's Basketball Rules," both in *A Century of Women's Basketball: From Frailty to Final Four,* ed. Joan S. Hult and Marianna Trekell (Reston: American Alliance for Health, Physical Education, Recreation and Dance, 1991), 19–36, 83–108. Hult and Trekell's work explores the role of physical educators in the growth and development of the rules and the game.

4. Susan K. Cahn, *Coming on Strong: Gender and Sexuality in Twentieth Century Women's Sport* (New York: Free Press, 1994). Cahn examines attempts to make the masculine sport of basketball compatible with womanhood.

5. "Bouncing into the Big Time," *Ms.* (April 1974): 73.

6. Helen Lenskyj, *Out of Bounds: Women, Sport and Sexuality* (Toronto: Women's Press, 1986).

7. Those playing five-on-five tended to be barnstorming semipro teams (who played men's teams) and industrial league teams whose players faced an uphill battle to be perceived as ladylike. Mary Jo Festle, *Playing Nice: Politics and Apologies in Women's Sport* (New York: Columbia University Press, 1996), 32–34. Festle also discusses the struggle for administrative and cultural control over women's basketball.

8. "Bouncing into the Big Time," 73.

9. See Janice A. Beran, *From Six-on-Six to Full Court Press: A Century of Iowa Girls' Basketball* (Ames: Iowa State University Press, 1993) for a history of the game and the cultural importance the state attached to it. When New York shifted to the full-court game in 1974, the number of girls playing increased. Laura Henning, "Girls' Basketball Is Gaining," *New York Times* 9 June 1974, 96.

10. The last of the baseball decisions, *Carnes v. Tennessee Secondary School Athletic Association,* 415 F. Supp. 569 (E.D. Tenn. 1976) (holding that if no girls' baseball team existed, girls had a right under the Equal Protection Clause to play on the boys' team) was decided by the same judge, Robert L. Taylor, who decided the first half-court basketball decision. Reassuringly, Taylor was consistent in his decisions.

11. Although *Clinton v. Nagy* was decided on Fourteenth Amendment grounds, *Darrin v. Gould,* 540 P.2d 882 (Wash. 1975) was decided on the Washington Equal Rights Amendment.

12. *Craig v. Boren,* 429 U.S. 190 (1976).

13. *Cape v. Tennessee Secondary School Athletic Assocation,* 424 F. Supp. 732 (E.D. Tenn. 1976).

14. Not until 1979 did the Supreme Court decide that Title IX had an implied right of action that allowed individuals to file suit, despite the fact that Title IX did not clearly state so. *Cannon v. University of Chicago,* 441 U.S. 677 (1979).

15. *Cape* at 737–38.

16. Ibid., 740–41.

17. Ibid., 742–44.

18. *Jones v. Oklahoma Secondary School Activities Association,* 453 F. Supp. 150 (W.D. Okla. 1977).

19. Ibid., 156.

20. *Cape v. Tennessee Secondary Schools Athletic Association,* 563 F. 2d 793, 795 (6th Cir. 1977) (hereafter *Cape II*).

21. *Cape II.*

22. *Jones,* 153.

23. "U.S. Denies Bias in Basketball," *New York Times* 27 Dec. 1978, 20; Byron Rosen, "Sextets Survive," *Washington Post,* 27 Dec. 1978, D6 (which emphasized the congressional efforts to obtain the announcement).

24. *Dodson v. Arkansas Acitivities Association,* 468 F. Supp. 394, 396–98 (E.D. Ark. 1979).

25. *Dodson,* 397.

26. Ibid., 399.

27. Janet J. Johnson, comment, "Half-Court Girls' Basketball Rules: An Application of the Equal Protection Clause and Title IX," *Iowa Law Review* 65 (1980): 766–98.

28. "Three File Class Action Suit," UPI Newswire, Des Moines, 30 Aug. 1983.

29. Lenskyj, *Out of Bounds.*

30. Quoted in Janice Kaplan, *Women and Sports* (New York: Viking Press, 1979), 69. Shelley Lucas's work on girls' basketball in Iowa explores the relationship between femininity and physicality. Shelley Lucas, "Iowa Girls' Basketball or Iowa Girls Playing Boys' Basketball? Examining Discourses on Femininity, Physicality and Location," paper presented at the North American Society for Sport History, State College, Pa., 21–24 May 1999.

31. Ironically, in 1982 Dr. Peter Wirtz, an Iowa orthopedic surgeon, wrote an article for the *Journal of the Iowa Medical Society* in which he claimed that six-on-six basketball was actually more dangerous than full-court basketball. Full-court ball, Wirtz maintains, strengthens leg muscles better than half-court ball, leaving a half-court player's knees more vulnerable to injury. Jump-stops to avoid crossing the half-court line in the girls' game cause more injury, in Wirtz's opinion, because of the lack of leg strength and the rules of the game requiring sudden stops. He recommends that Iowa girls play full-court ball to be safer. The Iowa Girls High School Athletic Union vehemently disagreed with Wirtz's conclusions. Mark Noblin, "Medical Study Suggests Abandoning Girls' Basketball Framework," UPI Newswire, 17 Mar. 1982

32. Dan Wilinsky, "Halfcourt Girls Basketball Format Is an Iowa Tradition," UPI Newswire, 11 Mar. 1982.

33. "Friday Nights Won't Be the Same in Iowa," *Des Moines Register,* 6 Feb. 1993, 8; Marc Hansen, "No More Reason for Restriction," *Des Moines Register,* 4 Feb. 1993, sports/business 1.

34. "Deep Six-on-Sixed," *Sports Illustrated,* 20 Mar. 1995, 15.

35. *Hoover v. Meiklejohn,* 430 F. Supp. 164 (D. Colo. 1977). For a more complete description of this case see chapter 5.

36. *Lavin v. Illinois High School Association,* 527 F. 2d 58 (7th Cir. 1975).

37. A trial court can issue summary judgment for one side or the other before the trial begins. "Summary judgment" means that in the eyes of the court, only an issue of law needs to be decided or no debate over relevant facts exist.

38. *Lavin,* 59.

39. This was the first of two basketball cases the Seventh Circuit heard. The second occurred in 1981 when the court decided that if a girls' basketball team existed, then a girl had no right to play on a boys' team. *O'Connor v. Board of Education,* 645 F. 2d 578 (7th Cir. 1981).

40. *Lavin,* 61.

41. One dissenting judge believed the affidavit was clear. The girls were cut because they were bad players, and talent should be the only criteria in making a team. He believed Rachel was using her gender and her attorneys to find a spot on the team that she did not deserve. Ibid., 62 (Pell, J., dissenting). On remand, her attempt to have her suit certified as a class action failed, and as a result she lost standing to file the suit. Because she was no longer affected by the rule (she had graduated four years before),

that is, she could not sue to change it. *Lavin v. Chicago Board of Education*, 73 R.F.D. 438 (N.D. Ill. 1977).

42. Although the OHSAA rule was similar to the Title IX enforcement regulations that would be announced in 1975, when the girls were banned from the competition the year was 1974.

43. *Yellow Springs Exempted Village School District Board of Education v. Ohio High School Athletic Association*, 443 F. Supp. 753 (S.D. Ohio 1978) (hereafter *Yellow Springs I*). The first thing the judge in this decision did was declare that the OHSAA was a state actor, unlike the *Magill* baseball court but like the majority of other gender and sport decisions.

44. U.S. Constitution, 14th Amend., sec. 1. (1868). Why the attorneys for Yellow Springs or Judge Rubin tried to rely on the Due Process Clause rather than the Equal Protection Clause is not clear from the record. They may have avoided the Equal Protection Clause because the Sixth Circuit had not looked favorably on that claim in the half-court basketball decision of *Cape II* in 1977 or because of the lack of clarity over which test to use in gender segregation under the Equal Protection Clause.

45. See Steven Emanuel, *Constitutional Law*, 9th ed. (New York: Emanuel Law Outlines, 1991) for a detailed explanation of due process.

46. *Goss v. Lopez*, 419 U.S. 565 (1975); *Albach v. Odle*, 531 F. 2d 983 (10th Cir. 1976) (no fundamental right to high school sports); *Board of Regents v. Roth*, 408 U.S. 564 (1972); *Parish v. National Collegiate Athletic Association*, 506 F. 2d 1028 (5th Cir. 1975); *Mitchell v. Louisiana High School Athletic Association*, 430 F. 2d. 1155 (5th Cir. 1970) (finding injury from lost media exposure and scholarships too speculative to form a property interest in high school sport).

47. *Yellow Springs I*, 756–57.

48. Ibid., 758.

49. For a complete examination of Babe's life, see Susan E. Cayleff, *Babe: The Life and Legend of Babe Didrikson Zaharias* (Urbana: University of Illinois Press, 1996).

50. *Yellow Springs Exempted Village School District Board of Education v. Ohio High School Athletic Association*, 674 F. 2d 651 (6th Cir. 1981) (hereafter *Yellow Springs II*), 654 citing OHSAA Rule I, § 6.

51. 45 C.F.R. § 86.41.

52. *Yellow Springs II*, 658.

53. *Morris v. Michigan State Board of Education*, 472 F. 2d 1207 (6th Cir. 1973).

54. *Cape v. Tennessee Secondary School Athletic Association*, 563 F. 2d 793 (6th Cir. 1977) (hereafter *Cape II*).

55. *Yellow Springs I*, 759.

56. *Yellow Springs II*, 654, citing OHSAA Rule I, § 6.

57. 45 C.F.R. § 86.41

58. *Yellow Springs II*, 656.

59. Ibid., 657–58.

60. *Cape II*.

61. *Yellow Springs II*, 657.

62. Ibid., 657–59.

63. Ibid., 662. Jones, however, agreed with the majority in concluding that the constitutionality of the Title IX regulations were not at issue because although the OHSSA's rule complied with the regulations, they were not parallel because the Title IX regulations never said that coeducational contact sports were prohibited, and the OHSSA did.

64. *Cape II; Morris v. Michigan State Board of Education*.

65. *Fortin v. Darlington Little League, Inc.*, 514 F2d 344 (1st Cir. 1975) and *Carnes*

v. Tennessee Secondary School Athletic Association, 415 F. Supp. 569 (E.D. Tenn. 1976) (about baseball); *Clinton v. Nagy,* 411 F. Supp. 1396 (N.D. Ohio 1974) (football); *Hoover v. Meiklejohn,* 430 F. Supp. 164 (D. Colo. 1977) (soccer, hereafter *Hoover*); *Leffel v. Wisconsin Interscholastic Association,* 444 F. Supp. 1117 (E.D. Wis. 1978) and *Brenden v. Independent School District 742,* 477 F. 2d 1292 (8th Cir. 1973) (noncontact sports).

66. *Yellow Springs II,* 662–66 (Jones, dissent).

67. *Hoover.*

68. *Yellow Springs II,* 666–67 (Jones, dissent).

69. *O'Connor v. Board of Education,* 545 F. Supp 376 (N.D. Ill. 1982) (hereafter *O'Connor III*).

70. Either Digger Phelps (then-coach of the men's basketball team of Notre Dame University) or Lou Henson (then-coach of the men's basketball team at the University of Illinois) rated her at their summer basketball camp, according to *O'Connor III.* The notation of the rating comes in *O'Connor v. Board of Education,* 449 U.S. 1301, 1302 (1980) (Stevens, Circuit Justice) (hereafter *O'Connor I*).

71. *O'Connor III,* 377–78.

72. George Vecsey, "Sports of the Times: At Twelve, She Wants to be a Celtic," *New York Times,* 6 Dec. 1981, sec. 5, 5.

73. *O'Connor III,* 378. In an unusual move the oral memo was attached to this decision as an appendix, hereafter referred to as *O'Connor III* (appendix), but in fact it was the first link in this chain.

74. *O'Connor III* (appendix), 384–85.

75. The basic level of scrutiny for equal protection claims was proving that the classification was rationally related to a legitimate goal. The evolving intermediate scrutiny asked if the classification was substantively related to an important goal. Suspect classifications (like race) needed to be necessary to attaining a compelling interest. Intermediate scrutiny for gender would not be widely accepted until 1981.

76. *O'Connor I,* 1301.

77. Each justice of the U.S. Supreme Court acts as a circuit justice for one of the Courts of Appeals. As circuit justice, the justice acts individually on cases requiring a speedy resolution, such as stays and injunctions because of pending deadlines.

78. *O'Connor I,* 1304–6.

79. The district court ordered an injunction against the rule prohibiting Karen from playing ball with the boys. Although the trial court rejected a stay of the injunction pending appeal, the stay was ultimately awarded. Thus the injunction was still in place saying Karen could play with the boys' team, but because of the stay she was not actually doing so. So far, no court had ruled on the merits of Karen's case; the rulings for the injunction and the stay had been based on her likelihood of success in a trial. The school board wanted to be rid of the injunction permanently.

80. *O'Connor v. Board of Education,* 645 F. 2d 578 (7th Cir. 1981) (hereafter *O'Connor II*).

81. Summary judgment means that the court rules that the other side cannot win in a trial because the evidence does not support that position, or if the case is an issue of law and not fact the court can make a legal decision and declare one side the winner before the trial even begins.

82. *O'Connor III,* 381.

83. Ibid., 380–81. At the trial, Karen O'Connor also tried to claim that her rights under the enforcement regulations of Title IX were violated. She knew she could not make a regular Title IX claim because basketball was excluded as a contact sport, but she claimed that the regulation reading that schools must provide "levels of competition effectively accommodating the interests and abilities of both sexes" as protecting her.

45 C.F.R. § 86.41(c)(1) (1981). The district court dismissed this desperate claim and cited legislative history indicating that HEW intended this section only to determine which teams to offer and not intending to exclude separate sport teams. *O'Connor III,* 383–84.

84. "Tennessee Rule Limiting Girls to Half Court," *New York Times,* 4 Oct. 1977, 46; Margaret Roach, "Women in Sports," *New York Times,* 23 Oct. 1977, 13.

85. "Girl Scores a Point, Joins a Boys' Quintet," *New York Times,* 4 Feb. 1978, 15.

86. "Girls Might Make Boys' Basketball Team" UPI Newswire, 7 Oct. 1983. The school district said that not enough seventh-grade girls showed an interest in basketball and therefore it could not form a girls' team. The school did allow girls to try out for the boys' team. No decision regarding this potential case was ever published, indicating that the school and the girl's parent reached a compromise.

Chapter 5: Soccer

1. For the rest of the world soccer is a highly gendered sport; in most of the world it is a masculine game. See, for example, Tony Mason, *Passion of the People? Football in South America* (London: Verso, 1995).

2. *Hoover v. Meiklejohn,* 430 F. Supp. 164 (D. Colo. 1977) (hereafter *Hoover*).

3. One other published decision regarding soccer and a girl exists. *Libby v. South Inter-Conference Association,* 704 F. Supp. 142 (N.D. Ill. 1988), 728 F. Supp. 504 (N.D. Ill. 1990), affirmed *Libby v. Illinois High School Association,* 921 F. 2d 96 (7th Cir. 1990). This case is discussed later in this chapter.

4. For a detailed description of the history of soccer in the United States, see Harvey Frommer, *The Great American Soccer Book* (New York: Atheneum, 1980), 54–86.

5. "Soccer Soars," *Time,* 24 May 1976, 39.

6. Frommer, *The Great American Soccer Book,* 76–78.

7. David Anable, "Soccer's U.S. Success Story," *Christian Science Monitor,* 8 Aug. 1977, 2.

8. Paul Gardner, "Making Soccer an American Sport," *Horizon,* Nov. 1977, 76–81.

9. Pete Axthelm, "The New Kick," *Newsweek,* 18 July 1977, 82–83.

10. Lowell Miller, "The Selling of Soccer-Mania," *New York Times Magazine,* 28 Aug. 1977, 12.

11. James C. Hyatt, "A Family Sport Is Threatened by Success," *Wall Street Journal,* 22 Aug. 1977, 10. This same column also bemoaned the fact that the Diplomats moved to the huge Robert F. Kennedy Stadium and that there was more pressure on the team to lure fans and win games. Hyatt warned of a day in the future when "the army of kids currently filling the neighborhood soccer fields will be up there in the stands, or parked in front of the t.v. with a beer, reminiscing about the good old days when soccer was new." He did not explain why he believed that a large fan base of people who had watched the game since childhood was a bad thing.

12. For a discussion of hooliganism among European soccer fans see Bill Buford, *Among the Thugs* (New York: Norton Press, 1992).

13. Jonathan Friendly, "Sandlot Soccer Teams Provide the Preliminary Kicks for Cosmos Fans," *New York Times,* 20 June 1977, 31.

14. Charles Osgood, "Rising Popularity of Soccer," *CBS Evening News with Walter Cronkite,* 22 July 1977, page 14 of transcript.

15. "Soccer Soars," 39.

16. James Mayo, "Early Starters Scrimmage, Get Kick out of Soccer," *Chicago Tribune,* 24 Sept. 1977, sec. N2, 12.

17. James O'Shea, "Soccer Catching on in Iowa," *Des Moines Register,* 9 Jan. 1977,

19, wrote that youths "shut out of the world of football because of size can excel at soccer," implying that, if bigger, they would play football instead.

18. Alex Vannis, "Soccer; Suburban Strongholds Getting Stronger," *New York Times*, 16 Oct. 1977, sec. 5, 13.

19. Tony Kornheiser, "Americans Have Adopted Soccer, No Longer an 'Immigrant' Sport," *New York Times*, 9 July 1977, 1.

20. Jeanne Clare Feron, "Connecticut Reverberates to the Soccer Boom," *New York Times*, 9 Oct. 1977, sec. 23, Connecticut Weekly, 1.

21. Jeanne Clare Feron, "It's a Whole New Ball Game," *New York Times*, 2 Oct. 1977, sec. 22, Westchester County Weekly, 1.

22. "From Kids to Pros . . . Soccer Is Making It Big in U.S.," *U.S. News & World Report*, 17 Oct. 1977, 100. See also Gramaine L. Jones, "Soccer Hits Stride as U.S. Sport," *Los Angeles Times*, 8 Oct., 1977, sec. 1, 1, noting that soccer costs about a third as much per player as football to a parent or a school.

23. Kornheiser, "Americans Have Adopted Soccer," 39.

24. Neil Milbert, "Pele Helped to Lure Blacks into Soccer," *Chicago Tribune*, 4 June 1977, sec. N2, 5.

25. Gardner, "Making Soccer an American Sport," 81.

26. The irony of the racist implications of the journalistic comments about the superiority of black athletes and the need for them to play soccer in order for the national U.S. team to be successful in international play seemed to have been lost on contemporary sources. The stereotype that black athletes are more naturally gifted than their white counterparts pervaded these 1977 articles. For a discussion of this stereotype see Jennifer Hargreaves, *Sporting Females: Critical Issues in the History and Sociology of Women's Sport* (London: Routledge, 1994): 256–60. In 1977 media accounts, the words *Latin* and *Hispanic* did not appear, as if America was only black and white. Soccer is still a predominantly white game. The U.S. National women's team won the 1999 World Cup with only two African American players on its roster.

27. Jonathan Evan Maslow, "At Home with the Syosset Under-Ten Traveling Team," *Saturday Review*, 29 Oct. 1977, 56.

28. Feron, "It's a Whole New Ball Game," 8.

29. Ibid.

30. Maslow, "At Home," 56.

31. Feron, "Connecticut Reverberates to the Soccer Boom," 1.

32. Ibid.

33. Gardner, "Making Soccer an American Sport," 78.

34. Feron, "Connecticut Reverberates to the Soccer Boom," 1.

35. Feron, "It's a Whole New Ball Game," 8.

36. O'Shea, "Soccer Catching on in Iowa," 18.

37. "Soccer Soars," 39. A professional women's soccer league (the Women's United Soccer Association) began play twenty-three years later, in the fall of 2000 and then shut down after the 2003 season for financial reasons.

38. Miller, "The Selling of Soccer-Mania," 12.

39. Gardner, "Making Soccer an American Sport," 77.

40. Friendly, "Sandlot Soccer," 31.

41. Steve Bogira, "Soccer: Resolving an Identity Crisis in Chicago," *Chicago Tribune*, 1 June 1977, sec. 5, 1; Steve Bogira, "Women Step into Soccer," *Chicago Tribune*, 1 June 1977, sec. 5, 1.

42. Alex Vannis, "Girls' Soccer Has a Long Way to Go," *New York Times*, 16 Oct. 1977, sec. 5, 13; Alex Vannis, "Soccer: Suburban Strongholds Getting Stronger," *New York Times*, 16 Oct. 1977, sec. 5, 13.

43. Lois Bryson, "Sport and the Maintenance of Masculine Hegemony," in *Women, Sport, and Culture,* ed. Susan Birrell and Cheryl L. Cole (Champaign: Human Kinetics, 1994), 47–64. Some theorists have discussed this noncompetitive ideal for women, debating over whether the male model of competitive sports can be reclaimed by feminists and other women. Several studies have argued that women are inherently less competitive than men. One described how, when the best team in a female softball league played the worst team, the best team rotated players away from their usual positions in order to equalize the game—much like youth soccer leagues. Susan Birrell and Diana M. Richter, "Is a Diamond Forever? Feminist Transformation of Sport," in *Women, Sport, and Culture,* ed. Susan Birrell and Cheryl L. Cole (Champaign: Human Kinetics, 1994), 221–44.

44. *Hoover,* 165.

45. Donna's soccer coach was placed on probation for one year because of his role in the episode. "Girl Soccer Player Files Bias Suit," *Denver Post,* 13 Oct. 1976, sec. B, 21. Donna was, in fact, allowed to practice with the team but not to play in games while the suit was pending. Whit Sibley, "Co-ed Soccer Teams Win Court Backing," *Denver Post,* 16 April 1977, sec. 1, 3.

46. 34 C.F.R. § 106.41 (d) (1991).

47. Ibid.

48. *Hoover,* 166, quoting Colorado High School Activities Association, Rule XXI § 3.

49. For a detailed discussion of the battle over coeducational noncontact sports, see Margo L. Anderson, "A Legal History and Analysis of Sex Discrimination in Athletics: Mixed Gender Competition, 1970–1987," Ph.D. diss., University of Minnesota, 1989.

50. *Hoover,* 166.

51. Ibid., 165.

52. A number of studies have compared male and female athletes and their injuries. Although some studies suggest that females are more prone to knee injuries, scientists do not believe that discouraging female athletics is the appropriate response. K. G. Harmon and M. L. Ireland, "Gender Differences in Noncontact Anterior Cruciate Ligament Injuries," *Clinical Sports Medicine* 19 (2000): 287–302. Other studies suggest that the increased injury rate of female athletes compared to male athletes in some sports is related to training differences. For example, inadequate strength and resistance training for female rowers was blamed for causing more rib stress fractures. D. L. Holden and D. W. Jackson, "Stress Fracture of the Ribs in Female Rowers," *American Journal of Sports Medicine* 13 (1985): 342–48. Studies of runners suggest that the most significant difference between male and female distance runners is not skeletal but rather hemoglobic, because males carry more oxygen in their blood than females. A. E. Ready, "Physiological Characteristics of Male and Female Middle Distance Runners," *Canadian Journal of Applied Sports Science* 9 (1984): 70–77.

53. *Hoover,* 166–67.

54. *Frontiero v. Richardson,* 411 U.S. 677 (1973).

55. *Hoover,* 169. The law article on which Matsch relies is J. Harvie Wilkinson III, "The Supreme Court, the Equal Protection Clause and the Three Faces of Constitutional Equality," *Virginia Law Review* 61 (1975): 945.

56. *Hoover,* 169.

57. A number of scholars have elaborated on the argument that sport is a male preserve and that a female intrusion into that preserve, just like an expanding social and political role for women, undermines the male hegemonic power system in society at

large. See, for example, Bryson, "Sport and the Maintenance of Masculine Hegemony," Michael A. Messner, "Sports and Male Domination: The Female Athlete as Contested Ideological Terrain," and Eric Dunning, "Sport as a Male Preserve: Notes on the Social Sources of Masculine Identity and Its Transformations," all in *Women, Sport, and Culture*, ed. Susan Birrell and Cheryl L. Cole (Champaign: Human Kinetics, 1994), 47–64, 65–80, 163–79.

58. Again, the existence of the Title IX enforcement regulations haunted this decision. The regulations did not require gender equality but comparability or gender equity (34 C.F. R. § 106.4[c][1991]). Matsch wrote that his ruling required "comparability, not absolute equality" for male and female athletes (*Hoover*, 170).

59. *Hoover*, 170–72.

60. Ibid., 166.

61. Those who wrote about it during the period around 1977 were divided over whether soccer is a contact sport. Gary Rosenthal, *Everybody's Soccer Book* (New York: Charles Scribner's Sons, 1981), 256, stated, "Soccer is a contact sport. While contact is not necessary or even part of the playing tactics, it inevitably occurs during the course of play." Jane A. Mott, *Soccer and Speedball for Women* (Dubuque: Wm. C. Brown, 1972), 5, noted with equal conviction that soccer is a "noncontact sport under the rules for women's play, and the incidence of injuries is relatively low."

62. Kevin Johnson, "In the Courtroom, Matsch Means Business," *USA Today*, 8 May 1997, 4A; Pete Slover, "Bombing Judge Values Privacy," *Dallas Morning News*, 10 Dec. 1995, 45A.

63. Margaret Roach, "A Westchester Girl's Battle to Compete in Soccer: She Finds Rules May Speak Louder than Ability," *New York Times*, 16 Oct. 1977, sec. 5, 5.

64. Ari L. Goldman, "Regents Let Girls Join Boys' Teams," *New York Times*, 19 Nov. 1977, sec. 1, 1.

65. Goldman, "Regents Let Girls Join Boys' Teams." Young Valerie's concern about how to deal with heterosexuality and sport reflects an extensive debate about the heterosexism and homophobia of sport. See, generally, Susan K. Cahn, *Coming on Strong: Gender and Sexuality in Twentieth-Century Women's Sport* (New York: Free Press, 1994).

66. Janice Kaplan, *Women and Sports* (New York: Viking Press, 1979), 187.

67. John DeWitt, *Coaching Girls' Soccer* (New York: Random House, 2001), x.

68. Jere Longman, *The Girls of Summer: The U.S. Women's Soccer Team and How It Changed the World* (New York: Perennial Press, 2000).

69. Bill Saporito, "Flat-Out Fantastic," *Time*, 19 July 1999, 60–67.

70. Mark Starr and Martha Brant, "It Went Down to the Wire and Thrilled Us All," *Newsweek*, 19 July 1999, 46–54.

71. Longman, *The Girls of Summer*, 27–47.

72. *Libby v. South Inter-Conference Association*, 704 F. Supp. 142 (N.D. Ill. 1988). She then filed a series of suits unsuccessfully seeking attorneys' fees. *Libby v. South Inter-Conference Association*, 728 F. Supp. 504 (N.D. Ill. 1990), *affirmed Libby v. Illinois High School Association*, 921 F. 2d 96 (7th Cir. 1990).

73. Patricia Schroeder, "A Dream Comes True for Title IX Pioneer," *Omaha World Herald*, 16 July 1999, 23.

74. Starr and Brant, "It Went Down to the Wire," 50.

75. Robert Sullivan, "Good-bye to Heroine Chic," *Time*, 19 July 1999, 62.

76. Donna De Varona, "Commentary," *USA Today*, 5 Aug. 1999, 3E.

77. Bob Hotakainen, "House Disputes Mars Soccer Team Honor," *Minneapolis Star-Tribune*, 17 July 1999, 1A.

Chapter 6: Wrestling

1. Wrestling in America can be divided into two different sports. Amateur wrestling, taught in schools and colleges, culminates in international amateur competitions like the Olympics. Professional wrestling is characterized by leagues like the World Wrestling Entertainment (WWE) in which performances are at least partially scripted and athletes are also actors playing characters. For convenience sake, in this book the generic term *wrestling* will be used to designate amateur wrestling, and pro wrestling will be designated as such. Generally, pro wrestling is beyond the scope of this discussion. For a history of pro wrestling in America see Gerald W. Morton and George M. O'Brien, *Wrestling to Rasslin: Ancient Sport to American Spectacle* (Bowling Green: Bowling Green University Popular Press, 1985). For a cultural analysis of pro wrestling see Michael R. Ball, *Professional Wrestling as Ritual Drama in American Popular Culture* (London: Edwin Mellen Press, 1990).

2. This section will refer to "female wrestling" to designate female wrestlers, regardless of whether they are competing against boys or other female wrestlers. "Single-sex wrestling" will refer to gender-segregated matches, and "coed" will refer to mixed-gender competition.

3. See Allen Guttmann, *Women's Sport: A History* (New York: Columbia University Press, 1991), 24–25, for an account of the eugenic justification. A discussion of the noneugenic theory appears in June Kennard and John Marshall Carter, "In the Beginning: The Ancient and Medieval Worlds," in *Women and Sport: Interdisciplinary Perspectives*, ed. D. Margaret Costa and Sharon R. Guthrie (Champaign: Human Kinetics, 1994), 20–21.

4. Guttmann, *Women's Sport*, 8.

5. Roberta J. Park, "From 'Genteel Diversions' to 'Bruising Peg': Active Pastimes, Exercise, and Sports for Females in Late Seventeenth- and Eighteenth-Century Europe," in *Women and Sport: Interdisciplinary Perspectives*, ed. D. Margaret Costa and Sharon R. Guthrie (Champaign: Human Kinetics, 1994), 31.

6. Guttmann, *Women's Sport*, 99–101.

7. Two suits were filed in the 1950s regarding gender and wrestling licenses. The first came after Rose Hesseltine was denied a wrestling permit in 1955 by the Illinois State Athletic Commission because she was female, and she sued claiming constitutional protection under the Equal Protection Clause. Both the trial court and the Illinois Supreme Court concluded that the commission had exceeded the scope of its powers and, without addressing Hesseltine's constitutional claim, ordered the commission to give her a permit and allow the state legislature to decide who could wrestle. *Hesseltine v. State Athletic Commission*, 126 N.E. 2d 631 (Ill. 1955). The second was *State v. Hunter*.

8. *State v. Hunter*, 300 P.2d 455, 458 (Ore. 1956).

9. *Goesaert v. Cleary*, 335 U.S. 464 (1948).

10. "'Legit' Wrestling for Women," *The Sportswoman* 2 (May–June 1974): 34–35.

11. Lawrence Feinberg, "D.C. Opens Football, Wrestling to Girls," *Washington Post*, 19 April 1979, A1.

12. "Two Oregon Girls Allowed Tryouts in Oregon," *New York Times*, 27 Nov. 1981, D12.

13. Tom Friend, "Where Else Could a Pretty Girl Make Her School's Wrestling Team and Pin a Loss on a Guy? Only in . . . America," *Los Angeles Times*, 12 Jan. 1986, sec. 3, 3.

14. *Saint v. Nebraska School Activities Association*, 684 F. Supp. 626 (D. Neb. 1988). Temporary restraining orders suspend the application of a rule until a trial on the merits

can be held, meaning that Stephani was allowed to wrestle at least until a trial. No evidence exists that a trial occurred, and most likely the NSAA changed its rule to avoid future litigation.

15. Scott Stocker, "CHSAA Ends Ban to Keep Girls Off Wrestling Teams," *Rocky Mountain News* (Denver), 1 Feb. 1994, 10B.

16. Tustin Amole, "Cherry Creek Schools Turn Down Boy vs. Girl Wrestling Matches," *Rocky Mountain News* (Denver), 20 July 1995, 5A

17. See, for example, "School Bans Female from Wrestling Team," *Arizona Republic*, 20 Dec. 1994, C2. Any legal settlements might have consisted of waivers for individual girls to compete, or perhaps no girls had the resources and the desire to pursue the matter to a published legal decision.

18. *Adams v. Baker*, 919 F. Supp. 1496 (D. Kan. 1996).

19. *Adams*, 1500–1502.

20. Frank Deford, "Now Georgy-Porgy Runs Away," *Sports Illustrated*, 22 April 1974, 28.

21. Joseph B. Treaster, "Town's Little League Reluctantly Signs Three Girls," *New York Times*, 27 April 1974, 33.

22. *Adams*, 1500–1501.

23. Ibid., 1504.

24. Holly Mullen, "Losing by Decision," *Dallas Observer*, 20 Feb. 1997.

25. Mullen, "Losing by Decision."

26. "Texas Wrestling Groups Say No to Boy-Girl Grappling," *New York Times*, 30 Dec. 1996, A9.

27. Mullen, "Losing by Decision."

28. "Refs Refuse Girl vs. Boy Wrestling," *Cincinnati Enquirer*, 26 Dec. 1996, D3.

29. Chris Newton, "Wrestling the Law," *Chattanooga Times*, 27 Dec. 1996, G5.

30. Newton, "Wrestling the Law," G5.

31. Mullen, "Losing by Decision."

32. Ibid.

33. David Lance, "Judge Rules against Girls Wrestling Team," *Fort Worth Star-Telegram*, 13 Feb. 1997, 10.

34. David Lance, "Wrestling Approved as UIL Sport; Girls Can Participate Separately," *Fort Worth Star-Telegram*, 12 April 1997, 1.

35. Lance, "Judge Rules," 10; *Barnett v. Texas Wrestling Association*, 1997 U.S. Dist. LEXIS 4875, Feb. 12, 1997.

36. *O'Connor v. Board of Education* (IL), 449 U.S. 1301 (1980); 645 F. 2d 578 (7th Cir. 1981); 545 F. Supp. 376 (N.D. Ill. 1982).

37. *Clark v. Arizona Interscholastic Association*, 695 F. 2d. 1126 (9th Cir. 1982) (excluding boy from girls' volleyball team); *Williams v. School District of Bethlehem*, 998 F. 2d 168 (3d Cir. 1993) (excluding boy from girls' field hockey team).

38. *Barnett v. Texas Wrestling Association*, 16 F. Supp. 2d 690, 695–96 (N.D. Tex. 1998).

39. Barnett, 693.

40. Theresa Walton's "Pinned By Gender Construction? Media Representations of Girls' and Women's Wrestling in the U.S.," presented at the North American Society for the Sociology of Sport, Colorado Springs, 9–11 Nov. 2000, examines the language of wrestling.

41. Susan K. Cahn, *Coming on Strong: Gender and Sexuality in Twentieth-Century Women's Sport* (New York: Free Press, 1994), discusses the twentieth-century assumption that talented female athletes were by definition mannish in appearance and/or lesbian.

42. Mullen, "Losing by Decision," describes a parent of a male wrestler referring to "these girls" who want to wrestle "our boys."

43. "Girl Barred from Boys' Wrestling Team," UPI Newswire, 11 Nov. 1986, A.M. Cycle.

44. Richard Roeper, "Wrestling Mat Is No Place for Boy-Girl Grappling," *Chicago Sun-Times*, 21 Jan. 1993, 11.

45. "Priest Is Opposed to Girl Wrestling Boys," *Minneapolis Star-Tribune*, 12 Jan. 1995, 2C.

46. Friend, "Where Else?" 3.

47. See Brian Pronger, *Arena of Masculinity: Sports, Homosexuality, and the Meaning of Sex* (London: GMP Publishers, 1996), 183–86, for a discussion of how many gay men find wrestling highly erotic and how a substantial amount of gay pornography focuses on wrestlers and the homoerotic possibilities of the sport. Allen Guttmann also explores the connection between homoeroticism and sport in general, as well as wrestling in particular, in *The Erotic in Sport* (New York: Columbia University Press, 1996).

48. Mullen, "Losing by Decision."

49. "Girl Barred from Boys' Wrestling Team."

50. See Pat Griffin, *Strong Women, Deep Closets: Lesbians and Homophobia in Sport* (Champaign: Human Kinetics, 1998) for a discussion of lesbians in sport, and Cahn, *Coming on Strong*, for a discussion of the assumption of lesbianism in female athletes.

51. For a discussion of these female apologetics, see M. Ann Hall, *Feminism and Sporting Bodies: Essays on Theory and Practice* (Champaign: Human Kinetics, 1996).

52. Christy True, "More High School Girls Find Wrestling Is One Sport They Can Pin Their Hopes On," *Seattle Times*, 11 Feb. 1998, B4.

53. See, for example, Susan Bickelhaupt, "Wrestling for Girls," *Boston Globe*, 24 Feb. 1999, C9.

54. Friend, "Where Else?" 3.

55. Guttmann, *Women's Sports*, 99–101.

56. *State v. Hunter*, 457.

57. Roeper, "Wrestling Mat Is No Place for Boy-Girl Grappling."

58. Mullen, "Losing by Decision." In the twenty-first century, professional wrestling changed its name to World Wrestling Entertainment (W.W.E.)

59. David Goricki, "Girl Overcomes Adversity to Qualify for Wrestling Finals," *Detroit News*, 2 Mar. 1999, E1.

60. True, "More High-School Girls Find Wrestling Is One Sport They Can Pin Their Hopes On."

61. David Goricki, "Wrestling: Organizers Pleased with First Girls Meet Results," *Detroit News*, 20 Mar. 1997, G4.

62. Nick Daschle, "Girls Wrestling: Grappling for Glory." *The Columbian* (Vancouver, BC), 26 Feb. 2004, B1.

63. Bickelhaupt, "Wrestling for Girls," C9.

64. Friend, "Where Else?" 3.

65. Ibid.

66. Ibid.

67. Mullen, "Losing By Decision."

68. Ibid.

69. Bickelhaupt, "Wrestling for Girls," C9.

70. Ibid.

71. Mullen, "Losing by Decision."

72. The case was dismissed in 2003. *National Wrestling Coaches Association v. United States Department of Education*, 263 F. Supp. 2d 82 (D.C., 2003).

73. Theresa A. Walton, "Pinned by Gender Construction? A Critical Analysis of Media Representation of Female Amateur Wrestling in the United States," Ph.D. diss,. University of Iowa, 2002, 31–34.

Chapter 7: Boxing

1. Joyce Carol Oates, *On Boxing* (Garden City: Doubleday, 1987), 73.

2. Jeffrey T. Sammons, *Beyond the Ring: The Role of Boxing in American Society* (Urbana: University of Illinois Press, 1988), examines the history of the sport in the twentieth century; see also Gerald Early, *Tuxedo Junction: Essays on American Culture* (New York: Ecco Press, 1989); Gerald Early, *The Culture of Bruising: Essays on Prizefighting, Literature, and Modern American Culture* (New York: Ecco Press, 1994); and Oates, *On Boxing.*

3. Mike Marquese, "Sport and Stereotype: From Role Model to Muhammad Ali," *Race and Class* 36 (1995): 1–29.

4. Theodore Roosevelt wrote about boxing being an important part of his time at Harvard University in *Theodore Roosevelt: An Autobiography* (New York: Charles Scribner's Sons, 1925), 36.

5. Elliott J. Gorn, *The Manly Art: Bare-Knuckle Prize Fighting in America* (Ithaca: Cornell University Press, 1986), 90.

6. In "Tribute to Title IX," aired on *ESPN Classic*, 25 June 2000, one commentator attributed the rise in female professional sports "from basketball to boxing" to Title IX.

7. Sammons, *Beyond the Ring*, 31. Although Gorn argues that slaves were too valuable to have been exposed to risk in such a manner, other accounts, including Sammons's, disagree with that position. Race played a prominent role in boxing from the beginning of its American history.

8. Ibid., 6, citing an 1876 Massachusetts Supreme Court decision upholding the prizefighting ban. Sammons's work clearly outlines the court battles that boxing fought to regain legality in America.

9. Gorn, *Manly Art*, 176–200.

10. Theodore Roosevelt, *The Strenuous Life* (New York: Review of Reviews, 1900), 137.

11. Roosevelt wrote that his only objection to prizefighting was the "crookedness" of the business surrounding the sport. *Theodore Roosevelt: An Autobiography*, 51.

12. Sammons, *Beyond the Ring*, 54–58

13. Susan Cahn, *Coming on Strong: Gender and Sexuality in Twentieth-Century Women's Sport* (New York: Free Press, 1994), 14.

14. John A. Lucas and Ronald A. Smith, *Saga of American Sport* (Philadelphia: Lea and Febiger, 1978), 305.

15. Sammons, *Beyond the Ring*, 49–60.

16. "Girls Boxing: Dallas' Missy Jr. Gloves," *The Sportswoman* 1 (Nov.–Dec. 1973): 31–33.

17. Janice Kaplan, "Lady Sluggers," *Seventeen* (May 1976): 30.

18. "Women Boxing Hurts 'Manhood,'" *The Sportswoman* 3 (May–June 1975), 13.

19. "Tonowanda Wins License," *The Sportswoman* 3 (Oct. 1975): 4.

20. Kaplan, "Lady Sluggers," 30.

21. In 1975 Dorothy L. Barnes wrote that she was surprised that "so little" had been written about rape. Her bibliography contained no section on date or acquaintance rape. Her 1991 update included both categories: *Rape: A Bibliography, 1976–1988* (Troy:

Whitston Publishing, 1991). The study of domestic violence increased in the 1980s after shelters were already being built. Edward W. Gondolf, *Research on Men Who Batter: An Overview, Bibliography, and Resource Guide* (Bradenton: Human Services Institute, 1988), 1.

22. *Lafler v. Athletic Board of Control*, 536 F. Supp. 104 (W.D. Mich. 1982). The decision released in 1993 was never published, and information about that case is therefore only available from media accounts of the oral decision. Whether a district court decision (especially regarding preliminary injunctions and temporary restraining orders) is published is, to a large extent, at the discretion of the judge making the decision.

23. *Lafler*, 107.

24. Ibid., 106–8.

25. "Judge Rules Bellingham Girl Eligible for Amateur Boxing Competition," *Seattle Post-Intelligence*, 8 May 1993, D6.

26. Kenny Lucas, "Golden Girls: Boxing Opens Its Ranks to Women," *New York Daily News*, 28 Mar. 1999, 110.

27. Information on Mike Tyson's career can be found at www.Britanica.com. For a cultural analysis of Tyson's conviction, see John M. Sloop, "Mike Tyson and the Perils of Discursive Constraints: Boxing, Race, and the Assumption of Guilt," in *Out of Bounds: Sport, Media, and the Politics of Identity*, ed. Aaron Baker and Todd Boyd (Bloomington: Indiana University Press, 1997).

28. Norm Frauenheim, "Girls Put on the Gloves," *Arizona Republic*, 23 July 1994, C1.

29. Frauenheim, "Girls Put on the Gloves."

30. Jayda Evans, "Male–Female Fights? Freak Show," *Seattle Times*, 7 Oct. 1999, A1.

31. *REAL Sports*, Home Box Office Productions, aired 28 July 2000.

32. "Man vs. Woman: Boxing Match or Freak Show," *Arizona Republic*, 9 Oct. 1999, B6.

33. Evans, "Male–Female Fights?" A1.

34. Frauenheim, "Girls Put on the Gloves," C1.

35. Mitch Sneed, "Fighters Don't Hit Like Girls in Exhibition," *Atlanta Journal and Constitution*, 21 Jan. 1996, 3E.

36. Lucas, "Golden Girls," 110.

37. Loren Ledin, "Sweet Science Gets Touch of Lass," *Rocky Mountain News* (Denver), 10 Dec. 1995, 30B.

38. Greg Rippee, "Hits and Misses: Police Program Teaches Girls the Ropes of Boxing," *Los Angeles Times*, 23 May 1997, B1.

39. Sharon Ginn, "The Girls Take a Jab at Learning Boxing," (Riverside, Calif.) *Press-Enterprise*, 25 Feb. 1993, B1.

40. See John Sugden, *Boxing and Society: An International Analysis* (New York: St. Martin's Press, 1996), 174–94, for an exploration of the ideas of boxing, civilization, and gender.

41. Oates, *On Boxing*, 30; Early, *Tuxedo Junction*, 188–95.

42. Bill Thompson, "Am I the Only One or Was It Weird Watching Two Girls in a Boxing Ring?" *Fort Worth Star-Telegram*, 23 Feb. 1997, 4.

43. Evans, "Male–Female Fights?" A1. See also www.womenboxing.com, accessed 21 April 2004, for a guide to female boxing.

44. Data accessed 3 Mar. 2002 from www.usaboxing.org.

Chapter 8: Boys on Girls' Field Hockey Teams

1. 34 C.F.R. § 106.41(b) (1991).

2. Ibid.

3. *Petrie v. Illinois High School Athletic Association*, 394 N.E. 2d 588 (Ill. 1979). On the other hand, another boy won a preliminary injunction to play volleyball because the district court ruled that volleyball was a noncontact sport and Title IX applied. *Gomes v. Rhode Island Interscholastic League*, 604 F. 2d 733 (1st Cir. 1979) (on appeal the case was dismissed as moot because the boy had graduated).

4. *Clark v. Arizona Interscholastic Association*, 886 F. 2d 1191 (9th Cir. 1989). Wade Clark's brother had also filed suit to gain access to the girls' volleyball team several years earlier and had also lost for the same reasons. *Clark v. Arizona Interscholastic Association*, 695 F. 2d 1126 (9th Cir. 1982), *cert. denied*, 464 U.S. 818 (1983). For a detailed analysis of noncontact sport lawsuits, see Margo L. Anderson, "A Legal History and Analysis of Sex Discrimination in Athletics: Mixed Gender Competition, 1970–87," Ph.D. diss., University of Minnesota, 1989.

5. Anderson, "A Legal History," 288–89.

6. *Attorney General v. Massachusetts Interscholastic Athletic Association*, 393 N.E. 2d 284 (Mass. 1979).

7. Opinion of the Justices to the House of Representatives, 371 N.E. 2d 426 (Mass. 1977).

8. *Attorney General v. MIAA*, 291–95.

9. The New Jersey state courts allowed the under-age plaintiff and his family to remain anonymous and referred to him only by his initials. The suit was filed in the boy's father's initials (B.C.), but the boy himself was denoted as C.C.

10. *B.C. v. Cumberland Regional School District*, 531 A.2d 1059 (N.J. Super. 1987) quoting *N.J.S.A.* 18A:11–15.

11. *B.C. v. Cumberland*, 1061–67.

12. *Lafler v. Athletic Board of Control*, 536 F. Supp. 104 (W.D. Mich. 1982).

13. *B.C. v. Cumberland*, 1065–67.

14. *Kleczek v. Rhode Island Interscholastic League*, 768 F. Supp. 951 (D.R.I. 1991) (hereafter *Kleczek I*).

15. *Kleczek I*, 952–53.

16. Ibid., 955.

17. *Kleczek v. Rhode Island Interscholastic League*, 612 A.2d 734 (R.I. 1992) (hereafter *Kleczek II*).

18. *Kleczek II*, 735–40.

19. *Williams v. School District of Bethlehem, PA*, 799 F. Supp. 513 (E.D. Penn. 1992) (hereafter *Williams I*).

20. 34 C.F.R. § 106.41(b) (1991).

21. Ibid. cited in *Williams I*, 515–16.

22. *Williams I*, 517–18.

23. Ibid., 519–22. The court addressed John's due process claim only in passing, noting that although his rights may have been violated the due process clause was not the most effective remedy in this instance.

24. John's career and court battles are summarized in "Court Upholds School Policy Banning Boy from Girls' Team," *Los Angeles Times*, 8 July 1993, C2.

25. *Williams v. School District of Bethlehem, PA*, 998 F. 2d 168 (3d Cir. 1993) (hereafter *Williams II*), *cert. denied*, 510 U.S. 1043 (1994).

26. *Williams II*, 173, citing 34 C.F.R. § 106.41(b) (1991).

27. Ibid., 173–74. In his concurring opinion Judge Anthony Scirica thought that field hockey was clearly a contact sport and that Judge Troutman was wrong in concluding otherwise. Scirica wrote that he would have granted the school district a summary judgment order excluding boys from field hockey under Title IX.

28. Ibid., 175.

29. Ibid., 176. Because the court of appeals concluded that the case should be remanded for trial on the issue of whether field hockey was a contact sport under the Title IX regulations, the court refused to address John's Fourteenth Amendment claims. If courts can make a decision on a legislative issue rather than a constitutional one they will usually do so. Constitutional decisions are to be made only if absolutely necessary.

30. *Williams II,* 179.

31. *Williams v. School District,* 510 U.S. 1043 (1994). Justice David Souter refused to issue a stay of the appellate court decision that would have allowed John to play his final season while appealing the decision to the full Supreme Court. "Court Foils Boy's Bid to Play Girls' Field Hockey," *Arizona Republic,* 11 Jan. 1994, D2.

32. *Williams II,* 180–81 (Scirica, J. concurring).

33. "Spotlight," *Milwaukee Journal-Sentinel,* 27 Aug. 1997, Sports 1.

34. Barry Svrluga, "Committee to Back Boy for Field Hockey," *Portland Press-Herald,* 5 Nov. 1997, 1D; Jason Wolfe, "Testimony Begins in Field Hockey Suit," *Portland Press-Herald,* 14 Jan. 1999, 1B; Matt DiFilippo, "Opinions Differ on Schoolboy Field Hockey Ban," *Kennebec* (County, Me.) *Journal,* 23 Jan. 1999, C1; Jason Wolfe, "Boys' Ban in Field Hockey Upheld," *Portland Press Herald,* 23 Jan. 1999, 1A.

35. Author survey of *Lexis-Nexis Academic Universe,* 1 Feb. 2000.

36. *B.C. v. Cumberland,* 1067.

37. *Williams I,* 517 n.3.

38. Interview with author, Iowa City, 7 May 1999.

39. *Williams II,* 180–81 (Scirica, J., concurring).

40. *Kleczek I,* 956.

41. *B.C. v. Cumberland,* 1061.

42. Barry Svrluga, "Impact Felt Where Boys Can Play Field Hockey," *Portland Press-Herald,* 14 Sept. 1997, 1A.

43. See Joan Verdon, "Girls' Teams Can Exclude Boys," (Bergan County) *Record,* 6 Sept. 1985, B5, quoting a local field hockey coach.

44. "Boys Banished from Field Hockey," UPI Newswire, 26 Sept. 1988.

45. George Snell, "Boys Causing Field Hockey Forfeits," *Worcester* (Mass.) *Sunday Telegram,* 5 Oct. 1997, B2.

46. Snell, "Boys Causing Field Hockey Forfeits."

47. Ibid.

48. *B.C. v. Cumberland,* 1062; see also "Boy on Board Keeps Chatham Girls off Field," *Minneapolis Star-Tribune,* 26 Oct. 1992, 2C; and Bob Holmes, "School Sports: Supreme Court Rules Boy Can't Play Field Hockey," *Boston Herald,* 11 Jan. 1994, 65.

49. *B.C. v. Cumberland,* 1062.

50. Bill Reynolds, "Ruling Could Wreck Girls Sports," *St. Louis Post Dispatch,* 8 Oct. 1991, 2B. St. Louis is one of the few midwestern cities that has a number of high school field hockey teams.

51. Colleen Roy, "It's Boys against Girls in Field Hockey Tomorrow," *Providence Journal-Bulletin,* 3 Nov. 1997, 1C. The results of the match, however, were not reported.

52. "Simsbury Girls' Field Hockey Team Practices with Kilted Boys," Associated Press Newswire, 23 Nov. 1998.

53. Svrluga, "Impact Felt," 1A.

54. Ron Kohl, "There's No Problem with Having Dave on This Team," *Allentown Morning Call*, 16 Oct. 1998, C3.

55. "Court Foils Boy's Bid to Play Girls' Field Hockey," *Arizona Republic*, 11 Jan. 1994, D2.

56. Dan Beyers, "Two Boys Skirt the Rules on Girls Field Hockey," *Washington Post*, 1 Nov. 1996, A1.

57. Beyers, "Two Boys Skirt the Rules."

58. "Simsbury Girls' Field Hockey Team Practices with Kilted Boys."

59. "Boy on Board," 2C.

60. Alexandra Clough, "Boys Shoot for Hockey Goal," *Washington Post*, 24 Aug. 1986, D1.

61. Vahe Gregorian, "Field Trial," *St. Louis Post-Dispatch*, 28 June 1994, 1B.

62. *Attorney General v. MIAA*, 296.

63. Ibid., 295.

64. Clough, "Boys Shoot," D1.

65. *O'Connor v. Board of Education*, 449 U.S. 1301 (1980) (Stevens, Circuit Justice).

66. Michael A. Messner, *Taking the Field: Women, Men, and Sports* (Minneapolis: University of Minnesota Press, 2002).

67. Clough. "Boys Shoot," D1.

68. Beyers, "Two Boys Skirt the Rules."

69. "Boy on Board," 2C.

70. Ibid.

71. "Bethlehem Boy Refused Permission to Play Girls' Field Hockey," UPI Newswire, 17 Oct. 1990.

Chapter 9: Wrapping Up Contact Sports

1. 34 C.F.R. § 106.41(b) (1991).

2. Or at least not litigated to the point of a published decision.

3. The magazine *Rugby*, in an annual yearbook/directory, keeps track of the number of clubs in America, dividing them by gender and age. Youth clubs became a separate category in 1995.

4. Field hockey is the one exception to schools excluding boys to redress past discrimination. Courts did not, however, prohibit school districts from creating separate boys' leagues but did not require the districts to let boys try out for the one female team.

5. Stephen Hardy, "Memory, Performance, and History: The Making of American Ice Hockey at St. Paul's School, 1860–1915," *International Journal of the History of Sport* 24 (1997): 97–115. St. Paul's School is in Concord, New Hampshire.

6. The title of the show has been appropriated by Richard Gruneau and David Whitson, *Hockey Night in Canada: Sport, Identities, and Cultural Politics* (Toronto: Garamond Press, 1993), in their examination of the history of hockey and its role in Canadian culture.

7. Survey of *TV Guide* throughout the 1999–2000 National Hockey League season.

8. Daniel S. Mason, "The International Hockey League and the Professionalization of Ice Hockey, 1904–1907," *Journal of Sport History* 25 (1998): 1–17. Mason notes that the league was played in five towns in northern parts of Michigan and Minnesota and the southern part of Ontario. The IHL failed because in 1906 the Eastern Canadian Amateur Hockey Association allowed professional players to play alongside amateurs, and many players went home to Canada. Most players in today's National Hockey

League (NHL) are not actually from the United States; many are from Canada. So few NHL players are from the United States that for several years the all-star game amounted to North American players versus those from the rest of the world—mostly Europe.

9. A search of the periodical and journal databases *SportDiscus* and *America: History and Life* revealed a two-to-one ratio of articles on Canadian hockey versus American hockey and no titles involving ice hockey and U.S. culture.

10. Nancy Theberge, *Higher Goals: Women's Ice Hockey and the Politics of Gender* (Albany: SUNY Press, 2000). Not surprisingly given the Canadian passion for the sport, the only lawsuit in North America about the right of a girl to play on a boys' hockey team arose in Canada. In 1987 an Ontario court ordered the local boys' league to allow Justine Blaney to try out, but the court added that women's hockey could exclude men because girls had been traditionally discriminated against in Canadian sport. Tracey Tyler, "Courts begin to Rule on Employment Equality," *Toronto Star*, 31 Jan. 1993, B7.

11. "Girls' Ice Hockey: Fast and Furious," *The Sportswoman*, 1 (Sept.–Oct. 1973): 9–10.

12. In a *Lexis-Nexis Academic Universe* search, the first reference is "Scouting," *New York Times*, 22 Jan. 1987, D28.

13. Bill and Nancy Gordon, "Girls in Ice Hockey," *San Diego Union-Tribune*, 21 Nov. 1985, B6 (an opinion piece supporting the girls and the sport).

14. "Scouting," D28.

15. A 2004 *Lexis-Nexis Academic Universe* search of U.S. news for "(girl or wom*n) and ice hockey" resulted in ten stories before 1990 and almost nine hundred after 1990.

16. Roman Augustoviz, "Gender Gap Still a Factor in State," (Minneapolis) *Star-Tribune*, 5 Oct 1995, 6C.

17. Jennifer Peck, "Goal Clear for Girls on the Ice," *Boston Globe*, 1 Mar. 1998, 11.

18. Andrea Simakis, "Bias Alleged in Keeping Girl Off Ice in Shaker Games," (Cleveland) *Plain-Dealer*, 10 Dec. 1999, 6B. No evidence exists that the suit was actually filed.

19. See Eric Dunning and Kenneth Sheard, *Barbarians, Gentlemen and Players: A Sociological Study of the Development of Rugby Football* (New York: New York University Press, 1979), for a history of the sport.

20. The players came from California because for a brief time the University of California and Stanford University played rugby instead of football. Roberta J. Park, "From Football to Rugby and Back, 1906–1919: The University of California–Stanford Response to the 'Football Crisis of 1905,'" *Journal of Sport History* 11 (1984): 5–40.

21. Mark Jenkins, "An American Coup in Paris," *American Heritage* 21 (July–Aug. 1989): 66–71. Rugby powerhouses like the countries that were part of the United Kingdom refused to play the French in Paris because of French fans' reputation for violence. Southern hemisphere teams such as New Zealand, Australia, and South Africa could not afford to travel to Paris. The French fans were, in fact, extremely violent and rioted when their team lost. As a result, the International Olympic Committee removed rugby from the games. Ibid.; see also John Lucas, "France Versus U.S.A. in 1924 Olympic Games Rugby: Efforts to Assuage Transnational Tension," *Canadian Journal of the History of Sport* 19 (1988): 15–27.

22. "Collegiate Rugby," *The Sportswoman* 2 (Nov.–Dec. 1974): 30.

23. Jamie Gold, "Women's Rugby," *Washington Post*, 2 Oct. 1981, 3.

24. Shannon Rose, "Girls Can Play Robust Sport of Rugby, Too," *Kansas City Star*, 20 July 1995, 10.

25. "Club Types by Territorial Union," *Rugby*, Feb.–Mar. 2000, 2.

26. Compiled from *Rugby*, Feb.–Mar. 1999.

27. For various discussions on masculinity and rugby outside the United States see Philip G. White and Anne B. Vagi, "Rugby in the Nineteenth-Century British Boarding-School System: A Feminist Psychoanalytic Perspective," in *Sport, Men, and the Gender Order: Critical Feminist Perspectives*, ed. Michael A. Messner and Donald F. Sabo (Champaign: Human Kinetics, 1990); John Nauright and Timothy J. L. Chandler, eds., *Making Men: Rugby and Masculine Identity* (Portland: Frank Cass, 1996); Timothy J. L. Chandler and John Nauright, eds., *Making the Rugby World: Race, Gender, and Commerce* (Portland: Frank Cass Press, 1999); and Dunning and Sheard, *Barbarians, Gentlemen, and Players*.

28. For a discussion of masculinity in American rugby see Steven P. Schacht, "Misogyny On and Off the 'Pitch': The Gendered World of Male Rugby Players," *Gender and Society* 11 (Feb. 1997): 69–87, and Kendal L. Broad, "Women's Rugby: Sport, Gender, and the Female Badass," M.A. thesis, Washington State University, 1993.

29. Alison Carle and John Nauright, "Crossing the Line: Women Playing in Rugby Union," in *Making the Rugby World: Race, Gender, and Commerce*, ed. Timothy L. J. Chandler and John Nauright (Portland: Frank Cass, 1999), 131–39.

30. Mary A. Boutilier and Lucinda SanGiovanni, *The Sporting Woman* (Champaign: Human Kinetics, 1983), 84, quoting Roger Angell, "Sharing the Beat," *The New Yorker*, 9 April 1978.

31. Bil Gilbert and Nancy Williamson, "Programmed to Be Losers," *Sports Illustrated*, 11 June 1973, 60–73.

32. *Plessy v. Ferguson*, 163 U.S. 537, 551 (1896).

33. *Missouri ex rel. Gaines v. Canada*, 305 U.S. 337 (1938) (holding that Missouri could not simply send a black law student out of state but must provide and an in state institution); *Sweatt v. Painter*, 339 U.S. 629 (1950) (holding that black students had to be admitted to the University of Texas School of Law because it was vastly superior to the black state law school); and *McLaurin v. Oklahoma State Regents*, 339 U.S. 637 (1950) (holding that forcing black students at a white university to sit in separate sections of the library, cafeteria, and classrooms impaired their ability to learn).

34. *Brown v. Board of Education*, 347 U.S. 483, 495 (1954).

35. *Vorchheimer v. School District of Philadelphia*, 532 F. 2d 880 (3d Cir. 1976), affirmed without comment 430 U.S. 703 (1977).

36. *Mississippi University for Women v. Hogan*, 458 U.S. 718 (1982).

37. *U.S. v. Virginia*, 518 U.S. 515 (1996).

38. *Virginia*, 596 (Scalia, dissenting).

39. *Kleczek v. Rhode Island Interscholastic League*, 768 F. Supp. 951 (D. R.I. 1991), 612 A.2d 734 (R.I. 1992).

40. *O'Connor v. Board of Education*, 545 F. Supp 376 (N.D. Ill. 1982), 384–85.

41. *Williams v. School District of Bethlehem, PA*, 799 F. Supp. 513 (E.D. Penn. 1992), rev'd 998 F. 2d 168 (3d Cir. 1993), cert. denied, 510 U.S. 1043 (1994).

42. Elizabeth Rush, "Diversity: The Red Herring of Equal Protection," *American University Journal of Gender and Law* 6 (1997): 43–58. Rush argues that racial minority groups should be allowed to have minority-only groups (like the United Negro College Fund) but that racial majority groups cannot specifically form or promote white groups (like the United White College Fund) because whites already have immeasurable privileges by virtue of being white. I have expanded on her idea to prohibiting dominant-only (male) teams while permitting nondominant-only (female) teams.

43. Tim Sullivan, "Co-ed Softball Team Clouds Gender Equity Arguments," *Cincinnati Enquirer*, 27 Aug. 2000, C15.

INDEX

SARAH K. FIELDS is an assistant professor at the University of Georgia on a visiting assistant professorship at the Ohio State University. She holds a J.D. and a Ph.D.

SPORT AND SOCIETY

The University of Illinois Press
is a founding member of the
Association of American University Presses.

———————————————————————

Composed in 9.5/12.5 Trump Mediaeval
by Jim Proefrock
at the University of Illinois Press
Manufactured by Thomson-Shore, Inc.

University of Illinois Press
1325 South Oak Street
Champaign, IL 61820-6903
www.press.uillinois.edu